Hugh and Jane Lowndes The Gawsworth, England Quakers

Howard G. Lownes Sr.

BALBOA.PRESS
A DIVISION OF HAY HOUSE

CONTENTS

DEDICATION

This book is being dedicated to my beloved wife, Verna, who passed away prior to me writing this book.

Verna M. Lownes

I also want to dedicate it to my son, Howard Jr., as he passed away prior to me completing the book.

Howard G. Lownes Jr.

I also want to deicate the book to my daughter, April Lynn (Lownes) Hostler, for her understanding and dedication in helping me with this effort.

PREFACE

I, Howard G. Lownes Sr., wrote the book, often referencing Charlotte Lownes Olewiler's work. Without her contribution this could not be as complete as it is. Charlotte's hard work back in the 1970s, before the internet, had to be a challenge. Early parts of her work that she wrote are reveled as part of this book. Without her dedication, it might have been more of a challenge to me, but she did a great job with what she contributed to this effort. Since she was several years older and I never met her, she had to be a beautiful, wonderful woman, with fortitude, and I wish I could have known her. Suzan and Conny, two of Charlotte's daughters, also inspired me and helped with the editing of the book. Our cousin, Thomas Lownes Jr., was also an inspiration and mentor to help with information about the family. I also want to thank Bette Ferris for her efforts in the George branch of the family. There was also Steve Lown from Ohio, Coral Heyl from Georgia, Mary Kaiser from North Carolina, and Randall Lownes from Lafayette Hills, Pennsylvania, not to mention Barbara Burke of the Springfield Historical Museum in Springfield, Pennsylvania.

This book is divided into generations; discussing various people and how they fit into the story I want to tell. In this way, we can step through the family of each branch as it unfolded through history. Provided are photographs of people, houses, and maps as they relate to the story. There are a number of missing people in some stories, making the stories incomplete. As you will see, there have been many famous people with whom our ancestors came in contact, as well as ancestors who became famous in their own right. We should all be proud of our ancestors and the hardships Hugh and Jane endured starting out in a world of turmoil in England and believing God as our savior, who guided them through the hardships while trusting God and never giving up.

Edward Lowndes (1566 – 7/5/1608) was our Hugh's Grandfather. He was born in Gawsworth Cheshire, England, and died in Odd Rode, Cheshire, England; Johanne (1568 – unk) was his Grandmother.

I have been able to trace back to a Thomas Lowndes with dates unknown. He had to have been born in the late 1300's since I did find his son John Lowndes being born in 1416. On pages 16 and 17 are trees showing early ancestors. Below is a dirct line up to our Hugh and Jane Lowndes.

Thomas Lowndes	unk – unk
John Lowndes	1416 – unk
Peter Lowndes	1459 – 4/3/1558
John Lowndes	1500 – 1591
Richard Lowndes	1/14/1510 – 9/3/1592
Hugh Lowndes	1532 – 4/15/1599
Edward Lowndes	1566 – 7/5/1608
Hugh Lowndes	5/22/1604 – 7/12/1680
Hugh Lowndes	5/3/1635 – 7/11/1680

As can be seen on page 3, the chart shows our Hugh Lowndes had eight siblings It shows a William Lowndes being born in 1663 and dieing in 1759. I have to assume that at age 17, he chose to stay in England rather than sailing to America with his mother and siblings..

This is as far back that is recorded in Ancestry.com

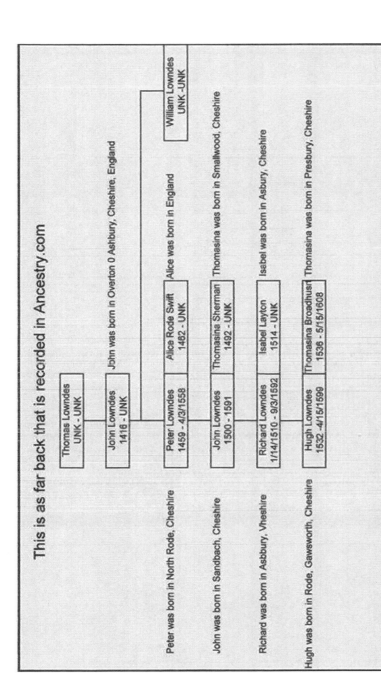

Thomas Lowndes
UNK - UNK

John Lowndes
1416 - UNK

John was born in Overton 0 Ashbury, Cheshire, England

William Lowndes
UNK - UNK

Peter Lowndes
1459 - 4/3/1558

Alice Rode Swift
1462 - UNK

Alice was born in England

Peter was born in North Rode, Cheshire

John Lowndes
1500 - 1591

Thomasina Sherman
1492 - UNK

Thomasina was born in Smallwood, Cheshire

John was born in Sandbach, Cheshire

Richard Lowndes
1/14/1510 - 9/3/1592

Isabel Layton
1514 - UNK

Isabel was born in Asbury, Cheshire

Richard was born in Assbury, Vheshire

Hugh Lowndes
1532 -4/15/1599

Thomasina Broadhust
1536 - 5/15/1608

Thomasina was born in Presbury, Cheshire

Hugh was born in Rode, Gawesworth, Cheshire

See the next sheet for the tree that shows those down through Generation Two

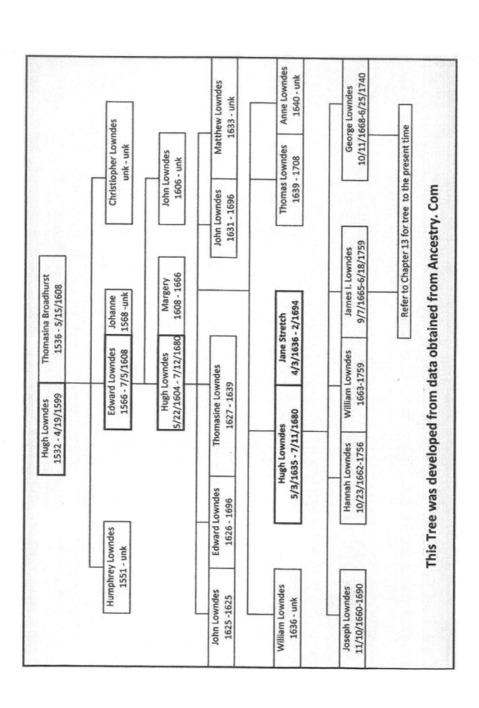

This Tree was developed from data obtained from Ancestry. Com

Hugh became acquainted with Jane Stretch, a Quaker, and sister to Thomas Stretch Hugh's best friend, who lived in the next village. As Hugh Lowndes and Thomas Stretch had been friends for a long time, and they had gone to another village on several occasions witnessing George Fox speak about the Lord.

It was believed that one evening after super, Hugh's father ordered him out of the house, since Hugh refused to sign the Oath of Abjugation because he followed the Quaker believes. Hugh went to Thomas's place for somewhere to go. Hugh then went to live in the back room of the bakery where he worked. Jane then joined him and they lived there for a short while. Hugh and Jane were married in Cheshire County, England, on October 2nd, 1658, at the home of William Davenport of Leeke Parish. Hugh and Jane both loved the Lord, their Savior, and adhered to the Quaker belief, although there were few Quakers in their village. In the early 1650s, the Quakers were stoned, flogged, and imprisoned for insisting that God dwelled within the believer in the person of the Holy Spirit. They believed that all men are equal in the sight of God. Their mission was to turn people from darkness to light by receiving Jesus Christ who died for all men as their Savior. They were attempting to help "build the Kingdom of Heaven on Earth." The grace of God who brings salvation teaches us to live godly, righteously-sober lives and deny ungodliness and worldly lusts. The Quakers refused to bear arms and tried to keep peace at any cost.

Many laws were passed in England to try to stop the spread of Quaker views. In 1655, everyone was required to take the Oath of Abjugation (an oath to give up their rights). Quakers refused to take the oath on scriptural principles (Matthew 5:35, 36). There were four laws passed which forbade the teaching of any but the Anglican catechism and forbade the assembling for the purpose of worship except the formal church. In 1661, the Quaker Act was announced,

Historian Green wrote, "The rectors and vicars driven out were the most learned and active of their order... with the expulsion of the Puritan clergy, all change, all efforts after reform, all rational development suddenly stopped...."

There was a spiteful refinement of cruelty in their expulsion. It was the day before the year's tithes would be paid. Thus, these godly men were cast adrift with no remuneration for their year's labor and no lodging for their loved ones.

Despite repeated fines and the responsibility of a growing family, Hugh continued to preach and live the teachings of the Gentle Way. He was a stubborn, faithful, persistent believer.

As strange as the Quaker doctrines may sound to our ears, surely we must agree that the early Quakers, at least the pioneer generation from 1650 to 1689, truly believed in the saving grace of God through the sacrifice of the Lord Jesus Christ for their sins. Today we call it being "born-again."

The famous William Penn and our humble Hugh Lowndes may likely have met in prison, possibly in 1669 (years later we shall see that Jane had another contact with Penn, much to her advantage).

Young William Penn, about the same age as Hugh, became a Quaker when he was a courtier in the court of King Charles II. He was convicted by the Holy Spirit at age twenty-three by the verse, "There is a faith that is overcome by the world and a faith that overcomes the world."

He wrote of his conversion, "Being ready to faint concerning my hope of the restitution of all things, it was at this time that the Lord visited me with a certain sound and testimony of His eternal word."

The qualities of the Quakers that fascinated Penn were their ability to judge lucidly and make forthright decisions, their integrity, their capacity for self-appraisal, and their absolute convincement.

Penn was attracted to George Fox because of the power of his message, that there was direct dealing between God and man. Writing of Fox, he said, "a most merciful man, as ready to forgive as unapt to take or give offense" and "a most engaging humility and moderation."

He came to know that, "Without a cross of suffering, there can be no crown of fulfillment." Penn also stated, "Ministers needed to be changed men themselves before they went about to change others."

William Penn was a great believer in discourse and communication. Most likely, he kept abreast of the steady stream of pamphlets and tracts printed by the Quakers. Most of them were arguments in defense of their faith or bitter denunciation of their detractors. Their titles were most extraordinary. One was called, "The Boasting Baptist Dismounted and the Beast Disarmed." A Quaker critic titled his tract, "The Quaker Quashed and his Quarrel Quelled."

Penn himself was an eloquent writer and pamphleteer. Possibly his most famous is "No Cross, No Crown," which he wrote when he was in the Tower of London in 1669 for his Anti-Trinitarianism doctrine. He was accused of elevating the Holy Spirit above the other members of the Trinity. Ordered to recant, he replied: "My prison shall be my grave before I shall budge a jot, for I owe my conscience to no mortal man."

After his conversion, Penn wrote that the main point of the Quaker belief was "the light of Christ written as God's gift for man's salvation."

This is followed by repentance from dead works to serve the living God… in other words, repent from the sight of sin, from the sorrow of sin, and make amendments for time to come. Following this, there is perfection from sin and finally eternal rewards and punishment.

Later he wrote that Quakers observe the following doctrine:

I	Communion and loving one another
II	To love one's enemies
III	Speak the truth with yea and nay without swearing

IV	No fighting
V	No title to a national church
VI	Not to respect persons (no flattering titles)
VII	Plain language (thee and thou)
VIII	Silence or few words
IX	Forbade drinking to people (no toasting)
X	That God alone can join two in marriage (no heathenish wedding ring but a simple self-wedding ceremony)
XI	No burial ceremony and no mourning dress (but a time to exhort the living)

The climax of all the persecution came in 1670. William Penn and William Meade were arrested for attending a meeting for worship at Grace Church Street, London, in defiance of the Conventicle Act. An unknown writer with the knowledge of shorthand took down the proceedings of the trial verbatim and published these immediately.

Meade and Penn were charged with causing a riot. Actually, they were preaching inside the locked doors of Grace Church Street Meeting House. The noise outside the place was so great; those people could not have known if the men were preaching or not. At the onset of the trial, Meade and Penn were trying to stay out of jail while defending the right of the Quakers to preach in public. But on September 1, 1670, by his skill, Penn set a precedent which established the independence of the jury systems forever.

John Sykes wrote a brief review of the matter in "The Quakers."

"William Penn and William Meade pleads 'Not Guilty,' and Penn spoke to such effect that he and Meade were ushered out of court, and the jury was instructed in their absence. Next, it was the jury's turn to offend. They returned, from the Crown's point of view, an unsatisfactory verdict. 'Gentlemen,' cried the recorder, 'you have not given in your verdict and you had as good day nothing. Therefore go and consider it once more ...,' They did so but again returned a verdict that would acquit Penn. 'Gentlemen,' pursued the recorder, now beside himself with rage, 'You shall not be dismissed 'till we have a verdict the Court will accept ....'

Penn, back at the bar, called out to fortify them, "You are Englishmen, mind your privilege, give not away your right."

"Nor will we ever do it," sturdily replied the jury foreman.

Nor did they. Shut up all night, bullied next day, finally thrown into Newgate, and fined for their pains, they still stood firm. Released on a writ of habeas corpus, they promptly sued the recorder for illegal imprisonment and won the case before a bench of twelve judges headed by the Lord Chief Justice and so established in English and American courts the right of independence of the jury. Bushel, the foreman, had nerved his colleagues, but the inspiration for the whole spirited stand had come from William Penn."

These were exciting but dreadful days in England. Hugh was in the midst of the controversy preaching and teaching from town to town, exhorting his Quaker brethren and possibly even writing pamphlets in defense of the Faith.

Hugh, Jane, and her brother, Thomas Stretch, had all been fined for holding Quaker meetings in nearby towns in northern England. They knew what they were doing. They knew the risks and the sure penalty. They also knew the spiritual rewards and their willingness, nay eagerness, to obey God far outweighed any possible fear of physical suffering.

The Act of Uniformity was viciously enforced in 1662. Perhaps it was at this time Hugh was jailed.

Imagine how Jane with her four children must have felt sailing for two months across the Atlantic in a boat like this. Their only hope was to have freedom from incarceration in England because of religious beliefs.

There must have been some personal contacts aboard the vessel, Friends Jane had known for years or met at other assemblies. Though the passage may have been crowded and difficult, surely there was rejoicing as they left the oppressions and bitterness of England for the promise of freedom in America.

Having arrived at Philadelphia, Jane and her family must have immediately made their way to Chester, a few miles south of the Philadelphia area. Possibly, Jane and her four children walked the entire twelve miles to Chester because even as late as 1724, only eight people owned carriages in Pennsylvania. Or perhaps they were fortunate enough to secure a barge or small boat to transport them down the beautiful Delaware River.

The name "Chester" alone would have drawn Jane there, since that is the name of the city where our beloved Hugh died in prison, but surely there were others from her corner of England already settled there.

Shortly afterward, Jane and her family walked to Springfield and found a beautiful spot of land with a gentle meadow, rolling hills, and a little stream later known as Lownes Run (much later, it was changed to Whiskey Run). They moved into a cave on this property, now known as Springfield. The Lenni Lenape Indians helped them find the cave and get through the first winter. Other families also lived in caves in this area, especially along the banks of the Delaware River.

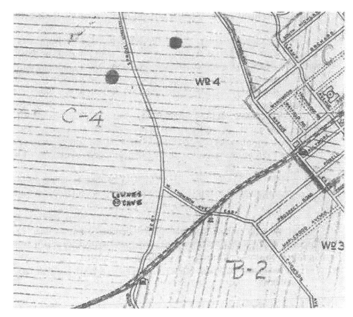

Old Map Showing Approximate Location of the Cave

Legend has it that Jane had a log cabin built first, and this has shown up in several documents, though not confirmed, before a stone house was built. It was stated that the log cabin was situated between Woodland Avenue and the house of Joseph Lownes Sr. The stone house was a one-over-one room house with the fireplace being in the lower level; it has been expanded into more than seventeen rooms and is the rectory for St. Kevin's Catholic Church located on Sproul Road behind the church. Part of the present house is the original building, and the one room still has the immense fireplace which was the heating system as well as the cook's stove. Jane had "more trouble with wildcats than the Indians" because she, as did the other Quakers in Pennsylvania, respected the rights of the aborigines and treated them with justice. Below is a picture of the fireplace in current times. You can see a kettle that could be similar to the one that Jane would have used.

Jane must have renewed her acquaintance with Mr. Penn at one of these meetings because on February 10, 1685, she patented one hundred fifty acres from William Penn, no doubt, the beautiful acreage surrounding her warm cave. William Penn was noted for not paying attention to details and may have had someone else file the papers for Jane's property.

Children of Hugh Lowndes and Jane Stretch (G 1)

Joseph Lowndes

Hugh Lowndes and Jane Stretch's first child was Joseph Lowndes, who never married. After arriving in America, he served as a juror in Chester County for four months in 1686 and was appointed constable for Springfield in 1687-1688. Later it is noted that Joseph drowned while fishing from a canoe when it capsized in the Darby Creek near Tinicum in 1690. Joseph Lowndes was born in England on November 10, 1660. No other information was available.

Hannah Lowndes

Hugh Lowndes and Jane Stretch's second child was Hannah Lowndes who married Thomas Collier at Darby in 1689. They had four children: Isaac Collier, Hannah Collier, Joseph Collier, and John Collier. Hannah Lowndes was born in England on October 23, 1662. No other information was available.

James I. Lowndes

Hugh Lowndes and Jane Stretch's third child was James I. Lowndes. He was born in England on September 7, 1665. He came to America with Jane and his two brothers and sister.

Jane must have been most pleased to know that her son James I. was made High Constable of Springfield Township, Chester County, in 1687 and 1688 at the age of twenty-two years old. Springfield Township is now part of Delaware County, Pennsylvania. Almost two hundred years later, another Lownes, a direct descendant named Walter B. Lownes Jr. was elected to serve twelve years as Justice of the Peace in Lower Merion Township, a few miles north of Chester. How history repeats itself.

James I. married Susannah Richards on October 9, 1692. Susannah's parents were Joseph and Jane Richards of Chichester, England. Joseph was a "Doctor of Fissicke." He moved to Philadelphia in about 1701. The Quaker records affirm that Susannah's father had his record of certificate entered in the Philadelphia Monthly Meeting in 1712. James I. and Susannah had six children: Joseph Lownes, Hannah Lownes, James Lownes, Susannah Lownes, Rebecca Lownes, and Mary Lownes.

Jane must have been most pleased that her son James I., at one point, must have traveled back to Chester. James was made Constable (probably Sheriff or Police Chief) of Chester in 1701 at the age of thirty-six. How long James I. remained High Constable is not recorded, but in 1711 at age forty-six, he moved his family twelve miles north, up the Delaware River to the city of Brotherly Love.

There were no more ties to the era of James's life in the cave. Jane died in 1694; Joseph was dead, and the other siblings remained in the Chester area. No doubt, his sister Hannah had married Thomas Collier and had her four children. What drew James I. to Philadelphia can only be surmised; Quaker records affirm that his and his family received a "Request of Certificate of Transfer" from Chester Monthly Meeting and was entered in the Philadelphia Quaker Monthly Meeting on January 31, 1712.

Philadelphia, at this time, was a fair city, full of busy industrious craftsmen. A young man named Benjamin Franklin had made his way from Boston to Philadelphia in 1723 when Joseph Lownes (G 3), Jane's grandson, was thirty years old.

James I. died at age ninety-four. The ledger also states his will was proved or filed in 1759 and that he died the same year. However, he lived long enough to see Joseph Lownes's generation three's eleven children born.

George Lowndes

Hugh Lowndes and Jane Stretch's fourth child was George Lowndes, who met a young woman by the name of Mary Bowers, daughter of Benanual and Elizabeth Bowers of Charlestown, Massachusetts. They were publicly whipped on the Boston Commons for possessing Quaker books. George Lownes and Mary Bowers declared their intention of marriage at Chester Monthly Meeting May 28, and on June 25, 1701, they were given permission to accomplish their marriage. They were married on June 25, 1701. Ironically, I, Howard G. Lownes Sr. married Verna M. Allebach, 259 years later on June 25, 1960. George Lownes and Mary Bowers had six children: Jane Lownes, Esther Lownes, Mary Lownes, Anne Lownes, George Lownes, and Benanuel Lownes.

George became owner of a homestead by deed dated November 18, 1715, and he and his wife built a house in 1717 at 61 W. Sproul Road, Springfield, Pennsylvania. The will of George Lownes was dated August 8, 1740, and proven December 5, 1740. To son George Lownes was given eighty acres of land where he lived. To son Benanuel Lownes, husband to Alice Williamson, was given one hundred fifty acres; to daughter Esther, wife of Samuel Ogden, was given £50; to daughter Anne, wife of George Maris, the interest of £100 was given during life, and the principal was to be divided amongst her children after her death. To daughter, Mary Lownes, was given £100, and grandson, Richard Maris, was given £5.

How pleased and content Jane must have been. Roots were going down in the new land. Jane was a true pioneer, tough and resilient but humble in the Lord. We know that her life and influence counted for much in early Springfield. Today there is a small wooded park there, named in her honor. The school children of the community learn about Jane Lownes, the persecuted Quaker lady who lived in the cave, and she is known as "The Pioneer Mother of Springfield."

In reviewing the generations of American Lownes's so far we note:

Generation 1.   Jane Lownes

2.   James, High Constable

It should be noted that after Jane with her children came to America they dropped the "d" from their name since they were the only Lownes family in America. Others came later as you will see.

Below will be some interesting facts about the Lownes family in those early years:

There is a park named in Jane's honor in a small sedtion of the origimal land patened from William Penn in 1685. Below is the entrance to that park.

On June 10, 2017, a Plaque was dedicated in Jane's honor. The plaque was dedicated telling her story, and was presented by a tenth generation, Howard G. Lownes Sr. and family.

This is a photograph of the plaque dedicated on June 10, 2017.

This plaque is mounted on one of the posts leading into the cemetery at the Springfield Meeting House property, in Springfield, Pennsylvania.

Jane was buried in the cemetery at the Springfield Friends Meeting House in Springfield, Pennsylvania.

This is the Springfield Friends Meeting House in Springfield, Pennslvania. The original was built in 1703 and was destroyed by a fire in 1737 and functioned as the meeting house for 113 years until it was replaced by the current structure in 1850.

This is a portion of a map of Philadelphia dated 1777, showing there once was a Lownes Alley that was south of Walnut Street, west of Second Street, east of Third Street, and between Pear and York which is part of an L- shaped street. It no longer exists as progress has torn down many buildings in Philadelphia for new high-rise buildings, etc.

In 1799, Jane's descendants placed a stone marker where the cave had been that Jane had lived in from 1684-1685. Below is a photograph of that marker.

This is the original stone marker where the cave was. It was moved to new location when that part of the property was being developed for new homes.

The original stone marker is now located in the Springfield Heritage Museum.

There is also a Lownes Lane in Springfield, Pennsylvania.

As we have noted, Jane bore the scars of her persecution. The memory of these scars touched her children, the second generation. But what did her grandchildren know of her suffering? How much did her children tell their children of the death of their father in prison?

How pleased and content Jane must have been! Her first grandson, Isaac Collier, was born on November 20, 1690. Her second grandson, Joseph Lownes, was born on January 30, 1693.

The records of the next few generations are sparse, but we do have the dates of births, marriages, and deaths of at least some of the sons and daughters of every generation down to the present (2020).

Later generations of Lowneses married Baptists and Lutherans, who had no impetus to keep detailed records as did the early Quakers. One cannot be too hard on these men. Great struggles were taking place in young America, and our Lownes ancestors were part of this growing country.

On a side note, it has been noted in several documents that there were at least two other branches of a Lowndes family here in the

United States, long after our Jane and her children came to America, both of whom came from Cheshire County, England. Since I have discovered fathers and grandfather's of our Hugh's family further back, but siblings of those men were not noted, it is possible that these two family's could still be related to our heritage. One is Christopher Lowndes of Bladensburg, Maryland, and the other, Rawlins Lowndes, settled in St. Kitts, British West Indies,then South Carolina.

The Baltimore sun on Sunday morning paper had an article about the Lowndes Family, distinguished Statesman in England and America. It was in the September 15, 22,and 29th and October 6, 1907 papers. It started by stating the Lowndes coat of arms as borne by William Lowndes of Bostock House in Hassall, in the county of Chester, son and heir of William Lowndes of Sandback, England. It goes on to state the coat of arms and crest by the Lowndes family's of North Carolina and Maryland, of which the late Governor Lowndes was a distinguished descendant are the same.

The English name of Lowndes is one of ancient origin and honorable record in England, and equally distinguished in the annuals of American statesmanship and in social life.

William Lowndes, of Bury Cheshire, made during his lifetime much research in England to several branches of the family. According to the pedigree of the Winslow branch, the first of the Lowndes name in England was William, Seigneur de Lounde, who accompanied William the Conqueror into Great Britain in 1006 and acquired large possessions in Buckinghamshire, North Hampttonshire, Lincolnshire and Bedfordshire in Middlewich and Sandbach, adjoining parishes in Cheshire, were early settled by the Lowndes family, which had become wealthy in the seventeenth century owing to success in operating salt mines upon their estates. From these mines worked for several centuries, an enormous amount of salt was sent out, both for home comsumption and foreign shipment.. Actually it was in 1066, and

William the conqueror became King of England on Christmas day of 1066.

There were many interesting Lowndes estates, including Bostock House and Hassall Hall, in Cheshire, There was also an estate in Overton Hall, located three milrs southeast of Bostock House. It is intesting to know that several of our ancestors where born in Bostock House and Overton Hall. Is there a connection? Not confirmed at this time, still researching.

The name Lowndes is variously spelled: Lounds, Lownes, Loundes, Lound, Lownde, Lownds, and Lowndes.

The article goes on through many generations of the Lowndes family in England. It states a Richard Lowndes, of Bostock House married Elizabeth Rawlins and a second marriage to Margery last name was unknown. There were four children by the first marriage, and one son John Lowndes by the second wife. It is interesting that John Lowndes shows up in our direct line back. Also a Richard Lowndes baptized in Sandbach.

These names and birth locations show up in the direct line of our ancestors. The Rawlins then was the Rawlins that went to St. Killis in the British West Indies. Rawlins then went to South Carolina where a son William Jones Lowndes became a distinguished lawyer and then representative of South Carolina.

These two have become famous in their own right.

The Lowndes family of South Carolina descends from Charles Lowndes, ninth child of John Lowndes, gentleman, of the Bostock House, in Cheshire. The Maryland Lowndes line descends from Richard Lowndes, of Bostock House, eldest son and heir of John Lowndes, gentleman, so that both familes descends from the same ancestor, John Lowndes, of Bostock House, with the Maryland branch having the distinction from the eldest son and heir.

The Maryland progenitor was Christopher Lowndes, fifth son of

Richard and Margaret (Poole) Lowndes, of Bostock House, in Hassall, Chester, England. He was the son of Richard Lowndes, eldest son and heir of John Lowndes, gentleman, of Bostock House. Christopher Lowndes was baptized at Sandbach, June 19, 1718, and died at Bladensberg, Prince George's County, MD., January 8, 1785

The Honorable Lloyd Lowndes was a graduate of the Law School of the University of Pennsylvania and early in life settled in Cunberland, Maryland. When he was only twenty eight years old he entered the forty-third Congress as its youngest member. He was the president of the Second National Bank of Cumberland and an officer in many important companies. He was a member and vestryman of the Episcopal Church, from which he was frequently sent as a delegate to the diocesan convention. He was a man of large wealth and a generous contributor to public and private enterprices.

Perhaps one of the most interesting branches of the Lowndes family now found in Maryland is the line whose earliest known ancestor, Hugh Lowndes, suffered death for conscience' sake. The father of Hugh Lowndes was either Christopher (Hugh) Lowndes, who, according to tradition, disinherited his son for his Quaker principles. All the family traditions link the South Carolina, the Maryland and the Virginia familes of the Lowndes name in the tie of kinship, and the date of their united settling in the American colonies and the recurrence of baptismal names common to all would indicate the same.The descendants of Hugh Lowndes came first to Pennsylvania and the story of their coming is best told by an inherited. Manuscript treasured in the family, which was written by James Lowndes, of Philadelphia, Pennsylvania, who died in the latter city, December, 1831, aged 91 years.

Lloyd Lowndes Jr. (February 21, 1845–January 8, 1905) was the son of Lloyd Lowndes and great-grandson of Christopher Lowndes (1703–1785) who settled in Bladensburg, Maryland. Christopher Lowndes was the fifth son of Richard Lowndes of Bostock House in Hassall, Cheshire, England. He was an early settler in Prince George County, Maryland, and the great-grandfather of Lloyd Lowndes Jr. Lloyd Jr. was a U.S. congressman and then governor of Maryland from January 8, 1896 – January 10, 1900.

Lloyd Lowndes Jr.

43rd Governor of Maryland

Rawlins Lowndes (January 6, 1721–August 24, 1800) was born on the island of St. Kitts in the British West Indies. At the age of twenty-one, he was appointed as the Provost-Marshall of South Carolina. On March 4, 1778, South Carolina General Assembly elected him president of South Carolina after John Rutledge. He first changed the title of president to governor of South Carolina on March 19, 1778. Since then South Carolina has dropped the title of president, to govenenor. His son, William Jones Lowndes (February 11, 1782–October 12, 1822), was elected to the U.S. Congress in 1811 to 1822. Lowndes Counties in Georgia (1825), Alabama

(1830), and Mississippi (1830) were created in his honor. On July 18, 1944, a Haskell-class attack transport ship was launched and acquired by the U.S. Navy during World War II and was named USS Lowndes Number 154, after the three states with Lowndes Counties.

USS Lowndes

USS Lowndes Haskill-class attack transport in Manila, Philippines

From here through the next number of generations will be separate chapters of each generation down to generation fifteen. Since records of Hugh and Jane's daughter Hannah have been difficult to locate, there is nothing more to add at this time.

CHAPTER THREE

Generation Three

Children of Hannah Lownes and Thomas Collier (G 2)

Isaac Collier

Hannah Lownes and Thomas Collier's first child was Isaac Collier, who was married (wife's name is unknown) in Darby, Pennsylvania. He and his wife had five children: Hannah Collier, Rebecca Collier, Isaac Collier, Elizabeth Collier, and James Collier. Isaac Collier was born on November 20, 1690. No other information was available.

Hannah Collier

Hannah Lownes and Thomas Collier's second child was Hannah Collier, who married Mordecai Thompson on September 28, 1741 in Darby, Pennsylvania. Hannah Collier was born on November 10, 1693. No other information was available.

Joseph Collier

Hannah Lownes and Thomas Collier's third child was Joseph Collier. He was born in 1696. No other information was available.

John Collier

Hannah Lownes and Thomas Collier's fourth child was John Collier. He was born in 1703. No other information was available.

THIS SECOND GROUP OF DESCENDANTS IS FROM THE JAMES I. LOWNES AND SUSANNAH RICHARDS'S BRANCH OF THE FAMILY

Children of James I. Lownes and Susannah Richards (G 2)

Joseph Lownes

James I. Lownes and Susannah Richards' first child was Joseph Lownes. Joseph Lownes was born on January 30, 1693. He was eight years old when the family moved from Chester, Pennsylvania, in 1701 to Philadelphia, Pennslvania. It was in bustling Philadelphia that Joseph entered the medical field. It may have been due to the influence of his maternal grandfather, Dr. Joseph Richards, that he soon became known as a "Practitioner of Physic." He probably spent ten years as an apprentice. Joseph followed his father and grandfather in the order process of the wedding tradition of the Quakers. At the age of twenty-eight he married twenty-one year old Sarah Tidmarch at the Philadelphia Monthly Meeting on April 30, 1721. Sarah's father was William Tidmarch of Chipping Norton, Oxfordshire, England.

Joseph Lownes and Sarah Tidmarch had eleven children: Ann Lownes, John Lownes, Susannah Lownes, Joseph Lownes, Sarah Lownes, Hannah Lownes, William Lownes, Rebecca Lownes, James Lownes, Mary Lownes, and Jane Lownes. James I. Lownes lived long enough to see Joseph's eleven children born.

It is entirely possible that Joseph's family read the *Philadelphia Gazette* that Benjamin Franklin purchased and published in 1729. (This magazine subsequently became known as the *Saturday Evening Post*). Three years later, Benjamin Franklin began publishing his famous *Poor Richard's Almanac*. This, too, the Lownes family may have read, unless the rigid Quaker teachings forbade reading this type of literature.

Hannah Lownes

James I. Lownes and Susannah Richards' second child was Hannah Lownes, who was reported married to Nehemiah Allen Jr. on August 31, 1718. Hannah Lownes was born on November 13, 1695. No other information was available.

James Lown Jr.

(note the "es" was dropped)

James I. Lownes and Susannah Richards' third child was James Lown Jr., who married Sarah Forester on June 27, 1736; was condemned due to marrying out of unity at the Philadelphia Monthly Meeting on June 27, 1736. They had one child, John Lown (James Lown had changed the spelling of the last name when he headed west). James Lown Jr. was born in 1697. No other information was available.

Susannah Lownes

James I. Lownes and Susannah Richards' fourth child was Susannah Lownes, who married out of unity at the Philadelphia Monthly Meeting on August 29, 1731; no husband's name was available. Susannah Lownes was born on June 13, 1703. No other information was available.

Rebecca Lownes

James I. Lownes and Susannah Richards' fifth child was Rebecca Lownes, who married Job Yarnall, son of Phillip Yarnall of Chester

County on August 13, 1737 at the Philadelphia Monthly Meeting. Rebecca Lownes was born on September 18, 1705. No other information was available.

Mary Lownes

James I. Lownes and Susannah Richards' sixth child was Mary Lownes, who married Phillips Coudemas, contrary to discipline on November 27, 1743. Mary Lownes was born on November 7, 1712. No other information was available.

—◆—

THIS THIRD GROUP OF DESCENDANTS IS FROM THE GEORGE LOWNES AND MARY BOWERS'S BRANCH OF THE FAMILY

Children of George Lownes and Mary Bowers' (G 2)

Jane Lownes

George Lownes and Mary Bowers' first child was Jane Lownes, who married Johanthan Maris; they had one child, Richard Maris. She then married Joseph Burn in 1744. She was born on January 10, 1702. No other information was available.

Esther Lownes

George Lownes and Mary Bowers' second child was Esther Lownes, who married Samuel Ogden on March 26, 1720. Esther Lownes was born on July 2, 1703. No other information was available.

Anne Lownes

George Lownes and Mary Bowers' third child was Anne Lownes, who married George Maris II on September 14, 1732. They had one child, Richard Maris. Ann Lownes was born on August 1, 1707. No other information was available.

George Lownes II

George Lownes and Mary Bowers' fourth child was George Lownes II, who married Elizabeth Mordegai Maddock on May 21, 1734. Elizabeth was the daughter of Mordecai Maddock of Springfield, Pennsylvania. They had eleven children: Slater Lownes, Rebecca Lownes, Curtis Lownes, George Bolton Lownes, Mary Lownes, James Lownes, Jean Lownes, Sarah Lownes, Rebecca Lownes, Francis Lownes, and Esther Lownes. George Lownes II was born on February 28, 1708. George was a blacksmith; he built his forge in the basement of the house. That house still stands and is located at 201 E. Thomson Ave. Springfield, Pennsylvania, at the corner of Thomson and Powell Roads. The house was built by a professional stone mason and in four stages. The first was a one-over-one structure with the original random width board, as well as the walk-in fireplace. The Lownes Tenant House was named "Stonelea" in 1929. There once was a winding stairway to the second floor that was removed during reconstruction to restore the house. Originally, there were only two windows having sixteen panes, as glass windows were expensive in the eighteenth century. The original size of the house was sixteen by fifteen feet. Over the years with the restoration, it was made larger. The property was part of a 108 acre tract that included a blacksmith shop operated by his father, George Lownes. The land on which the house stands was in the Lownes family from 1718 to 1920. A woman named Emily Pollard bought the property in 1929 and restored it, adding new additions, and she named it "Stonelea" in the English custom.

"Stonelea"/Lownes Tenant House
(201 East Thomson Ave.)

Benanuel Lownes

George Lownes and Mary Bowers' fifth child was Benanuel Lownes, who married Alice Williamson on May 20, 1744; she was the daughter of John and Sarah Williamson of Newtown. They were married at the Goshen Meeting House, Chester County, Pennsylvania. They had eight children: Benanuel Lownes, Sarah Lownes, Alice Lownes, Mary Lownes, George Lownes III, Joseph Lownes, Hannah Lownes, and Hugh Lownes. Benanuel Lownes was born in 1720.

The grandson of Springfield's pioneer mother, Mrs. Jane Lownes, owned the house known as "The Happiness House," the quaint stone cottage on Paper Mill Rd. Springfield, Pennsylvania, at Lownes Run (now called Whiskey Run). Benanuel Lownes was the first owner of the house, and he selected a site not far from where his grandmother established a home, in a cave, when she came to America from England. It was nestled against a wooded hill and was once a grist mill. Records show that there were many births there, but no one died

in it since it was built in 1751. The natural setting is peaceful, in spite
of the nearness to Baltimore Pike, and the creek babbles over rocky
ledges fringed with ferns and overhanging aspens. The ancient stone
walls of the house are the gems of early craftsmen, and the mellowed
quaintness is typical of a well loved dwelling. George Bolton Lownes
had a blade mill there too. It has been stated that it was originally a
grist mill where corn was ground. It also was known as the Jones' Mill.
It later became a wheel house to pump water to the house on top of the
hill. Pipes are still buried in the hill. (This data came from Ethel McNeil
Wolf dated 12-7-1986). She lived there for sixty–two years.

"HAPPINESS HOUSE," home of Mr. and Mrs. John Wolff, 27 E. Paper Mill Road, once
the Jones Mill. Mill machinery is still in the cellar. It was built by Samuel Lownes in
1752.

Benanuel Lownes, the grandson of Springfield's "Pioneer Mother,"
Mrs. Jane Lownes, owned "Happiness House," the quaint stone
cottage on Paper Mill Road beside Whiskey Run. In his will of 1772, he
mentioned it as "my new house."

The Delaware County Turnpike, or Baltimore Pike as it is identified
today, was laid out in 1701. Conestoga wagons on their way southward
traversed it, and at one time, the pike was paved with wooden planks.

Folks in the "Happiness House" must have climbed the winding lane in the early days to wave to occasional stage coaches that passed, and weary travelers must have rested at the junction of the run and Crum Creek near the house. Long before the building was erected, there was a large Indian wigwam near the run and others along the creek.

The house was believed to be built by Benanuel Lownes, although the caption states Samuel Lownes. The house's deeds have been removed from the court house; it was owned at one time by William and Anna Garnett, his wife.

Both Benanuel Lownes and Alice Lownes are buried at Springfield Friends Meeting Cemetery.

CHAPTER FOUR

Generation Four

THIS FIRST GROUP OF DESCENDANTS IS FROM HANNAH LOWNES AND HOMAS COLLIER'S BRANCH OF THE FAMILY

Children of Hannah Lownes and Thomas Collier (G 3)

Isaac Collier

Hannah Lownes and Thomas Collier's first child was Isaac Collier who married (name was not available) they had five children: Hannah Collier, Rebecca Collier, Isaac Collier, Elizabeth Collier, and James Collier. Isaac Collier was born on November 20, 1690. No other information was available.

Hannah Collier

Hannah Lownes and Thomas Collier's second child was Hannh Colllier, who married Mordecai Thompson on September 28.1741. Hannah Lownes was born on November 10, 1693. No other information was available.

Joseph Collier

Hannah Lownes and Thomas Collier's third child was Joseph Collier. He was born in 1696 and died in 1748. No other information was available.

John Collier

Hannah Lownes and Thomas Collier's fourth child was John Collier. He was born in 1703 and died in 1755. No other information was available.

THIS SECOND GROUP OF DESCENDENTS IS FROM THE JAMES I. LOWNES AND SUSANNAH RICHARDS'S BRANCH OF THE FAMILY

Children of Joseph Lownes and Sarah Tidmarch (G 3)

Ann Lownes

Joseph Lownes and Sarah Tidmarch's first child was Ann Lownes, who married John Page, son of George Page, on March 24, 1744 at the Philadelphia Monthly eting. There were no children recorded. After John died, Ann Lownes married Thomas James. No other information was available.

John Lownes

Joseph Lownes and Sarah Tidmarch's second child was John Lownes. He was a Philadelphia seaman and active in the relief of impoverished ship captains; he married Agnes Cowpland, daughter of Caleb and Sarah Cowpland, on August 24, 1753, at the Chester Monthly Meeting. Agnes received certification from Chester Monthly Meeting on December 31, 1753. They had ten children: Caleb Lownes, Sarah Lownes, Joseph Lownes, David Lownes, Grace Lownes, John Lownes, Agnes Lownes, Agnes Lownes, Elizabeth Lownes, and Hannah Lownes. No other information was available.

Susannah Lownes

Joseph Lownes and Sarah Tidmarch's third child was Susannah Lownes, who married James Lindley of Philadelphia, Peensylvania on July 12, 1745. She was reported to have married out of unity. No other information was available.

Joseph Lownes

Joseph Lownes and Sarah Tidmarch's fourth child was Joseph Lownes, who married Hannah Robinson, daughter of Edward Robinson, on December 15, 1757 at the Philadelphia Monthly Meeting. They had one son, James Lownes. No other information was available.

Sarah Lownes

Joseph Lownes and Sarah Tidmarch's fifth child was Sarah Lownes, who married Jonathan Shoemaker, son of Jacob Shoemaker of Philadelphia, on October 20, 1757 at the Philadelphia Monthly Meeting. They had one child, Joseph Shoemaker. No other information was available.

Hananah Lownes

Joseph Lownes and Sarah Tidmarch's sixth child was Hannah Lownes, who married Joshua Pancoast son of Samuel Pancoast on May 7, 1761, at the Philadelphia Monthly Meeting. They had two children: Ann Pancoast and Hannah Pancoast. No other information was available.

William Lownes

Joseph Lownes and Sarah Tidmarch's seventh child was William Lownes, who married Rebecca Elwell, daughter of David Elwell of Philadelphia, on May 6, 1762, at the Philadelphia Monthly Meeting. They had five children: Joseph Lownes, Mary Lownes, Daniel Lownes, William Lownes Jr. and James Lownes. He then married Rachel Fell on May 13, 1784. They had no children. Rachel died September 1, 1784. He then married Mary Whitson on December 16, 1790; she died August 23, 1807. They had no children. No other information was available.

Rebecca Lownes

Joseph Lownes and Sarah Tidmarch's eighth child was Rebecca Lownes, who married Caleb Ash on April 20, 1768. They had eight children: Joshua Ash, Joseph Ash, Sarah Ash, Alice Ash, Caleb Ash, Thomas Ash, Elizabeth Ash, and William Ash. Rebecca was condemned for marrying contrary to discipline. One child died at fifty, two others about sixty, two over eighty, one eighty-seven, one eighty eight and one age ninety five. No other information was available.

James Lownes

Joseph Lowndes and Sarah Tidmarch's ninth child was James Lownes. He, no doubt, grew up in the Philadelphia area, but a young lady from Burlington, New Jersey, Sarah Pancoast, captured his heart, and they were married on November 3, 1763, at the Philadelphia Monthly Meeting which was held in Burlington, New Jersey. Sarah was the daughter of William Pancoast. This marriage took place two years after Sarah's older brother, Joshua Pancoast, married James's sister, Hannah Lownes.

James was a tanner in Passyunk, New Jersey (Passyunk is now Audubon, New Jersey). The couple stayed in New Jersey until after the Revolutionary War ended. James and Sarah had ten children: Mary Lownes, Sarah Lownes, Hyatt Lownes, John Lownes, Deborah Lownes, James Lownes, Caleb Lownes, Jane Lownes, Joseph Lownes, and William Lownes . The family was granted certificate to transfer to Hopewell, Virginia, on December 31, 1779. From there, they reported to transfer to Fairfax, Virginia, on December 22, 1792. At one point, they occupied the property in Richmond, Virginia, where the Richmond Court House is located. When in Richmond, it was known that he had one thousand slaves on that property. Later, James married Ann Robinson, a widow, on July 14, 1803. Ann died on June 6, 1833. James and his son, Caleb, returned to Philadelphia; apparently, the other children remained in Virginia. This Caleb was a cousin of Caleb, the engraver.

On January 9, 1832, *Poulsona American Daily Advertiser* printed the following obituary for James Lownes:

> "Died in this city, on December 10, 1831, James Lownes, in the ninety first year of his age. He married early in life and settled in Philadelphia, where he was a native. About the year 1779, he removed with his family to Winchester, Virginia and afterward to Richmond, Virginia. As a resident of Richmond, Virginia, he was deservedly respected by all of the inhabitants, particularly by his fellow members of the Society of Friends, for the general consistency of his conduct and demeanor and his undeviating attachment to the principles and institutions of the society.
>
> He set an example which he set in regularity in attendance of its religious meetings. In autumn of 1830, he, with his wife, spent the remainder of his life in this city, surrounded by his relatives and descendants, including a number of the third and fourth generations. His general health had declined considerably, yet not to prevent the enjoyment of frequent visits to his relations, and especially to a beloved sister, even more advanced in years than him.
>
> He likewise continued to attend religious meetings, unless when prevented by indisposition or by inclement weather, although hard of hearing, he was able to

collect the sense of anything verbally communicated; as on one occasion, he signified to an acquaintance, this seeming disadvantage was more than made up to him, by mental participation of the spiritual refreshment which is beyond all mere words. It became obvious to those in habits of intercourse with him, that his mind, for some time past, was secretly preparing for the final change, of the near approach of which he seemed in daily anticipation, and at the last visit he made to the sister before mentioned, on going away, he affectionately embraced her, intimating it would be the last time they should see each in mutability, but that he trusted they would surely meet again in another and better world.

With the exception already mentioned, his understanding and faculties, in a remarkable degree remained unimpaired. His last illness was short but without alarm. Toward the close his nurse reminding him of taking medicine, he said that he needed no more, and in answer to an inquiry by her, he further said, in substance, that his confidence was in Jesus Christ his Saviour and Redeemer, and that his peace was made and his work was done.

James died at Rebecca's residence in Christian St. Southwark on the morning of the eleventh ultimo in the ninety-fourth year of her age. Rebecca Ash also a respected member of the Society of Friends, sister to the above named James Lownes and widow of Caleb Ash, grazier, who died of yellow fever in 1797 in the same house, in the manner as the above James Lownes."

Mary Lownes

Joseph Lownes and Sarah Tidmarch's tenth child was Mary Lownes, who married John Bacon, a British officer and son of John and Elizabeth Bacon, on February 24, 1764, at the Philadelphia Monthly Meeting. They had two children: John Lownes, and another child un-named. No other information was available.

Jane Lownes

Joseph Lownes and Sarah Tidmarch's eleventh child was Jane Lownes, who was never married. No other information was available.

Children of James Lownes and Sarah Forester (G 3)

John Lown

(Note the "es" was dropped from the name)

James Lownes and Sarah's only child was John Lown, who married Catherine Baumgartine in 1789. They had a farm in Cherry Run, Virginia. John died in Martinberg, Virginia (now Martinsburg, West Virginia). John Lown signed a loyalty oath of Allegian in 1778 in York, Pennsylvania. The document was #414. No other information was available.

It should be noted that John, as he ventured west, dropped the "es" from the last name for reasons unknown.

This Second Group of Descendants is From the George Lownes and Mary Bowers's Branch of the Family

Children of George Lownes II and Elizabeth Mordegai Maddock (G 3)

Slater Lownes

George Lownes II and Elizabeth Mordegai Maddock's first child was Slater Lownes, who married Eleanor Cox on August 31, 1778. They had one child, Clarissa Lownes. No other information was available.

Rebecca Lownes

George Lownes II and Elizabeth Mordegai Maddock's second child was Rebecca Lownes, who was "a venerable lady" and remained unmarried, dying about 1845. She is buried at St. Paul's Cemetery in Chester, Pennsylvania. No other information was available.

Curtis Lownes

George Lownes II and Elizabeth Mordegai Maddock's third child was Curtis Lownes, who married Grace Lownes on December 21, 1794 they had two children: John Lownes and Agnes Lownes. Curtis was a scythe maker and operated a stone mill which later became a carding mill in 1816. He died of cancer and is buried at St. Paul's Church in Chester, Pennsylvania. When Grace died in 1813 leaving him with two children, Curtis moved Philadelphia to Springfield. He lived with his sister in the old Lownes/Powell homestead at the corner of Thompson and Powell Road for the rest of his life. No other information was available.

George Bolton Lownes

George Lownes II and Elizabeth Mordegai Maddock's fourth child was George Bolton Lownes, who was born in a little room on the first floor on the west corner of the Lownes' homestead on Thompson Road, part of the original property owned by his father, George.

The story of the origination of the name Bolton was told to Joseph Lownes by George B. "Samuel Bolton of Maryland was a friend of George B's father. When he was born, his father gave him his friend's name as a middle name, hence George Bolton Lownes." George Bolton Lownes married Hannah Lawrence, daughter of Joshua Lawrence of Springfield. Hannah was buried with her family at the Springfield Friends Meeting. George owned one thousand acres in Springfield, Pennsylvania.

Below is a picture of George Bolton Lownes's farm house called the Shady Bank Farm, or sometimes it was called the Clover Crest Farm.

George was an overseer of the poor and did much good with his money, donating two acres of land from part of his farm for The Blue Church, which he founded in 1832. He planned and built a solid structure of native blue limestone, unpretentious, but beautiful in its simplicity and built to endure. He protected it from external misuse by a stone wall surrounding it and of a creed which he had hung in a prominent place in the interior. It was free for all to use who would comply with this deed of trust, hence its name, "Lownes' Free Church." Because of the blue tint of the limestone, the church was known almost from the time of its construction as The Blue Church. (The Lownes Free Church is located on Baltimore Pike in Springfield, Pennsylvania).

George Bolton Lownes's tombstone is in a small cemetery plot near the entrance of the church, and it reads, "An honest man and a useful citizen." He left his home farm of 122 acres to his namesake, George Bolton II, when young George was nine years old. George B. Lownes II owned the property from 1834 to 1923, when he died at ninety eight years old.

This picture of The Blue Church was taken in 2017.

This is the grave marker of George Bolton Lownes, located in front of The Blue Church on Baltimore Pike, Springfield, Pennsylvania.

Children of Benanuel Lownes and Alice Williamson (G 3)

Benanuel Lownes

Benanuel Lownes and Alice Williamson's first child was Benanuel Lownes, was born in Springfield, Pennsylvania, who never married. Benanuel Lownes was born on October 20, 1773 and he died on November 29, 1773. No other information was available.

Sarah Lownes

Benanuel Lownes and Alice Williamson's second child was Sarah Lownes, who married Ebenezer Reynolds; they had one son, name unknown. No other information was available.

Alice Lownes

Benanuel Lownes and Alice Williamson's third child was Alice Lownes, who married William Temple; they had four children: Thomas Temple,

Mary Temple, William Temple, and Alice Temple. She then married John Pennock; they had two children: Marshall Pennock and Ruth Pennock. No other information was available.

Mary Lownes

Benanuel Lownes and Alice Williamson's fourth child was Mary Lownes, who married William Levis; they had two children: Alice Levis and William Levis. Then she married Joseph Taylor; they had three children: Joseph Taylor, Sarah Taylor, and Lownes Taylor. Joseph Taylor was the bother of Elizabeth Taylor. No other information was available.

George Lownes III

Benanuel Lownes and Alice Williamson's fifth child was George Lownes III, a Quaker who married Elizabeth Taylor on July 29 sister of Joseph Taylor, 1780; they had three children: George Lownes IV who was granted certificate to Wilmington Monthly Meeting, Maria Lownes, and Sarah Lownes. 1860 census listed Elizabeth Lownes owning a farm worth $4,200 and personal property worth $12,000. No other information was available.

Joseph Lownes

Benanuel Lownes and Alice Williamson's sixth child was Joseph Lownes. Joseph was a Quaker, although he was a major in 6th Company, 3rd Battalion in the Revolutionary War on May 14, 1777. He was dismissed from the Quaker meeting but reinstated after the war.

There is a story about a sword that he carried in the war. It was sold at George Bolton's sale to Ira Burdsall, who owned the Oakdale Store (across from the present site of the Springfield Mall on Baltimore Pike in Springfield, Pennsylvania).

Hannah Lownes

Benanuel Lownes and Alice Williamson's seventh child was Hannah Lownes. No other information was available.

Hugh Lownes

Benanuel Lownes and Alice Williamson's eighth child was Hugh Lownes, a Quaker who married Rebecca Rhodes; they had four children: Benanuel Lownes III who never married, Elizabeth Lownes II who never married, Sydney Lownes who never married, and Joseph Lownes. Hugh was a tanner and also was dismissed from meeting in 1784 for military action in the Revolutionary War. No other information was available.

Sarah Lownes

Benanuel Lownes and Alice Williamson's ninth child was Sarah Lownes, who never married. No other information was available.

Alice Lownes

Benanuel Lownes and Alice Williamson's tenth child was Alice Lownes, who married, (name was not available). No other information was available.

Mary Lownes

Benanuel Lownes and Alice Williamson's eleventh child was Mary Lownes, who married, (name was not available), they had one child; Alice Lownes. No other information was available.

CHAPTER FIVE

Generation Five

THIS FIRST GROUP OF DESCENDANTS IS FROM THE JAMES I. LOWNES AND SUSANNAH RICHARDS'S BRANCH OF THE FAMILY.

Children of John Lownes and Agnes Cowpland (G 4)

Caleb Lownes

John Lownes and Agnes Cowpland's first child was Caleb Lownes, who married Margaret Robeson on December 31, 1790. They had four children: Edward Lownes, George Bolton Lownes, John Lownes, and Catherine Lownes.

Caleb Lownes, Margaret (Robeson) Lownes, and their children, Edward, George, and John, were granted certificate to the North Division Monthly Meeting on December 30, 1796. (Catherine died before this date). Caleb was a Quaker and an iron merchant at 16 North Street and 21 South Wharves in Philadelphia, Pennsylvania, where he had connections with Thomas Jefferson. Caleb was supplying him with iron for his nail-making until Thomas Jefferson found him unreliable in his deliveries and switched suppliers in 1796.

At the age of twenty-one, Caleb designed the "New Plan for Boston Harbor." As an engraver, he made a definite contribution to the creation and development of the Commonwealth of Pennsylvania's Coat of Arms in 1778; it was officially adopted by the Legislature on

March 17, 1875. The commission appointed reported: "They have adopted the arms as represented by Caleb Lownes in 1778." There is a stone depicting the coat of arms surmounting the doorway of Congress Hall (6th and Chestnut Streets) in Philadelphia. It was home to the U.S. Congress from 1790 to 1800, when Philadelphia served as the temporary capital of the United States. Several historic achievements happened within Congress Hall, including the establishment of the First Bank of the United States, the Federal Mint and the Department of the Navy, as well as the ratification of Jay's Treaty with England.

It is unknown for sure who carved it or how it was made, but the coat of arms was an early version of Caleb's work.

The following is a picture showing the stone.

Photo of original bas-relief of the Coat of Arms of Pennsylvania created by Caleb Lownes

This is the stone over the doorway of the Congress Hall at 6th and Chestnut Street in Philadelphia.

This is Caleb's early design. Notice the position of the horses' heads, the ship in the middle, and that the plow and eagle's wings are different than the adopted coat of arms. The Adopted Coat of Arms was derived from this design.

This can be verified by going on the internet and looking up "The Coat of Arms of Pennsylvania." It states that the adopted Coat of Arms was derived from Caleb's design.

Caleb Lownes was a selfless public servant of his day, working as an Indian agent for the Federal government in Indian Territory with headquarters at Vincennes, Indiana. He was a man of many talents.

He was a prison reformer who participated in and managed for ten years the affairs of the Walnut Street Jail in Philadelphia, Pennsylvania, the city's jail from 1773 to 1838. In 1790, the penitentiary was added. The word penitentiary came from the Pennsylvania Quakers' belief in penitence and self-examination as a means to salvation. This became a new and permanent form of combating crime through the practice of solitary confinement, which was adopted at the Eastern State Penitentiary when it became the first state prison in the United States. Active in civic affairs, Caleb became a penal reformer who, in the 1790s, played a leading role as a creator and administrator of the innovative state penitentiary on Walnut Street. He served as secretary of the citizens' committee which cared for the sick for Mayor Matthew Clarkson's tenure; Clarkson took charge of the city during the yellow fever plague of 1793.

Caleb was charged not only to carry on the affairs of the stricken city but also to deal with all phases of relief work. He also supervised the pest-house at Bush Hill under the personal direction of Steven Girard, a noted ship-owner and philanthropist. He also dealt with the burial of the dead, collection of food, articles needed at the hospital, and, above all, money to take care of the endless requests for help. A heavy burden fell on Caleb Lownes. It was his job to execute orders and translate the resolutions into actions. He kept a perfect record of every person admitted to the pest-house and went about the city seeking beds. It was, for instance, Lownes who directed the activities of Stephen Girard and others who slaved at the make-shift hospital-pest-house.

Caleb Lownes was also a charter member of the Philadelphia Society for Alleviating the Miseries of Public Prisons. He was one of the thirty-seven who signed its constitution at its first meeting on the evening of May 7, 1787. One other notable fact was that Caleb Lownes was given credit in another form, far from Philadelphia. At the Third International Penal and Penitentiary Congress, held in Rome in 1885, a souvenir volume was presented to the delegates attending. One of the features of this ornate work, bound in white leather and dedicated to President Grover Cleveland, was a list of the "masters" in the fields of criminology, penology, and administration. The great and near great are listed, and among them is Caleb Lownes.

Sarah Lownes

John Lownes and Agnes Cowpland's second child was Sarah Lownes; she was born on June 18, 1756, and died on September 17, 1757. No other information was available.

Joseph Lownes

John Lownes and Agnes Cowpland's third child was Joseph Lownes, who married Esther Middleton, daughter of Abel and Mary Middleton at the Philadelphia Monthly Meeting on January 12, 1786. Joseph became a silversmith, founding the Philadelphia SilverSmith Company; Joseph was in partnership with his son Josiah from 1817-1820.

Below are some of the pieces that Joseph Lownes the silverswith produced in his lifetime.

Tradecard, c 1790 advertised in the *Federal Gazettwe,* April 2, 1792, announcing"Joseph Lownes, Goldsmith, No. 130 South Front street, near the Drawbridge.

Cup, c 1795

Caddy spoon, c 1800

Teapot, c 1800

Creamer, c 1810

Soup tureen, c 1810
Part of a nine suite of serving dishes commissioned
by Secretary of the Navy Benjamin Crownshield

Tankard, c 1810

Joseph was a partner in 1816 with Henry Erwin in Philadelphia, Pennsylvania as LOWNES & ERWIN. Joseph later was a partner from 1817 to 1820 with Josiah Hewes Lownees his son, in Philadelphia, Pennsylvania..

Joseph Lownes and Esther were granted certificate at Southern District Monthly Meeting. Later, Joseph Lownes received certificate at the Northern Monthly Meeting on December 23, 1800.

Joseph and Esther had four children: Agnes Lownes, Josiah Lownes, Esther Lownes, and Martha Lownes.

David Lownes

John Lownes and Agnes Cowpland's fourth child was David Lownes; he was allegedly unmarried but had three children: Rebecca Lownes, Edmond Lownes, and Hannah Lownes. David was disjoining others in military expeditions. There is a record of "An essay of a certificate for David Lownes directed to the Monthly Meeting of Friends of Grace Church Street or elsewhere in London being prepared and approved and signed by the Meeting." This was at the Philadelphia Monthly

Meeting on October 5, 1790. David Lownes was born on January 16, 1760. No other information was available.

Grace Lownes

John Lownes and Agnes Cowpland's fifth child was Grace Lownes, who married her cousin, Curtis Lownes, on December 21, 1794, of the George Lownes's branch. Curtis was a scythe-maker. They had two children: John Lownes and Agnes Lownes. Grace was disowned due to marrying out of unity. Grace was born on January 226, 1762. No other information was available.

John Lownes

John Lownes and Agnes Cowpland's sixth child was John Lownes. He was born December 20, 1763, and died August 11, 1765. No other information was available.

Agnes Lownes

John Lownes and Agnes Cowpland's seventh child was Agnes Lownes. She was born on August 21, 1766, and died on July 27, 1788. No other information was available.

Agnes Lownes

John Lownes and Agnes Cowpland's eighth child was Agnes Lownes. She was born August 21, 1773, and died September 22, 1793. No other information was available.

Elizabeth Lownes

John Lownes and Agnes Cowpland's ninth child was Elizabeth Lownes, who married Samuel Huggins on May 4, 1820. They had four children: Curtis Huggins, Emily Huggins, Margaret Huggins, and Esther Huggins.

Elizabeth Lownes was born on December 19, 1798. She died two days old. No other information was available.

Hannah Lownes

John Lownes and Agnes Cowpland's tenth child was Hannah Lownes. She was born on February 21, 1799, and died two days later. No other information was available.

Child of Joseph Lownes and Hannah Robinson (G 4)

James Lownes

Joseph Lownes and Hannah Robinson child was James Lownes. No other information was available.

Child of Sarah Lownes and Jonathan Shoemaker (G 4)

Joseph Shoemaker

Sarah Lownes and Jonathan Shoemaker's child was Joseph Shoemaker. Joseph Shoemaker and (wife name was not available) had one child, Elizabeth Shoemaker. No other information was available.

Children of Hannah Lownes and Joshua Pancoast (G 4)

Ann Pancoast

Hannah Lownes and Joshua Pancoast's first child was Ann Pancoast, who married Luke Morris; they had one child, Hannah Morris. No other information was available.

Hannah Pancoast

Hannah Lownes and Joshua Pancoast's second child was Hannah Pancoast, who married Buckley (first name was not available). They had no children. No other information was available.

Children of William Lownes and Rebecca Elwell (first wife) (G 4)

Joseph Lownes

William Lownes and Rebecca Elwell's first child was Joseph Lownes. He was born April 25, 1765; he went to Ohio. No other information was available.

Mary Lownes

William Lownes and Rebecca Elwell's second child was Mary Lownes, who married Robert Knowles. Mary Lownes was born November 10, 1768. No other information was available.

Daniel Lownes

William Lownes and Rebecca Elwell's third child was Daniel Lownes. Daniel Lownes was born May 28, 1771; he lived in Philadelphia. No other information was available.

William Lownes Jr.

William Lownes and Rebecca Elwell's fourth child was William Lownes Jr., who married Mary (last name was not available). He then married Susanna Stokes in 1795. He then married Sarah Canby in 1800. William and Sarah Canby had ten children: Mary Lownes, Thomas Lownes, Samuel Lownes, Beulah Lownes, Rebecca Lownes, Joseph Lownes, Joshua Lownes, Susanna Lownes, William Lownes, and Elizabeth

Lownes. William Lownes was born on September 4, 1776. No other information was available.

James Lownes

William Lownes and Rebecca Elwell's fifth child was James Lownes, who married Marcy Betts on March 13, 1802. James was disowned due to marriage out of unity on May 23, 1797. They had eight children: Eliza Lownes, William Lownes, Mary Biles Lownes, Hannah P. Lownes, Thomas Betts Lownes, Esther Lownes, Sarah A. Lownes, and Rebecca Lownes. James Lownes was born on October 16, 1775. No other information was available.

Children of Rebecca Lownes and Caleb Ash (G 4)

Joshua Ash

Rebecca Lownes and Caleb Ash's first child was Joshua Ash, who was unmarried. No other information was available.

Joseph Ash

Rebecca Lownes and Caleb Ash's second child was Joseph Ash, who married Frances Penrose; they had three children: Joseph Ash, Penrose Ash, and Rebecca Ash. No other information was available.

Sarah Ash

Rebecca Lownes and Caleb Ash's third child was Sarah Ash, who married Alex Elmslio. They had five children: Rebecca Elmslio, Thomas Elmslio, William Elmslio, Ann Elmslio, and Elizabeth Elmslio. No other information was available.

Alice Ash

Rebecca Lownes and Caleb Ash's fourth child was Alice Ash, who married Benjamin Jones Jr. They had two children: Elizabeth Jones and Alice Jones. No other information was available.

Caleb Ash

Rebecca Lownes and Caleb Ash's fifth child was Caleb Ash, who was unmarried. No other information was available.

Thomas Ash

Rebecca Lownes and Caleb Ash's sixth child was Thomas Ash, who married Sarah Chapman. No other information was available.

Elizabeth Ash

Rebecca Lownes and Caleb Ash's seventh child was Elizabeth Ash, who died young. No other information was available.

William Ash

Rebecca Lownes and Caleb Ash's eighth child was William Ash, who died young. No other information was available.

Children of James Lownes and Sarah Pancoast (G 4)

Mary Lownes

James Lownes and Sarah Pancoast's first child was Mary Lownes, who married Thomas Chapman. Thomas was an officer in the Revolutionary War. Mary was disowned due to marrying out of unity. They had seven children: Marianna Chapman, Charles Chapman, Elizabeth Chapman, Charlotte Chapman, John Chapman, Sarah Chapman, and

Louise Chapman. Mary Lownes was born on August 6, 1764. No other information was available.

Sarah Lownes

James Lownes and Sarah Pancoast's second child was Sarah Lownes was transferred to Fairfax, Virginia on August 2, 1783, who married John Scott Pleasants, son of Jacob Pleasants, on April 29, 1790, at Alexandria Monthly Meeting. They had ten children: Sarah Pleasants, George Pleasants, Mary Hewes Pleasants, Fredrick Woodson Pleasants, Eliza Ann Pleasants, Charles Scott Pleasants, Louisa Plasants, James Pleasants, Fitzhenry Pleasants, and Cyrus Rodaphus Pleasants. Sarah Lownes was born on August 17, 1766. No other information was available.

Hyatt Lownes

James Lownes and Sarah Pancoast's third child was Hyatt Lownes, who married Elizabeth Emmery; they were granted certificate to Fairfax, Virginia, on August 2, 1793. They had six children: George Emmery Lownes, James Pancoast Lownes, John Lownes, Margaret Lownes, Elias Lownes, and Betsy Ann Lownes. Hyatt Lownes was born on August 26, 1769. No other information was available.

John Lownes

James Lownes and Sarah Pancoast's fourth child was John Lownes, who was unmarried. John Lownes was born September 21, 1771, and died August 1, 1800. No other information was available.

Deborah Lownes

James Lownes and Sarah Pancoast's fifth child was Deborah Lownes, who was granted certificate to Fairfax, Virginia, on August 2, 1783. She married

Samuel Pleasants on July 18, 1795. Deborah was disowned due to marring contrary to discipline on June 4, 1796. They had nine children: Lucinda Pleasants, Sally Ann Pleasants, Samuel Madison Pleasants, Christian Pleasants, Madison Pleasants, Edwin Chapman Pleasants, Ellen Pleasants, Charlotte Pleasants, and Mary Galego Pleasants. Deborah Lownes was born on February 20, 1774. No other information was available.

James Lownes Jr.

James Lownes and Sarah Pancoast's sixth child was James Lownes Jr., who married Sarah Donaldson, niece of the famous Betsy Ross and daughter of William and Sarah Donaldson on May 26, 1797. James was granted a certificate of transfer to Fairfax, Virginia, on August 2, 1783. James was a hatter. James and his brother Caleb received certificate from Fairfax, Virginia, on December 22, 1792. James Jr. and Sarah had four children: Caleb Pancoast Lownes, Sarah Lownes, Lydia Lownes, and William Lownes.

In December 1792, James Sr. sent James Jr. and his brother Caleb to Philadelphia, where they were both placed in apprentices, one with Joseph Shoemaker (hatter,) the other with Thomas Savery in 1793. The Philadelphia record notes: "A certificate of church records membership was produced for James and Caleb Lownes from the Monthly Meeting of Fairfax, Virginia." James Jr. and Caleb made their fortunes in Philadelphia. James Jr. must have been reasonably successful there because he had his own hat business for three years.

Both James Jr. and Caleb participated in the Quaker assembly at least for a while. Then James Jr. fell in love with Sarah Donaldson. The faithful Quaker records tell us James Jr. was "disowned for marrying out of unity at the Monthly Meeting on May 26, 1797." Alas, Sarah Donaldson was not a Quaker. In fact, this union marks the end of Quaker participation by the Lowneses. One might say that the "fires of convincement" lasted for five generations. But along the way, Quaker practices and beliefs were changing also. Soon it became common for adherents of the early faiths to intermarry.

It is assumed that James Jr. and Sarah were married immediately prior to the date of May 26, 1797. It is believed they were married in Richmond, Virginia, where they raised four children. Naturally, little else is recorded about James Jr. The Quakers disassociated themselves literally and physically when a fellow Friend was condemned. Perhaps this was the reason James Jr. and Sarah moved to Virginia, or perhaps Sarah had relatives there. James Lownes Jr. was born on August 21, 1776.

Today, if one visits the gift shop adjacent to the restored Betsy Ross home in Philadelphia; you will find a large copy of the Grissom Family tree on the wall, ancestors of Betsy Grissom Ross. On the lower left-hand corner of this document are several branches referring to five or six different Lowneses, starting with the marriage of our James Jr. to Sarah Donaldson.

Eventually James Jr. retired to Philadelphia and died on August 20, 1820. Sarah remarried and produced six more children. Her second husband was David McCord.

One further note of interest is that Betsy Ross's third husband, John Claypool, was a direct line descendant of Lady Claypoole, Cromwell's favorite daughter. It is reported that she, too, was a Quaker.

Caleb Lownes

James Lownes and Sarah Pancoast's seventh child was Caleb Lownes, who married Jane Steele, daughter of George Steele, on May 21, 1807, This marriage was undoubtedly dismissed from the Philadelphia Friends Meeting July 2, 1807, as they stated "accomplished his marriage by the assistance of hiring a minister with a woman, not in profession with Friends and without the consent of his father." They had seven children: Andrew Jackson Lownes, James Lownes, George Steel Lownes, Ann Lownes, Levin Birkhead Lownes, Samuel Pleasants Lownes, and Araminta Steel Lownes. Caleb may be the only child of James who returned to Philadelphia with him from Virginia 1792. Caleb Lownes was born on August 17, 1778. No other information was available.

Jane Lownes

James Lownes and Sarah Pancoast's eighth child was Jane Lownes, who was granted certificate to Fairfax, Virginia, on August 2, 1783. Jane Lownes was born on June 30, 1780. No other information was available.

Joseph Lownes

James Lownes Sarah Pancoast's ninth child was Joseph Lownes, who was granted certificate to Fairfax, Virginia, on August 2, 1783. Joseph Lownes was born on February 21, 1783. He died unmarried. No other information was available.

William Lownes

James Lownes and Sarah's tenth child was William Lownes, who married Arian Wormly Glynn. William was granted certificate to the White Oak Swamp Monthly Meeting, Virginia, on August 23, 1794. They had ten children: Josiah Hewes Lownes, Mary Glenn Lownes, Charles Lownes, Chapman Lownes, Virginia Radcliffe Lownes, Jane Dado Lownes, John Henry Augustus Lownes, Margaret Ann Lownes, William Lownes, and Sarah Lownes. William Lownes was born on March 23, 1785. No other information was available.

Children of John Lown and
Catherine Baumgartine (G 4)

(note the "es" was dropped from the name)

John Lown

John Lown and Catherine Baumgartine's first child was John Lown Jr. He was born in 1791, and his death is unknown. No other information was available.

It should be noted that John, as his parents had ventured west, dropped the "es" from the last name. No other information was available.

Henry Lown

John Lown and Catherine Baumgartine's second child was Henry Lown, who married Esther High in 1815. They had ten children: John Lown, James Lown, Phillip Lown, Katherine Lown, Lewis Lown, Mary Ann Lown, Jane Lown, Henry Lown Jr., Martha Lown, and Jacob Lown. Henry Lown was born in 1794. Henry Lown was in the war of 1812. No other information was available.

Nancy Lown

John Lown and Catherine Baumgartine's third child was Nancy Lown. The only records available are that she may have married a man with the last name of Synder. Nancy Lown was born in 1796, and her death is unknown. No other information was available.

Frances Lown

John Lown and Catherine Baumgartine's fourth child was Frances Lown. She may have married a man with the last name of McBride.

Frances Lown was born in 1798, and her death is unknown. No other information was available.

Martha Lown

John Lown and Catherine Baumgartine's fifth child was Martha, who married a man with the last name of Smith. Martha Lown was born in 1798, and her death is unknown. No other information was available.

THIS SECOND GROUP OF DESCENDANTS IS FROM THE GEORGE LOWNES AND MARY BOWERS'S BRANCH OF THE FAMILY

Child of Slater Lownes and Eleanor Cox (G 4)

Clarissa Lownes

Slater Lownes and Eleanor Cox's only child was Clarissa Lownes. Her birth is unknown, but she died March 24, 1837, and is buried at The Blue Church. No other information was available.

Children of Curtis Lownes and Grace Lownes (G 4)

John Lownes

Curtis Lownes and Grace Lownes's first child was John Lownes, who married Rebecca Crosby, daughter of John and Sarah Crosby of Ridley, on January 13, 1820; they had three children: Curtis Lownes, Sarah Crosby Lownes, and Hannah Lane Lownes. Curtis Lownes was born in 1759 and died at age three. John Crosby was a farmer. No other information was available.

Agnes Lownes

Curtis Lownes and Grace Lownes's second child was Agnes, who married Edwin Levis in 1821, they had one child; Elizabeth Levis. Agnes Lownes was born on May 13, 1797. No other information was available.

Children of Esther Lownes (G 4)

Joseph Lownes

Esther Lownes's first child was Joseph Lownes. He was a jeweler. No other information was available.

Curtis Lownes

Esther Lownes's second child was Curtis Lownes who married Agnes (no last name listed). No other information was available.

Children of Alice Lownes and William Temple (first marriage) (G4)

Thomas Temple

Alice Lownes and William Temple's first child was Thomas Temple. No other information was available.

Mary Temple

Alice Lownes and William Temple's second child was Mary Temple. No other information was available.

William Temple

Alice Lownes and William Temple's third child was William Temple. No other information was available.

Alice Temple

Alice Lownes and William Temple's fourth child was Alice Temple. No other information was available.

Children of Alice Lownes and John Pennock (second marriage) (G 4)

Marshall Pennock

Alice Lownes and John Pennock's first child was Marshall Pennock. No other information was available.

Ruth Pennock

Alice Lownes and John Pennock's second child was Ruth Pennock. No other information was available.

Children of Mary Lownes and William Levis (First Marrage) (G 4)

Alice Levis

Mary Lownes and William Levis's first child was Alice Levis, who married Mr. Thomas. No other information was available.

William Levis

Mary Lownes and William Levis's second child was William Levis. No other information was available.

Mary Lownes and
Joseph Taylor (Second Marriage) (G 4)

Joseph Taylor

Mary Lownes and Joseph Taylor's first child was Joseph Taylor. No other information was available.

Sarah Taylor

Mary Lownes and Joseph Taylor's second child was Sarah Taylor. No other information was available.

Lownes Taylor

Mary Lownes and Joseph Taylor's third child was Lownes Taylor. No other information was available.

Children of George Lownes III
and Elizabeth Taylor (G 4)

George Lownes IV

George Lownes and Elizabeth Taylor's first child was George Lownes IV, who was granted a certificate to the Willington Monthly Meeting on February 24, 1814.

No other information was available.

Maria Lownes

George Lownes and Elizabeth Taylor's second child was Maria Lownes. No other information was available.

Sarah Lownes

George Lownes and Elizabeth Taylor's third child was Sarah Lownes. No other information was available.

Children of Hugh Lownes and Rebecca Rhodes (G 4)

Benanuel Lownes III

Hugh Lownes and Rebecca Rhodes's first child was Benanuel Lownes III. He never married. No other information was available.

Elizabeth Lownes II

Hugh Lownes and Rebecca Rhodes's second child was Elizabeth Lownes II. She never married. No other information was available.

Sydney Lownes

Hugh Lownes and Rebecca Rhodes's third child was Sydney Lownes. She never married. No other information was available.

Joseph Lownes

Hugh Lownes and Rebecca Rhodes's fourth child was Joseph Lownes, who married Rachel Massey; they had seven children: Rebecca Lownes III, Hugh Lownes III, William Lownes, Phineas Lownes, Massey Lownes, Joseph Lownes, and George Bolton Lownes II. Rachel died about 1830. Joseph then married Priscilla Pratt, and they had one child, Elizabeth Pratt Lownes. Joseph was a farmer and a teacher at Springfield Central School (a one room school house) and a school director for several years. Joseph Lownes was born on January 17, 1797. No other information was available.

CHAPTER SIX

Generation Six

THIS FIRST GROUP OF DESCENDANTS IS FROM THE JAMES I. LOWNES AND SUSANNAH RICHARDS'S BRANCH OF THE FAMILY

Children of Caleb Lownes and Margaret Robeson (G5)

Edward F. Lownes

Caleb Lownes and Margaret Robeson's first child was Edward F. Lownes (a Quaker), who married Hannah Pancoast Byrnes, a Quaker of Wilmington, Delaware, on October 2, 1816, at the Pine Street Meeting, and they received certificate from the South Division Monthly Meeting on February 26, 1817. Hannah Pancoast Bynes was the daughter of Thomas Byrnes and Sarah Pancoast. They had one child, Hannah Ann Lownes. Edward's second wife was Elizabeth Richlo, the daughter of William Richlo, a tanner. They had a son named William Lownes. Edward's will was drawn up on August 20, 1834, and probated as Philadelphia Wills 1834 Number 138. Edward F. Lownes was disowned due to marrying out of unity on February 26, 1829.

Edward F. Lownes was a silversmith in the firm of Lownes and Henry Erwin from 1816 to 1817, as the Lownes & Edwin with their shop at 161 South Street.. Eward remained his practice at that location until 1821, and then moved his shop to 123 Chestnur Street Philadelphia, Pennsylvania. Edward Lownes was a silversmith until 1834. Below is a picture of a Cruet that is located in the New York Metropolitan Museum in New York City. The description states:

Cruet with Bottles,
Marked by Edward Lownes (1792 – 1834
Philadelphia, 1820 – 25
Silver and cut glass
Lent by a Private Collection (L.2006.561a-1)

Cruit with Bottles Silver and cut Glass

Another piece from his collection was a Covered bowel and stand made in 1820, and is 7 ½ " high and 6 " in diameter.

Covered bowel and stand made in 1820

Another piece from his collection was a pitcher made in 1827.

Edward F. Lownes was one of the founding members of the Franklin Institute in Philadelphia. He was buried in front of The Blue Church on Baltimore Pike, Springfield. Edward was born in 1792. No other information was available.

George Bolton Lownes

Caleb Lownes and Margaret Robeson's second child was George Bolton Lownes, (not to be confused with the George Bolton Lownes in Chapter Four) who married Mary Paul of Valley Forge, daughter of Joseph Paul who owned Washington's Headquarters. George Bolton Lownes and Mary Paul had a daughter, Margaret, who died at the age of six months. George Bolton Lownes was born in 1796. No other information was available.

John Lownes

Caleb Lownes and Margaret Robeson's third child was John Lownes, who married, but the wife's name is unknown; they had a son, George Lownes. They were married in Louisville, Kentucky, and moved west. No other information was available.

Catherine Lownes

Caleb Lownes and Margaret Robeson's fourth child was Catherine Lownes, and she only lived about six months (Northern Lib Meeting's records). No other information was available.

Children of Joseph Lownes and Esther Middelton (G 5)

Agnes Lownes

Joseph Lownes and Esther Middelton's first child was Agnes Lownes, who married Isaac Harvey on December 7, 1814; they had 100 wittness's at their wedding. They had one child, Josiah Harvey. Agnes Lownes was born on November 18, 1786. No other information was available.

Josiah Hewes Lownes

Joseph Lownes and Esther Middelton's second child was Josiah Hewes Lownes, who was unmarried. He was a silversmith and in the partnership of J. & J. H. Lownes with his father, Joseph Lownes, from 1817 to 1820. Josiah Hewes Lownes was born on Decmber 8, 1791. No other information was available.

Esther Lownes

Joseph Lownes and Esther Middelton's third child was Esther Lownes, who married Michael Newbold on January 31, 1821. They had four children: Martha Newbold, Alexander Newbold, Josiah Newbold, and Helen Newbold. Esther Lownes was born on September 3, 1795. No other information was available.

Martha Powell Lownes

Joseph Lownes and Esther Middelton's fourth child was Martha Powell Lownes. She was born on January 7, 1798, and her death is unknown. No other information was available.

Children of David Lownes (allegedly unmarried) (G 5)

Rebecca Lownes

David Lownes's first child was Rebecca Lownes. She was born in 1799, and she died on April 19, 1829. No other information was available.

Edmond Lownes

David Lownes's second child was Edmond Lownes. He was born on April 21, 1801, and he died on June 21, 1805. No other information was available.

Hannah Lownes

David Lownes's third child was Hannah Lownes. She was born in 1805, and she died on June 8, 1829. No other information was available.

Children of Grace Lownes and Curtis Lownes (G 5)

John Lownes

Grace Lownes and Curtis Lownes's (of the George Lownes branch of the family) first child was John Lownes, who married Rebecca Crosby, daughter of John and Sarah Lane Crosby of Ridley, on January 13, 1820. They were married in Louisville, Kentucky. John was a farmer in Springfield, Pennsylvania. John and Rebecca had three children: Curtis Lownes, Sarah Lownes, and Hannah Lane Lownes. John Lownes was born on March 10, 1796. No other information was available.

Agnes Lownes

Grace Lownes and Curtis Lownes's second child was Agnes Lownes, who married Edward Levis in June, 1821. They had one child, Elizabeth. Agnes Lownes was born on May 13, 1797. No other information was available.

Children of Elizabeth Lownes and Samuel Huggins (G 5)

Curtis Huggins

Elizabeth Lownes and Samuel Huggins's first child was Curtis Huggins. He was born September 19, 1803, and died April 2, 1821. He was a twin to his sister Emily. No other information was available.

Emily Huggins

Elizabeth Lownes and Samuel Huggins's second child was Emily Huggins. She was born September 19, 1803, and died in January 1804. She was a twin to her brother Curtis. No other information was available.

Margaret Huggins

Elizabeth Lownes and Samuel Huggins's third child was Margaret Huggins. She was born on February 17, 1805, and she died on October 21, 1821. No other information was available.

Esther Huggins

Elizabeth Lownes and Samuel Huggins's fourth child was Esther Huggins. She was born on October 12, 1810, and her death is unknown. No other information was available.

Child of Joseph Shoemaker (no wife's name was available) (G 5)

Elizabeth Shoemaker

Joseph Shoemaker's only child was Elizabeth Shoemaker, who married Richard Paxon; they had five children: Richard Paxon, Lashbrook Paxon, Anna Paxon, Sarah Paxon, and Elizabeth Paxon. No other information was available.

Child of Ann Pancoast and Luke Morris (G 5)

Hannah Morris

Ann Pancoast and Luke Morris's only child was Hannah Morris, who married Effingham Buckley; they had one child, Ann Buckley. No other information was available.

Children of William Lownes Jr. and Sarah Canby (G 5)

Mary Lownes

William Lownes Jr. and Sarah Canby's first child was Mary Lownes. She was born on October 9, 1800, and she died on October 4, 1831. No other information was available.

Thomas Lownes

William Lownes Jr. and Sarah Canby's second child was Thomas Lownes. He was born on January 29, 1804, and he died on May 10, 1864. No other information was available.

Samuel Lownes

William Lownes Jr. and Sarah Canby's third child was Samuel Lownes. He was born on March 11, 1806, and he died on June 24, 1806. No other information was available.

Beulah Lownes

William Lownes Jr. and Sarah Canby's fourth child was Beulah Lownes. She was born on March 13, 1807, and she died on May 15, 1888. No other information was available.

Rebecca Lownes

William Lownes Jr. and Sarah Canby's fifth child was Rebecca Lownes. She was born on February 2, 1809, and she died on July 24, 1891. No other information was available.

Joseph Lownes

William Lownes Jr. and Sarah Canby's sixth child was Joseph Lownes, who married Sarah Ann Fly on March 14, 1832; they had four children: Henry Ely Lownes, Mary Lownes, Elias Lownes, and Joseph Lownes. After Joseph died, Sarah married Samuel Cooper. No other information was available.

Joshua Lownes

William Lownes Jr. and Sarah Canby's seventh child was Joshua Lownes. He was born December 16, 1811, and he died on August 19, 1825. No other information was available.

Susannah Lownes

William Lownes Jr. and Sarah's eighth child was Susannah Lownes. She was born December 25, 1813, and she died on February 4, 1900. No other information was available.

William Elwell Lownes

William Lownes Jr. and Sarah's ninth child was William Elwell Lownes. He was born December 7, 1816, and he died at a young age. No other information was available.

Elizabeth Lownes

William Lownes Jr. and Sarah's tenth child was Elizabeth Lownes. She was born December 15, 1820, and she died on April 12, 1821. No other information was available.

Children of James Lownes and Marcy Betts (G 5)

Eliza Lownes

James Lownes and Marcy Betts's first child was Eliza Lownes. She was born on September 21, 1802, and she died on January 15, 1892. No other information was available.

William Lownes

James Lownes and Marcy Betts's second child was William Lownes. He was born on December 22, 1804, and he died on August 30, 1830. No other information was available.

Mary Biles Lownes

James Lownes and Marcy Betts's third child was Mary Biles Lownes. She was born on January 15, 1807, and she died on April 7, 1893. No other information was available.

Hannah P. Lownes

James Lownes and Marcy Betts's fourth child was Hannah P. Lownes. She was born on December 18, 1808, and she died on September 10, 1869. No other information was available.

Thomas Betts Lownes

James Lownes and Marcy Betts's fifth child was Thomas Betts Lownes. He was born May 25, 1811, and he died on December 24, 1880. No other information was available.

Esther Lownes

James Lownes and Marcy Betts's sixth child was Esther Lownes. She was born on July 21, 1813, and she died on May 28, 1838. No other information was available.

Sarah A. Lownes

James Lownes and Marcy Betts's seventh child was Sarah Lownes, who married Samuel Cooper, and they had one child, Rachel Cooper. Sarah A. Lownes was born on July 14, 1815. No other information was available.

Rebecca Lownes

James Lownes and Marcy Betts's eighth child was Rebecca. No husband's name was available. Rebecca had one child, Susannah Rebecca Lownes. Rebecca Lownes was born on July 7, 1818.No other information was available.

Children of Joseph Ash and Frances Penrose (G 5)

Joseph Ash

Joseph Ash and Frances Penrose's first child was Joseph Ash, who married Marie Ashmoad. No other information was available.

Penrose Ash

Joseph Ash and Frances Penrose's second child was Penrose Ash; he was unmarried. No other information was available.

Rebecca Ash

Joseph Ash and Frances Penrose's third child was Rebecca Ash; she was unmarried.

No other information was available.

Children of Sarah Ash and Alex Elmslio (G 5)

Rebecca Elmslio

Sarah Ash and Alex Elmslio's first child was Rebecca Elmslio; she was unmarried. No other information was available.

Thomas Elmslio

Sarah Ash and Alex Elmslio's second child was Thomas Elmslio; he was unmarried. No other information was available.

William Elmslio

Sarah Ash and Alex Elmslio's third child was William Elmslio; he was unmarried. No other information was available.

Ann Elmslio

Sarah Ash and Alex Elmslio's fourth child was Ann Elmslio; she was unmarried. No other information was available.

Elizabeth Elmslio

Sarah Ash and Alex Elmslio's fifth child was Elizabeth Elmslio; she was unmarried. No other information was available.

Children of Alice Ash and Benjamin Jones Jr. (G 5)

Elizabeth Jones

Alice Ash and Benjamin Jones Jr.'s first child was Elizabeth Jones, who married Robert Taylor; they had four children: Benjamin James Taylor, Anthony Taylor, Alice Jones Taylor, and Sarah Taylor. No other information was available.

Alice Jones

Alice Ash and Benjamin Jones Jr.'s second child was Alice Jones, who married Benjamin (no last name was available). No other information was available.

Children of Mary Lownes and Thomas Chapman (G 5)

Marianna Chapman

Mary Lownes and Thomas Chapman's first child was Marianna Chapman. She was born September 1, 1784, and her death is unknown. She was unmarried. No other information was available.

Charles Chapman

Mary Lownes and Thomas Chapman's second child was Charles Chapman, who married Charlotte Christte. They had three children: Charlotte Chapman, Charles Chapman, and Fredrick Wiltshire Chapman who died in India. Charles was born on September 21, 1785, and died on August 27, 1821, also in India. No other information was available.

Elizabeth Chapman

Mary Lownes and Thomas Chapman's third child was Elizabeth Chapman, who married Samuel Harvey; they had two children: Thomas Harvey and Louise Harvey. Elizabeth Chapman was born on March 2, 1787. No other information was available..

Charlotte Chapman

Mary Lownes and Thomas Chapman's fourth child was Charlotte Chapman, who married Thomas Ingalls. Charlotte Chapman was born on April 23, 1788. Thomas died in 1812. No other information was available.

John James Chapman

Mary Lownes and Thomas Chapman's fifth child was John James Chapman, who was unmarried. John Chapman was born on January 10, 1790. No other information was available.

Sarah Chapman

Mary Lownes and Thomas Chapman's sixth child was Sarah Chapman, who married Thomas Ash; they had four children: Mary Ash, Joshua Ash, Charlotte Ash, and Charles Ash. Sarah Chapman was born on August 12, 1792. No other information was available.

Louise Chapman

Mary Lownes and Thomas Chapman's seventh child was Louise Chapman, who was unmarried. Louise Chapman was born on May 24, 1794. No other information was available.

Children of Sarah Lownes and John Scott Pleasants (G 5)

Sarah Pleasants

Sarah Lownes and John Scott Pleasants's first child was Sarah Pleasants. No other information was available.

George Pleasants

Sarah Lownes and John Scott Pleasants's second child was George Pleasants. No other information was available.

Mary Hewes Pleasants

Sarah Lownes and John Scott Pleasants's third child was Mary Hewes Pleasants. No other information was available.

Fredrick Woodson Pleasants

Sarah Lownes and John Scott Pleasants's fourth child was Fredrick Woodson Pleasants. No other information was available.

Eliza Ann Pleasants

Sarah Lownes and John Scott Pleasants's fifth child was Eliza Ann Pleasants. No other information was available.

Charles Scott Pleasants

Sarah Lownes and John Scott Pleasants's sixth child was Charles Scott Pleasants. No other information was available.

Louisa Pleasants

Sarah Lownes and John Scott Pleasants's seventh child was Louisa Pleasants. No other information was available.

James Pleasants

Sarah Lownes and John Scott Pleasants's eighth child was James Pleasants. No other information was available.

Fitzhenry Pleasants

Sarah Lownes and John Scott Pleasants's ninth child was Fitzhenry Pleasants No other information was available..

Cyrus Pleasants

Sarah Lownes and John Scott Pleasants's tenth child was Cyrus Pleasants. No other information was available.

Children of Hyatt Lownes and Elizabeth Emmery (G 5)

George Emmery Lownes

Hyatt Lownes and Elizabeth Emmery's first child was George Emmery Lownes. No other information was available.

James Pancoast Lownes

Hyatt Lownes and Elizabeth Emmery's second child was James Pancoast Lownes. No other information was available.

John Lownes

Hyatt Lownes and Elizabeth Emmery's third child was John Lownes. No other information was available.

Margaret Lownes

Hyatt Lownes and Elizabeth Emmery's fourth child was Margaret Lownes. No other information was available.

Elias Lownes

Hyatt Lownes and Elizabeth Emmery's fifth child was Elias Lownes. No other information was available.

Betsy Ann Lownes

Hyatt Lownes and Elizabeth Emmery's sixth child was Betsy Ann Lownes. No other information was available.

Children of Deborah Lownes and
Samuel Pleasants (G 5)

Lucinda Pleasants

Deborah Lownes and Samuel Pleasants's first child was Lucinda Pleasants. No other information was available.

Sally Ann Pleasants

Deborah Lownes and Samuel Pleasants's second child was Sally Ann Pleasants; she had an infant, no name was avilable. No other information was available.

Samuel Madison Pleasants

Deborah Lownes and Samuel Pleasants's third child was Samuel Madison Pleasants. No other information was available.

Christian Pleasants

Deborah Lownes and Samuel Pleasants's fourth child was Christian Pleasants. No other information was available.

Madison Pleasants

Deborah Lownes and Samuel Pleasants's fifth child was Madison Pleasants. No other information was available.

Edwin Chapman Pleasants

Deborah Lownes and Samuel Pleasants's sixth child was Edwin Chapman Pleasants. No other information was available.

Ellen Pleasants

Deborah Lownes and Samuel Pleasants's seventh child was Ellen Pleasants. No other information was available.

Charlotte Pleasants

Deborah Lownes and Samuel Pleasants's eighth child was Charlotte Pleasants. No other information was available.

Mary Gelego Pleasants

Deborah Lownes and Samuel Pleasants's ninth child was Mary Gelego Pleasants. No other information was available.

Children of James Lownes Jr. and Sarah Donaldson (G 5)

Caleb Pancoast Lownes

James Lownes Jr. and Sarah's first child was Caleb Pancoast Lownes. At the age of thirty-four, he married Ann Minges on January 2, 1826 (whose brother was a noted Baptist minister). Caleb Pancoast Lownes and his wife Ann had six children: Thomas Chapman Lownes, Catherine Lownes, Robert Lownes, William Lownes, Mary Lownes, and James Roach Lownes. James Jr. must have held a great affection for his brother Caleb to name his first son after him.

Caleb was a baker by trade and lived in Baltimore, Maryland. How he settled there is not known. In 1834 at age forty two, Caleb, made a journey to the Midwest, probably to purchase flour for his bakery business and was not heard from again. There is a legend that he was killed by the Indians, but an old diary cast a new light on the plight of Caleb Lownes. It was determined that along the way he had decided to be in the cattle business instead.

Taken from the D.E. Ledger of Ida Eckle (or the Mrs. George W. Cope), a descendant of Sarah Griscom and William Donaldson (the original was in possession of Mr. Ed. Durkerley, Philadelphia) on July 20, 1903 in Pottsville, Pennsylvania: "Caleb Lownes, my grandfather's brother, was killed at the battle of the Alamo, a building. He was a victim of the massacre by the Mexicans in the Mexican war, when of the 400 not one soul escaped." The diary further states that "Caleb had decided to change business from baker to cattle dealer, and he traveled west to seek cattle." Even then, Texas was cattle country, and Caleb may simply have been in the right place at the wrong time. It has not been determined that he was in the service of his country at the time. A copy of the pages from that diary is located in the back of the book listed as "Diary."

The Grolier Book of Knowledge states:

> Another mission which later played a tragic part in the history of Texas was San Antonio de Valero, often called the Alamo (cottonwood) Mission because of the grove of trees in which it stood. It was founded in 1718, and the City of San Antonio has grown up around it. Within a century after it was founded, the Indians disappeared from the region around the mission, and it was abandoned. Then the chapel was sometimes used as a fort. In 1836, during the war of Texas Independence, about 180 Texans, including W. B. Travis, James Bowie, and David Crockett, were besieged within the Alamo Chapel by several thousand Mexicans. When the besiegers forced an entrance, after nearly two weeks, only five of the defenders were left alive. These five were killed by the victors. Afterward, "Remember the Alamo" was the battle cry of Texans. The Alamo is today one of the great heroic shrines of

Texas and the United States because of the brave men
who died there.

It should be noted the above account states one hundred eighty Texans died there, and the old diary says four hundred were present. The difference, no doubt, was made up of non-Texans like our great, great grandfather Caleb Lownes.

Wouldn't it be interesting to know more about the character of this man?

Ann and their six children continued living in Baltimore for a time. When Ann's money was running out, she knew she had to make plans for a life without Caleb. Soon she and her six small children went north to live with her brother, Robert Minges, a noted Baptist minister, in a remote area between Center Point and Center Square, near Philadelphia, Pennsylvania.

I, Howard G. Lownes Sr., along with my daughter, April Lownes Hostler, went to San Antonio, Texas, in January 2018 to see if there were any records there of our Caleb. We spoke with two people: one had a spreadsheet which was not shown to us, but it indicated there wasn't any Caleb Lownes listed, and the other had a book which listed those who they knew were killed there. Neither had our Caleb Lownes listed. They had numerous books in the gift shop; one described that when the Mexicans stormed the Alamo over the wall, there was hand-to-hand combat, and after the Mexicans killed all those that were left, they put them in a pile in the compound and set them on fire. That accounts for the difference in the number being killed and who to be unknown since there were some Mexicans that were killed and burned with those that were identified as being there. From the internet there was a listing of numerous people and their rank in the service, from many states and countries that fought in this battle. Our Caleb was not listed, but there were many others as well.

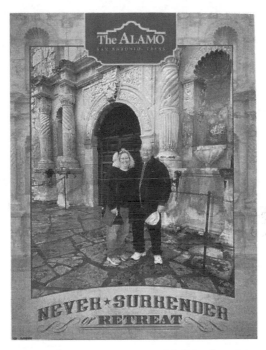

This is Howard G. Lownes Sr. with his daughter, April
Lownes Hostler, at the Alamo in January 2018.

Sarah Lownes

James Lownes Jr. and Sarah Donaldson's second child was Sarah
Lownes, who married William Wencks. No other information was
available.

Lydia Lownes

James Lownes Jr. and Sarah Donaldson's third child was Lydia Lownes,
who married Herman Keller. No other information was available.

William Donaldson Lownes

James Lownes Jr. and Sarah Donaldson's fourth child was William
Donaldson Lownes, who married Hannah Low (they lived in Norristown,
Pennsylvania). William was granted certificate at Alexandria, Virginia,

on May 2, 1803. William was a ship merchant and owned a large vessel. He also fought in the Revolutionary War and was captured and put in Mill Prison in England. He was released and exchanged when Cornwallis surrendered. He came back on the ship with John Claypole when the exchange took place. William and Hannah had four children: Jane Eliza Lownes, Amanda Lownes and two un named sons.. William was the grandfather of a son of Jake Eckel and Jane Eliza Lownes. The son, Benjamin Barker Eckel, wrote the diary that has been mentioned before and referred to as "The D.E. Ledger of Ida Eckel."

Children of Caleb Lownes and Jane Steel (G 5)

It is to be noted that this branch of the family that headed south reinstated the "d" in the name.

Andrew Jackson Lowndes

Caleb Lownes and Jane Steel's first child was Andrew Jackson Lowndes, who married Mary Ann Bucknall on January 7, 1846, in Baltimore County, Maryland. They had one child, Mary Lowndes. Andrew Jackson Lowndes was born on August 23, 1822, in Richmond, Virginia, and died in Baltimore, Maryland.

James Lowndes

Caleb Lownes and Jane Steel's second child was James Lowndes. No other information was available.

George Steel Lowndes

Caleb Lownes and Jane Steel's third child was George Steel Lowndes, who married Kate Williams. No other information was available.

Ann Lowndes

Caleb Lownes and Jane Steel's fourth child was Ann Lowndes. No other information was available.

Kevin Birkhead Lowndes

Caleb Lownes and Jane Steel's fifth child was Kevin Birkhead Lowndes. No other information was available.

Samuel Pleasants Lowndes

Caleb Lownes and Jane Steel's sixth child was Samuel Pleasants Lowndes, who married Julia Catherine Dougherty; they had six children: Mary Ellen Lowndes, Jennie Lowndes, Henry Lowndes, James Lowndes, Sarah Lowndes, and Rueben Lowndes. Samuel Pleasants Lownes was born in 1816. No other information was available.

Araminta Steel Lowndes

Caleb Lownes and Jane Steel's seventh child was Araminta Steel Lowndes, who married Francis J. Barnes; they had eight children: Alice Barnes, Jane E. Barnes, Fannie M. Barnes, Addie Barnes, Ella Barnes, George Barnes, Bella Barnes, and Ella G. Barnes. Araminta Steel Lownes was born in 1828. No other information was available.

Children of William Lownes and Arian Wormly Glynn (G 5)

Josiah Hewes Lownes

William Lownes and Arian Wormly Glynn's first child was Josiah Hewes Lownes, who married Arrabella Sinton on May 14, 1834; they had five children: Joseph Henry Lownes, Sarah Lownes, Josiah Hewes

Lownes Jr., Chas Lownes, and Danison Lownes. No other information was available.

Mary Glenn Lownes

William Lownes and Arian Wormly Glynn's second child was Mary Glenn Lownes, who married G. L. Donison on May 12, 1831. No other information was available.

Charles Lownes

William Lownes and Arian Wormly Glynn's third child was Charles Lownes. No other information was available.

Chapman Lownes

William Lownes and Arian Wormly Glynn's fourth child was Chapman Lownes. No other information was available.

Virginia Radcliffe Lownes

William Lownes and Arian Wormly Glynn's fifth child was Virginia Radcliffe Lownes who married F. G. Annen on November 18, 1834. No other information was available.

Jane Dado Lownes

William Lownes and Arian Wormly's sixth child was Jane Dado Lownes who married Mr. Root (no first name was available). No other information was available.

John Henry Augustus Lownes

William Lownes and Arian Wormly Glynn's seventh child was John Henry Augustus Lownes. No other information was available.

Margaret Ann Lownes

William Lownes and Arian Wormly Glynn's eighth child was Margaret Ann Lownes. No other information was available.

Williamna Lownes

William Lownes and Arian Wormly Glynn's ninth child was Williamna Lownes who married Mr. Miller (no first name was available). No other information was available.

Sarah Lownes

William Lownes and Arian Wormly Glynn's tenth child was Sarah Lownes. She had one child, Laura Beth Lownes. No other information was available.

Child of John Lownes (no wife name was available) (G 5)

Mary Ann Lownes

John Lownes and (no wife's name was available) child was Mary Ann Lownes. No other information was available.

Children of Henry Lown and Esther High (G 5)

(It is to be noted here that this branch changed the spelling of the last name going west by removing the "es' from the name. No explanation has been determined.)

John Lown

Henry Lown and Esther High's first child was John Lown. He was born in 1817. No other information was available.

James Lown

Henry Lown and Esther High's second child was James Lown. He was born in 1821. No other information was available.

Phillip Lown

Henry Lown and Esther High's third child was Phillip Lown, who married Martha Van Velset in 1848. They had one child, Frank Lown. Phillip Lown was born in 1824 and died in 1900. No other information was available.

Katherine Lown

Henry Lown and Esther High's fourth child was Katherine Lown who married Elwin Highley in 1846. Katherine Lown was born in 1827. No other information was available.

Lewis Lown

Henry Lown and Esther High's fifth child was Lewis Lown. He was born in 1829. No other information was available.

Mary Ann Lown

Henry Lown and Esther High's sixth child was Mary Ann Lown who married Abram Wright in 1853. Mary Ann Lown was born in 1831. No other information was available.

Jane Lown

Henry Lown and Esther High's seventh child was Jane Lown. No other information was available.

Henry Lown Jr.

Henry Lown and Esther High's eighth child was Henry Lown Jr who married Mary W. Hughes in 1865. He was born in 1835. No other information was available.

Martha Lown

Henry Lown and Esther High's ninth child was Martha Lown who married David Rees in 1858. Martha Lown was born in 1837. No other information was available.

Jacob Lown

Henry Lown and Esther High's tenth child was Jacob Lown, who married Mary Ann Rees on May 27, 1866. Jacob Lown served in the Civil War, 113 Regiment Ohio Volunteer Infantry Company F. They had three children: Albert "Bert" Lown, Sarah J. Lown, and Rees Rees Lown. Jacob Lown served in the Civil War 113 Regiment Ohio Volunteer Infantry Co. F. No other information was available.

THIS SECOND GROUP OF DESCENDANTS IS FROM THE GEORGE LOWNES AND MARY BOWERS'S BRANCH OF THE FAMILY

Children of John Lownes and Rebecca Crosby (G 5)

Curtis Lownes

John Lownes and Rebecca Crosby's first child was Curtis Lownes. Curtis was born in 1820 and died at the age of three. No other information was available.

Sarah Crosby Lownes

John Lownes and Rebecca Crosby's second child was Sarah Crosby Lownes, who married Crosby P. Morton on September 19, 1839. They had one child, Susannah Crosby Morton. No other information was available.

Hannah Lane Lownes

John Lownes and Rebecca Crosby's third child was Hannah Lane Lownes, who married William W. Maddock on March 10, 1843. They had two children: Lownes Maddock and William Maddock. No other information was available.

Child of Agnes Lownes and Edward Levis (G 5)

Elizabeth Levis

Agnes Lownes and Edward Levis's only child was Elizabeth Levis, who married Phillip Brooks. They had one child, Agnes Brooks. Elizabeth Levis was born on April 5, 1819. No other information was available.

Children of Joseph Lownes and Rachel Massey (First Marriage) (G 5)

Rebecca Lownes III

Joseph Lownes and Rachel Massey's first child was Rebecca Lownes III. She was born on September 4, 1809. She never married. No other information was available.

Hugh Lownes III

Joseph Lownes and Rachel Massey's second child was Hugh Lownes III. He was born on October 11, 1811. He never married. No other information was available.

William Lownes

Joseph Lownes and Rachel Massey's third child was William Lownes. He was born on June 4, 1814. He never married. No other information was available.

Phineas Lownes

Joseph Lownes and Rachel Massey's fourth child was Phineas Lownes, who married Emily Lewis; they had three children: Anna Lownes, Phineas William Lownes, and Emily Lownes. Phineas Lownes was born on April 1, 1816. No other information was available.

Massey Lownes

Joseph Lownes and Rachel Massey's fifth child was Massey Lownes, who married John Jackson (her second cousin); they had five children: Deborah Jackson, Elizabeth Jackson, John Jackson, Israel Jackson, and Harlum Jackson. Massey Lownes was born on September 23, 1819. No other information was available.

Joseph Lownes

Joseph Lownes and Rachel Massey's sixth child was Joseph Lownes, who married Minerva Webb on November 9, 1852. Joseph was a teacher at Springfield High Scool. Joseph Lownes was born on October 12, 1827 and is buried at Springfield Meeting house. No other information was available.

George Bolton Lownes II

Joseph Lownes and Rachel Massey's seventh child was George Bolton Lownes II, who married Rachel (Rebecca) Webb on January 12, 1849. They had five children: William Henry Lownes, George Bolton Lownes III, Mary Lownes, Hannah Darlington Lownes, and Joseph Lownes. George Bolton Lownes II was born on January 25, 1825. George was said to be the oldest land-owner in Pennsylvania. He worked his farm until he was nearly ninety years old. At the age of eighty-nine while operating a hay cutter, he suffered severe injuries when the machine overturned. He was ill for nearly a year, but finally recovered.

He was the first juror called in a criminal case when the old Media, Pennsylvania court house opened in 1850. He attributed his longevity to freedom from worry. He was known as "the grand old man" of Delaware, County. Of the many complements he was a member of the Springfield Meeting of the Society of Friends and a founder of the Morton Building and Loan Association and served several terms as supervisor and school director of his district. He was buried at the Springfield Meeting House graveyard. He died on August 21, 1923.

Child of Joseph Lownes and
Priscilla Pratt (Second Marriage) (G 5)

Elizabeth Pratt Lownes

Joseph Lownes and Priscilla Pratt's only child was Elizabeth Pratt Lownes. The only record available is that she was born on November 22, 1841, and she died on November 7, 1886. No other information was available.

CHAPTER SEVEN

Generation Seven

Child of Edward F. Lownes and Hannah Pancoast Byrnes (first wife) (G 6)

Hannah Ann Lownes

Edward F. Lownes and Hannah Pancoast Byrnes's only child was Hannah Ann Lownes, who married William Ellis, a Philadelphia druggist. They have three children: Catherine Ellis, Edward Ellis, and Rebecca Ellis. Hannah Ann Lownes was born on May 12, 1820. No other information was available.

Child of Edward F. Lownes and Elizabeth Richlo (second wife) (G 6)

William Edward Lownes

pEdward F. Lownes and Elizabeth Richlo's only child was William Edward Lownes. No other information was available.

Child of George Bolton Lownes and Mary Paul (G 6)

Margaret R. Lownes

George Bolton Lownes and Mary Paul's child was Margaret R. Lownes. She died at the age of six months in September 26, 1825. No other information was available.

Child of John Lownes (no wife's name was available) (G 6)

George Lownes

John Lownes and wife's name not available only child was George Lownes. No other information was available.

Child of Agnes Lownes and Issac Harvey (G 6)

Josiah Harvey

Agnes Lownes and Issac Harvy's only child was Josiah Harvey. He was married but no name was available. They had one child; Alex Elmslio Harvey. No other information was available.

Children of Esther Lownes and Michael Newbold (G 6)

Martha Newbold

Esther Lownes and Michael Newbold's first child was Martha Newbold, who married Thomas Mummy. No other information was available.

Alexander Newbold

Esther Lownes and Michael Newbold's second child was Alexander Newbold. No other information was available.

Josiah Newbold

Esther Lownes and Michael Newbold's third child was Josiah Newbold. No other information was available.

Helen Newbold

Esther Lownes and Michael Newbold's fourth child was Helen Newbold. No other information was available.

Children of John Lownes and Rabecca Crosby (G 6)

Curtis Lownes

John Lownes and Rebecca Crosby's first child was Curtis Lownes who was born on July 18, 1829 and died in 1831. No other information was available.

Sarah Crosby Lownes

John Lownes and Rebecca Crosby's second child was Sarah Crosby Lownes, who married Crosby P. Morton on September 19, 1839. They had one child; Susannah Crosby Morton. No other information was available.

Hannah Lene Lownes

John Lownes and Rebecca Crosby's third child was Hannah Lane Lownes, who married William J. Maddock on March 10, 1843.They had two children: Lownes Maddock, and William Maddock. No other infrpmation was available.

Child of Agnes Lownes and Edward Levis (G 6)

Elizabeth Levis

Agnes Lownes and Edward Levis's only child was Elizabeth Levis, who married Philip Brooke; they had one child, Elizabeth Levis was born on August 5, 1819. They had one child; Agnes Levis Brooke. No other information was available.

Children of Elizabeth Shoemaker and Richard Paxon (G 6)

Richard Paxon

Elizabeth Shoemaker and Richard Paxon's first child was Richard Paxon. No other information was available.

Lashbrook Paxon

Elizabeth Shoemaker and Richard Paxon's second child was Lashbrook Paxon. No other information was available.

Anna Paxon

Elizabeth Shoemaker and Richard Paxon's third child was Anna Paxon, who married Joshua Pancoast. They had two childrem: Richard Pancoast and Henry Pancoast. No other information was available.

Sarah Paxon

Elizabeth Shoemaker and Richard Paxon's fourth child was Sarah Paxon, who married Allen (no last name was available). No other information was available.

Elizabeth Paxon

Elizabeth Shoemaker and Richard Paxon's fifth child was Elizabeth Paxon, who married Chas Pickering. No other information was available.

Child of Hannah Morris and Effingham Buckley (G 6)

Ann Buckley

Hannah Morris and Effingham Buckley's only child was Ann Buckley, who married Israel W. Morris; they had one child, Effingham Morris. No other information was available.

Children of Joseph Lownes and Sarah Ann Ely (G 6)

Henry Ely Lownes

Joseph Lownes and Sarah Ann Ely's first child was Henry Ely Lownes, who married Sarah Jane Walton on January 10, 1855. They had two children: Marianna Lownes and Sarah Elizabeth Lownes. Henry Ely Lownes was born on February 23, 1833. No other information was available.

Mary Lownes

Joseph Lownes and Sarah Ann Ely's second child was Mary Lownes; she had one child, Marianna Lownes. Mary was born on April 3, 1837. There was no husband named. No other information was available.

Elias Paxsen Lownes

Joseph Lownes and Sarah Ann Ely's third child was Elias Paxsen, who married Margaret Norcross on December 23, 1898. They had three children: Martha Conrad Lownes, Beulah Lownes, and William Elias Lownes. Elias Paxsen Lownes was born on April 22, 1842. No other information was available.

Joseph Lownes

Joseph Lownes and Sarah Ann Ely's fourth child was Joseph Lownes, who married Margaret Ann Scully on March 26, 1874. They had nine children: Samuel Cooper Lownes, John Scully Lownes, Fanny Edith Lownes, Sarah Ann Lownes, George Mahan Lownes, Hannah Lownes, Helen Jones Lownes, Joseph Ewell Lownes, and Thomas Russell Lownes. Joseph Lownes was born on November 4, 1847. No other information was available.

Child of Sarah A. Lownes and Samuel Cooper (G 6)

Rachel Cooper

Sarah A. Lownes and Samuel Cooper's child was Rachel Cooper, who married William Pidcuck. No other Information was available.

Child of Rebecca Lownes and (husband's name was not available) (G 6)

Susannah Rebecca Lownes

Rebecca Lownes and (husband's name was not available) child was Susannah Rebecca Lownes, who married Frank Daniels; they had one child, Ruth Daniels. Frank died in Florida. Susannah Rebecca Lownes was born on July 12, 1880. No other information was available.

Children of Elizabeth Jones and Robert Taylor (G 6)

Benjamin James Taylor

Elizabeth Jones and Robert Taylor's first child was Benjamin James Taylor. He was unmarried. No other information was available.

Anthony Taylor

Elizabeth Jones and Robert Taylor's second child was Anthony Taylor, who married Caroline F. Johnson. No other information was available.

Alice Jones Taylor

Elizabeth Jones and Robert Taylor's third child was Alice Jones Taylor, who was unmarried. No other information was available.

Sarah Taylor

Elizabeth Jones and Robert Taylor's fourth child was Sarah Taylor. No other information was available.

Children of Charles Chapman and Charlotte Christte (G 6)

Charlotte Chapman

Charles Chapman and Charlotte Christte's first child was Charlotte Chapman. No other information was available.

Charles Chapman

Charles Chapman and Charlotte Christte's second child was Charles Chapman. No other information was available.

Fredrick Wiltshire Chapman

Charles Chapman and Charlotte Christte's third child was Fredrick Wiltshire Chapman. His birth is unknown; he died in 1821 in India. No other information was available.

Children of Elizabeth Chapman and Samuel Harvey (G 6)

Thomas Harvey

Elizabeth Chapman and Samuel Harvey's first child was Thomas Harvey. No other information was available.

Louise Harvey

Elizabeth Chapman and Samuel Harvey's second child was Louise Harvey. No other information was available.

Children of Sarah Chapman and Thomas Ash (G 6)

Mary Ash

Sarah Chapman and Thomas Ash's first child was Mary Ash. No other information was available.

Joshua Ash

Sarah Chapman and Thomas Ash's second child was Joshua Ash. No other information was available.

Charlotte Ash

Sarah Chapman and Thomas Ash's third child was Charlotte Ash. No other information was available.

Charles Ash

Sarah Chapman and Thomas Ash's fourth child was Charles Ash. No other information was available.

Child of Sally Ann Pleasants and husband (name unknown) (G 6)

Infant

Sally Ann Pleasants and an unknown husband's (name unknown) child was an infant. No name was found. No other information was available.

Children of Caleb Pancoast Lownes and Ann Minges (G 6)

Thomas Chapman Lownes

Caleb Pancoast Lownes and Ann Minges's first child was Thomas Chapman Lownes, who married Sarah Frick. It is to be noted that Thomas Chapman Lownes, sometimes called "Casper," was born May 22st, 1827 in Baltimore, Maryland where his father had his bakery business. Young Thomas was seven years old when his father disappeared out west. Thomas was the oldest of six children. He and his siblings were raised by their mother in Center Square. No doubt this is where he learned the blacksmith trade.

At age twenty-three, Thomas married Sarah Frick on April 25th, 1850, and they continued living in Center Square. (A lengthy notation concerning the grandparents of Sarah Frick, the Van Fossens, who founded Germantown, Pennsylvania, and built the original Mennonite Church there, will be found at the close of this document).

When the Civil War broke out, thirty-four year old Thomas enlisted in "Company E. 4th Regiment, Penna. Volunteers, Gar: 1861 in the service of the United States," At the time, he was a father of three children while serving his country. He served in six of the 2400 battles of the Civil War; he was mustered in April 20th, 1861. He went to Philadelphia on April 21st then to Perryville, and Annapolis, MD. From there, they moved to Washington, D.C. near Bladensburg and to Shutter's Hill. They advanced to Manassas, VA. In July 16-21, then they went to Bull Run on July, 21st. Three months later, he was discharged from the service of the United States this twenty-seventh day of July, 1861. The reason for discharge was listed as "Time of Enlistment Expires." His official record also states that he was a musician and that he was five feet, eight inches tall, with light complexion, blue eyes and brown hair. Isn't that strange; one of his great grand-sons is five feet, eight inches tall, blue eyes, and at one time had brown hair; that was me, Howard G. Lownes Sr. It is also noted that Thomas Chapman Lownes was buried at St. John Lutheran Church in Center Square, Pennsylvania. There is a walk of memory there leading into the cemetery, and Howard G. Lownes Sr. had purchased a brick in his memory which is now in that walk.

This is the brick in the memory walk at St. John Lutheran Church

Above is the grave stone and marker for Thomas Chapman Lownes
at St John's Lutheran Church in Center Square, Pennsylvania

This is a close-up of the marker for Thomas Chapman Lownes

Following Thomas's return from the service, twins (a boy and a girl)
where born on July 1st, 1861 and five more children were born to this

household making a total of ten children. Thomas Chapman Lownes and Sarah Frick's children: Adaline Lownes, Henry Lownes, Charles Thomas Lownes, Anna Frick Lownes, Samuel Lownes, Lewis Lownes, Robert Lownes, Ida Lownes, Walter B. Lownes, and Morris Lownes.

About 1877, Thomas (Casper) moved his large family from Center Square, Pennsylvania, to the outskirts of Iron Bridge in Western Pennsylvania where he rented a blacksmith shop. During this period, Anna and one of the twins went to live with her grandparents, Henry and Catherine Van Fossen Frick, for a couple of years. However, two years later Thomas was able to open a blacksmith shop in the Village of Iron Bridge, next to St. John's Lutheran Church, where he was a sexton. At this time, Anna came home to live with the family again. (It was Anna's daughter, Myrtle, who supplied Charlotte Lownes Olewiler with most of the early background material about the Lowness).

Thomas Chapman Lownes and Sarah had almost fifty wonderful years of marriage together in the most beautiful rural part of Pennsylvania before they died. They lived to see most of their grandchildren including Dr. John Barton Lownes, a noted urologist and one of the founders of the Philadelphia Urological Society.

Catherine Lownes

Caleb Pancoast Lownes and Ann Minges's second child was Catherine Lownes. No other information was available.

Robert Lownes

Caleb Pancoast Lownes and Ann Minges's third child was Robert Lownes. No other information was available.

William Lownes

Caleb Pancoast Lownes and Ann Minges's fourth child was William Lownes.

No other information was available.

Mary Lownes

Caleb Pancoast Lownes and Ann Minges's fifth child was Mary Lownes. No other information was available.

James Roach Lownes

Caleb Pancoast Lownes and Ann Minges's sixth child, was James Roach Lownes, who married Euphemia Bisbing; they had seven children: Sarah Lownes, Herbert Lownes, Anna Lownes, James Oscar Lownes, Milton Markley Lownes, Elia Lownes, and, Herbert Lownes. James Roach Lownes was born in 1830. No other information was available

Children of William Donaldson Lownes and Hannah Low (G 6)

Jane Eliza Lownes

William Lownes and Hannah Low's first child was Jane Eliza Lownes, who married John Eckel. They had nine children: Benjamin Barker Eckel, Caroline Eckel, Edwin Eckel, Sarah Ellen Eckel, Lilla Eckel, Earl Eckel, Mary Eckel, John Eckel, and Christina Eckel. The only record available is, Benjamin Barker Eckel was the man that wrote the diary on July 20th, 1903. These diary pages are at the end of the book. No other information was available.

Amanda Lownes

William Lownes and Hannah Low's second child was Amanda Lownes, who married Benjamin F. Baker. No other information was available.

Two Sons

William Lownes and Hannah Low had two other sons and no names where available. No other information was available.

Child of Andrew Jackson Lowndes
and Mary Ann Bucknall (G 6)

(Note the "d" was reinstated).

Mary Lowndes

Andrew Jackson Lowndes and Mary Ann Bucknall's child was Mary Lowndes, who married Albert Sidney Johnson Owens on August 23rd, 1887 in Baltimore, Maryland. Mary Ann was born in Baltimore, Maryland and died in Baltimore, Maryland. Albert Sidney Johnson Owens was born in Smithville, Calvert County, Maryland, and died in Baltimore, Maryland. Mary Lowndes was born on January 25, 1859. They had one child; Mary Lownes Owens. No other information was available.

Children of Samuel Pleasants Lowndes and Julia
Catherine Dougherty (G 6)

Mary Ellen Lowndes

Samuel Pleasants Lowndes and Julia Catherine Dougherty's first child was Mary Ellen Lowndes, who married Lester Arrowsmith, they had three children: Lester Arrowsmith, Halstead Arrowsmith, and Jennie Arrowsmith. Mary Ellen Lowndes was born on October 12, 1845. No other information was available.

Jennie Lowndes

Samuel Pleasants Lowndes and Julia Catherine Dougherty's second child was Jennie Lowndes. No other information was available.

Henry Lowndes

Samuel Pleasants Lowndes and Julia Catherine Dougherty's third child was Henry Lowndes. No other information was available.

James Lowndes

Samuel Pleasants Lowndes and Julia Catherine Dougherty's fourth child was James Lowndes. No other information was available.

Sarah Lowndes

Samuel Pleasants Lowndes and Julia Catherine Dougherty's fifth child was Sarah Lowndes. Sarah Lowndes was born in 1863. No other information was available.

Reuben Lowndes

Samuel Pleasants Lowndes and Julia Catherine Dougherty's sixth child was Reuben Lownes, who married Nellie Verbeck, of Budapest, Prussia. They had three children: Raymond Gerald Lowndes, Albert Lowndes, and George Lowndes. Reuben Lowndes was born in 1872. No other information was available.

Children of Araminta Steel Lowndes
and Francis J. Barnes (G 6)

Alice Barnes

Araminta Steel Lowndes and Francis J. Barnes's first child was Alice Barnes. No other information was available.

Jane E. Barnes

Araminta Steel Lowndes and Francis J. Barnes's second child was Jane E. Barnes. She was born in 1839. No other information was available.

Fannie M. Barnes

Araminta Steel Lowndes and Francis J. Barnes's third child was Fannie M. Barnes. She was born in 1843. No other information is available.

Addie Barnes

Araminta Steel Lowndes and Francis J. Barnes's fourth child was Addie Barnes. She was born in 1847. No other information was available.

Ella Barnes

Araminta Steel Lowndes and Francis J. Barnes's fifth child was Ella Barnes. She was born in 1849. No other information was available.

George Barnes

Araminta Steel Lowndes and Francis J. Barnes's sixth child was George Barnes. He was born in 1831. No other information was available.

Bella Barnes

Araminta Steel Lowndes and Francis J. Barnes's seventh child was Bella Barnes. She was born in 1855. No other information was available.

Elia G. Barnes

Araminta Steel Lowndes and Francis J. Barnes's eighth child was Elia G. Barnes. She was born in 1856. No other information was available.

Children of Josiah Hewes Lownes
and Arabella Sinton (G 6)

Joseph Henry Lownes

Josiah Hewes Lownes and Arabella Stinson's first child was Joseph Henry Lownes. No other information was available.

Sarah Lownes

Josiah Hewes Lownes and Arabella Stinson's second child was Sarah Lownes. No other information was available.

Josiah Hewes Lownes Jr.

Josiah Hewes Lownes and Arabella Stinson's third child was Josiah Hewes Lownes Jr. No other information was available.

Chas Lownes

Josiah Hewes Lownes and Arabella Stinson's fourth child was Chas Lownes. No other information was available.

Danison Lownes

Josiah Hewes Lownes and Arabella Stinson's fifth child was Danison Lownes, who married Nancy Catherine Gamble, they had eight children: Robert Lownes, Glynn Lownes, Chas Lownes, Henry Grattan Lownes, Edward Brackinridge Lownes, Elise Gamble Lownes, Cary Gamble Lownes, and Letitia Edwards Lownes. No other information was available.

Child of Sarah Lownes and (Husband's name was not available) (G 6)

Laura Beth Lownes

Child of Sarah Lownes and husband's name was not available, was Laura Beth Lownes. She died at the age of six. No other information was available.

Child of Phillip Lown and Martha Van Velset (G 6)

(Note that the "es" has been dropped)

Frank Lown

Phillip Lown and Martha Van Velset's child was Frank Lown, who married Nora Naden in 1915. They had two children: Frank Phillip Lown, and Wendall Naden Lown No other information was available..

Children of Jacob Lown and Mary Ann Rees (G 6)

Albert "Bert" Lown

Jacob Lown and Mary Ann Rees's first child was Albert "Bert" Lown, who married Maud Eschleman. They had three children: Floyd Lown, Glenna Lown, and Pauline Lown. Jacob Lown was born in 1840. No other information was available.

Sarah J. Lown

Jacob Lown and Mary Ann Rees's second child was Sarah J. Lown, who married Wilson Brooks in 1887. They had eight children: Ocar Brooks, Ernest Brooks, Jay Brooks, Ralph Brooks, Helen Brooks, Alice Brooks, Mary Brooks, and Harold Brooks. Sarah J. Lown was born in 1867. No other information was available.

Rees Rees Lown

Jacob Lown and Mary Ann Rees's third child was Rees Rees Lown, who married Olive Lanah Mason, on October 31, 1894. They had two children; Benie Colman Lown, and Emory Lester Lown. Rees Ress Lown was born in 1870. No other information was available.

THIS SECOND GROUP OF DESCENDANTS IS FROM THE GEORGE LOWNES AND MARY BOWERS'S BRANCH OF THE FAMILY

Child of Sarah Crosby Lownes and Crosby P. Morton (G 6)

Susannah Crosby Morton

Sarah Crosby Lownes and Crosby P. Morton's child was Susannah Crosby Morton, who married J. Frank Black, of Chester on February 16, 1865. No other information was available.

Children of Hannah Lane Lownes and William W. Maddock (G 6)

Lownes Maddock

Hannah Lane Lownes and William W. Maddock's first child was Lownes Maddock, who married Elizabeth Worrall, of Ridley, Pennaylvania on January 22nd, 1872. No other information was available.

William Maddock

Hannah Lane Lownes and William W. Maddock's second child was William Maddock, who married M. Hannah (no first name was available). They had one child; Willie Maddock. No other information was available.

Child of Elizabeth Levis and Philip Brooks (G 6)

Agnes Brooks

Elizabeth Levis and Philip Brooks's child was Agnes Brooks. She was born July 23, 1844, she died in 1914. No other information was available.

Children of Phineas Lownes and Emily Lewis (G 6)

Anna Lownes

Phineas Lownes and Emily Lewis's first child was Anna Lownes. She was born on December 19, 1816. No other information was available.

Phineas William Lownes

Phineas Lownes and Emily Lewis's second child was Phineas William Lownes, who married Eunice Stevens, they had three children: Edward Phineas Lownes, Edith B. Lownes, and Harry P. Lownes. Phineas William Lownes was born on November 16, 1851. No other information was available.

Emily Lownes

Phineas Lownes and Emily Lewis's third child was Emily Lownes, who married Dr. Walter Browing. They had two children: Walter Browing Jr., and Eleanor Browing. Emily Lownes was born on July 3, 1855. No other information was available.

Children of Massey Lownes and John Jackson (G 6)

Deborah Jackson

Massey Lownes and John Jackson's first child was Deborah Jackson. No other information was available.

Elizabeth Jackson

Massey Lownes and John Jackson's second child was Elizabeth Jackson. No other information was available.

John Jackson

Massey Lownes and John Jackson's third child was John Jackson, who married Massey Lownes. No other information was available.

Israel Jackson

Massey Lownes and John Jackson's fourth child was Israel Jackson, who married Joseph Taylor. They had one child; Joseph Taylor. No other information was available.

Harlum Jackson

Massey Lownes and John Jackson's fifth child was Harlum Jackson. No other information was available.

Childern of George Bolton Lownes II and Rachel (Rebecca) Webb (G6)

William Henry Lownes III

George Bolton Lownes II and Rachel (Rebecca) Webb's first child was William Henry Lownes III, who married Florence Ida Thayer, daughter of Nathan Thayer of Boston, on October 13th, 1881. They had four children: Nathan Thayer Lownes, Rebecca Lownes, Emily Lownes and Charlotte Lownes. William Henry Lownes was born on January 9, 1850. No other information was available.

George Bolton Lownes III

George Bolton Lownes II and Rachel (Rebecca) Webb's second child was George Bolton Lownes III, who married Elizabeth Commings. They had no children. After she died, George Bolton Lownes III, married Mary Datesman, they had two children: Edward Datesman Lownes, and George Bolton Lownes IV. George Bolton Lownes was born on August 9, 1851. No other information was available.

Mary Moore Lownes

George Bolton Lownes II and Rachel (Rebecca) Webb's third child was Mary Moore Lownes, who married S. Edgar Levis, of Clifton Heights, Pennsylvania. They had four children: Florence Levis, Ogborn Levis, George B. Levis, and Hannah Darlington Levis. Mary Moore Lownes was born on August 24, 1854. No other information was available.

Hannah Darlington Lownes

George Bolton Lownes II and Rachel (Rebecca) Webb's fourth child was Hannah Darlington Lownes, who was never married. She is buried at the Springfield Friends Meeting House. Hannah Darlington Lownes was born on April 6, 1856. She passed away at her home at 255 Woodland Avenue, located on the old Lownes homestead farm when she was seventy four years old. No other information was available.

Edward Lownes

George Bolton Lownes II and Rachel (Rebecca) Webb's fifth child was Edward Lownes, who married Viola Healy. They had one child; Viola Healy Lownes. Edward Lownes graduated from the University of Pennsylvania. Edward Lownes was born on August 22, 1860. He is buried in Media, Pennsylvania. No other information was available.

Rebecca Lownes

George Bolton Lownes II and Rachel (Rebecca) Webb's sixth child was Rebecca Lownes, who never married. She was born on November 24, 1861. No other information was available.

Francis "Frank" Lownes

George Bolton Lownes II and Rachel (Rebecca) Webb's seventh child was Francis "Frank" Lownes, who married Eliza Rogers on October 21, 1896. They had two children: John "Jack" Lownes (a Quaker), and Margaret Lownes (a Quaker). Frances "Frank" Lownes was born on July 6, 1863. No other information was available.

Minerva Webb Lownes

George Bolton Lownes II and Rachel (Rebecca) Webb's eighth child was Minerva Webb Lownes, who never married. Minerva Webb Lownes graduated from the Friends School in Philadelphia. She lived in the Woodland Avenue house until her brother Joseph Lownes and his wife Grace moved in. Minerva Webb Lownes was born on June 7, 1865. No other information was available.

Jane Carpenter Lownes

George Bolton Lownes II and Rachel (Rebecca) Webb's ninth child was Jane Carpenter Lownes, who married John Webster. John Webster graduated from University of Pennsylvania in the same class as Edward Lownes. They had five children: Edward Webster, Mary Rebecca Webster, Harold Smedley Webster, Lydia Smedley Webster, and John Webster Jr. Jane Carpenter Lownes was born on April 16, 1867. No other information was available.

Joseph Lownes

George Bolton Lownes II and Rachel (Rebecca) Webb's tenth child was Joseph Lownes, who married Jennie Worrell Powell in 1905. Jennie Worrell Powell was the daughter of Charles H. Powell, a Springfield Quaker farmer, and Emma J. Worrell, also a Quaker from Springfield. Charles and Emma Powell owned the house at 540 W. Springfield Road next to the Haldeman Field in Springfield. Joseph had a large truck farm on Crum Creek Road in Marple, Township. One day a week, they drove in their horse and buggy to the Farmers Market on 52nd Street in Philadelphia to sell their fresh produce, homemade pies, jams and pickles. They had to leave at the wee hours of the morning to get there by 7 AM. Joseph Lownes and Jennie Worrell Powell had one child Joseph Lownes Jr. Joseph Lownes was born on July 24, 1858. He died on November 9, 1943 and is buied at the Springfield Meeting House. No other information was available.

CHAPTER EIGHT

Generation Eight

THIS FIRST GROUP OF DESCENDANTS IS
FROM THE JAMES I. LOWNES AND SUSANNAH
RICHARDS'S BRANCH OF THE FAMILY

Children of Hannah Ann Lownes
and William Ellia (G 7)

Caterinc Ellis

Hannah Ann Lownes and William Ellis's first child was Christine Ellis.
No other information was available.

Edward Ellis

Hannah Ann Lownes and William Ellis's second child was Edward Ellis.
No other information was available.

Rebecca Ellis

Hannah Ann Lownes and William Ellis's third child was Rebeca Ellis.
No other information was available.

Child of Josiah Harvey & (wife name was no avilable) (G7)

Alex Elmslio Harvey

Josiah Harvey and (wife's name was not available) only child was Alex Elmslio Harvey, who married Rachel Wister. They had two children: the first name was not available, and Esther Wister Harvey. No other information was available.

Child of Sarah Crosby Lownes and Crosby P. Morton (G 7)

Susannah Crosby Morton

Sarah Crosby Lownes and Crosby P. Morton's child was Susannah Crosby Morton, who married Frank Black of Chester, Pennsylvania, on February 16, 1865. They did not have any children. No other information was available.

Children of Hannah Lane Lownes and William J. Maddock (G 7)

Lownes Maddock

Hannah Lane Lownes and William J. Maddock's first child was Lownes Maddock, who married Elizabeth Worrall of Ridley, Pennsylvania, on January 22, 1872. They did not have any children. No other information was available.

William Maddock

Hannah Lane Lownes and William J. Maddock's second child was William Maddock, who married M. Hannah (no first name was available). They had one child, Willie Maddock, who died in infancy. No other information was available.

Child of Elizabeth Levis and Phillip Brooke (G 7)

Agnes Brooke

Elizabeth Levis and Phillip Brooke's only child was Agnes Levis Brooke. She was born on July 23, 1844 and died in 1914. No other information was available.

Children of Anna Paxon and Joshua Pancoast (G 7)

Richard Pancoast

Anna Paxon and Joshua Pancoast's first child was Richard Pancoast. No other information was available.

Henry Pancoast

Anna Paxon and Joshua Pancoast's second child was Henry Pancoast. No other information was available.

Child of Ann Buckley and Israel W. Morris (G 7)

Effingham Morris

Ann Buckley and Israel W. Morris's child was Effingham Morris, who married Ellen Burroughs. No other information was available.

Children of Henry Ely Lownes
and Sarah Jane Walton (G7)

Marianna Lownes

Henry Ely Lownes and Sarah Jane Walton's first child was Marianna Lownes, who married J. Russell Lownes of California in 1876. Mariana Lownes was born on July 1, 1857, and she died on December 4, 1899. No other information was available.

Sarah Elizabeth Lownes

Henry Ely Lownes and Sarah Jane Walton's second child was Sarah Elizabeth Lownes, who married Charles B. Hellyer on December 1, 1888; they had five children: Rebecca Morris Hellyer, Marianna Hellyer, Elizabeth Roach Hellyer, Charles Henry Hellyer, and Robert Conrad Hellyer. Sarah Elizabeth Lownes was born on August 14, 1859; she died on July 28, 1941. Charles died on January 10, 1942. No other information was available.

Child of Mary Lownes and (no husband
name was avilable) (G 7)

Marianna Lownes

Mary Lownes and no husband's name was available, child was Marianna Lownes. Marianna Lownes was born on April 2, 1857; she died on December 4, 1899. No other information was available.

Children of Elias Paxsen Lownes and Margaret Norcross (G 7)

Martha Conrad Lownes

Elias Paxsen Lownes and Margaret Norcross's first child was Martha Conrad Lownes. She was born on September 5, 1860; she died on May 11, 1959. No other information was available.

Beulah Lownes

Elias Paxsen Lownes and Margaret Norcross's second child was Beulah Lownes. She was born on December 13, 1873; she died on June 30, 1875. No other information was available.

William Elias Lownes

Elias Paxsen Lownes and Margaret Norcross's third child was William Elias Lownes. He was born on January 11, 1876; he died on April 12, 1968. No other information was available.

Children of Joseph Lownes and Margaret Ann Scully (G 7)

Samuel Cooper Lownes

Joseph Lownes and Margaret Ann Scully's first child was Samuel Cooper Lownes, who married Susan McDowell. They had one child, Dorothy Lownes. Samuel Cooper Lownes then married Elizabeth, no last name was avilable. They had six children: Margaret Lownes, Elizabeth Lownes, Samuel Lownes Jr., Robert Lownes, Donald Lownes, and Frances Lownes. Samuel Cooper Lownes was born on March 6, 1875; he died on September 8, 1948. No other information was available.

John Scully Lownes

Joseph Lownes and Margaret Ann Scully's second child was John Scully Lownes, who married Cora German; they had one child, Harriet German Lownes. John Scully Lownes was born on October 8, 1877; he died on February 19, 1948. No other information was available.

Fanny Edith Lownes

Joseph Lownes and Margaret Ann Scully's third child was Fanny Edith Lownes, who died of walking typhoid. Fanny Edith Lownes was born on September 5, 1880; her death date was not given. No other information was available.

Sarah Ann Lownes

Joseph Lownes and Margaret Ann Scully's fourth child was Sarah Ann Lownes. She was born on July 17, 1882; she died on July 7, 1892. No other information was available.

George Mahan Lownes

Joseph Lownes and Margaret Ann Scully's fifth child was George Mahan Lownes, who married Florence Worrell. They had four children: Alfred Russell Lownes, Wilmer Atkinson Lownes, Helen Eleanor Lownes, and George M. Lownes Jr.. George Mahan Lownes was born on November 8, 1884; he died on February 14, 1959. No other information was available.

Hannah Lownes

Joseph Lownes and Margaret Ann Scully's sixth child was Hannah Lownes, who married husband's name was not available. They had one child; Margaret Elizabeth Lownes. Hannah Lownes was born on October 17, 1886; she died of tuberculosis on September 16, 1927. No other information was available.

Helen Jones Lownes

Joseph Lownes and Margaret Ann Scully's seventh child was Helen Jones Lownes, who married Albert Cornell; they had one child, James Martin Cornell. Helen and Albert divorced. After seventeen years of teaching, Helen married Roscoe L. Horner, a funeral director living in Langhorne, Pennsylvania. Roscoe L. Horner's child from a previous marriage was Florence, who married Kjell Christiansen. Hjell was a surgeon at Bryn Mawr Hospital in Bryn Mawr, Pennsylvania. Helen Jones Lownes was born on April 17, 1894. No other information was available.

Joseph Ewell Lownes

Joseph Lownes and Margaret Ann Scully's eighth child was Joseph Ewell Lownes, whose wife's name was not avilable. They had three children. The first two daughter's names are unknown; the third one was Margaret Evelyn Lownes. Joseph Ewell Lownes was born on September 4, 1896 he died on October 3, 1973. Joseph Ewell Lownes is a twin to Thomas Russell Lownes. No other information was available.

Thomas Russell Lownes

Joseph Lownes and Margaret Ann Scully's ninth child was Thomas Russell Lownes, who married Laura Lownes. They had two children; their names were not avilable. Thomas Russell Lownes was born on September 4, 1896; he died on November 15, 1973. Thomas Russell Lownes is a twin to Joseph Ewell Lownes. No other information was available.

Child of Susanna Rebecca Lownes
and Frank Daniels (G 7)

Ruth Daniels

Susanna Rebecca Lownes and Frank Daniels's only child was Ruth Daniels, who married Art McCollion. They had one child, Jane Ellen McCollian. No other information was available.

Children of Thomas Chapman Lownes
and Sarah Frick (G 7)

Adaline Lownes

Thomas Chapman Lownes and Sarah Frick's first child was Adaline Lownes, who married William J. Thompson on November 17, 1877. They had one child, William Thompson. Adaline Lownes was born on June 29, 1851; she died on August 16, 1906. No other information was available.

Henry Lownes

Thomas Chapman Lownes and Sarah Frick's second child was Henry Lownes. Henry Lownes was born on February 6, 1854; he died on August 20, 1861. No other information was available.

Charles Thomas Lownes

Thomas Chapman Lownes and Sarah Frick's third child was Charles Thomas Lownes, who married Mary C. Heist on September 8, 1880. They had two children: Morris Lownes and John Barton Lownes. Charles Thomas Lownes was born on September 8, 1856; he died on August 21, 1927. No other information was available.

Anna Frick Lownes

Thomas Chapman Lownes and Sarah Frick's fourth child was Anna Frick Lownes, who married Irvin Peltz Williams on January 11, 1882. They had two children; Bertha L. Williams and Myrtle Williams. Anna Frick Lownes was a twin to Samuel Lownes. Anna Frick Lownes was born on July 1, 1861; she died on December 2, 1949. It's ironic that my parents, Irvin Lownes and Dotrthey Deihm were married fifty years later on January 11, 1932. No other information was available.

Samuel Lownes

Thomas Chapman Lownes and Sarah Frick's fifth child was Samuel Lownes, who married Lillian Perch. They had two children: Florence Lownes and Elmer Lownes. Samuel was a twin to Anna Frick Lownes. Samuel Lownes wa a twin to Anna Frick Lownes. Samuel Lownes was born on July 1, 1861, he died on November 29, 1932. No other information was available.

Lewis M. Lownes

Thomas Chapman Lownes and Sarah Frick's sixth child was Lewis M. Lownes, who was unmarried. Lewis was born on August 15, 1867, in Center Square on the family homestead. He was educated at the public schools of the townships and at Loller Academy, a famous school at Hatboro, Pennsylvania. He served an apprenticeship to hat making in West Perkiomen Township. He went to Fall River, Massachusetts, where he was employed for several years in manufacturing hats at one of the extensive establishments in the area and later was similarly engaged working in Newark, New Jersey, and Orange Valley, Connecticut, remaining there some time, all of which was spent in his occupation of hat making.

In 1890, Lewis came to Norristown, Pennsylvania his native county, and opened an establishment for manufacturing hats on East

Main Street, where he purchased property and turned it into one of the most eligible business places in Norristown. He was successful in his business, having provided himself with the latest machinery for doing first class work. He had acquired an excellent reputation for the products he turned out because of his up-to-date methods in hat making. He was not only a thoroughly wide-awake business man, but he was also an inventor of considerable notes, and many patents have been granted to him in this and other countries for his improvements in the manufacturing of hats.

In politics; Lewis was an active Republican, never missing an election, although he was too much devoted to his business interests to seek an official position. He was unmarried. Fraternally, he was a member of the Order of Knights of the Golden Eagle and the Junior Order of United American Mechanics. He was a Lutheran in religion.

This is a picture of Lewis M. Lownes copied from
a book in the Montgomery County Historical
Museum in Norristown, Pennsylvania.

Robert C. Lownes

Thomas Chapman Lownes and Sarah Frick's seventh child was Robert C. Lownes, who married Anna C. Bean, daughter of Henry K. Bean of Norristown. They had two children: Clarence Lownes and Harry Lownes, who died young. Robert Lownes then married Susan Trumbower Gotals in 1898, widow of John Godshall. They had one child, Ruth Lownes.

Robert C. Lownes was born on April 24, 1869, in Center Square on the family homestead in Whitpain Township, Montgomery County, Pennsylvania. He was educated in the common schools of the neighborhood until he was sixteen years of age. He learned the trade of blacksmithing, and after his apprentaship he followed blacksmithing at Skippack for ten or eleven years. He purchased the hotel at Center Point in Worcester Township, conducting it for five years. He next purchased a hotel at West Point in Gwynedd Township that he successfully operated for two years. At the end of that time, he moved to Lansdale and purchased the Norwood Hotel that he operated for many years. He made many improvements so that it ranked with the finest hotels of Montgomery County.

Ida Parker Lownes

Thomas Chapman Lownes and Sarah Frick's eighth child was Ida Parker Lownes, who married William Blackwood Thomason on August 1, 1900. They had no children. Ida Parker Lownes was born on March 11, 1870; she died on October 18, 1930. No other information was available.

Walter B. Lownes

Thomas Chapman Lownes and Sarah Frick's ninth child was Walter B. Lownes, who married Anna Clark in 1894; they had seven children: Walter Bowen Lownes Jr., Myrtle Lownes, Thomas Lownes, Edna Lownes, Charles Lownes, Laura Lownes, and Irvin Lownes.

Here is an excerpt from Charlotte Lownes Olewiler's book, *The*

Gawsworth Quakers Hugh and Jane Lowndes, she is my cousin and Walter B. Lownes Jr.'s daughter.

Walter B. Lownes was born on September 25, 1872, on the family homestead in Center Square. Walter lived during the peaceful and prosperous time known as "the turn of the century." He saw the bustle give way to daring skirts that showed the ankle. He saw the horse and buggy exchanged for trolleys and automobiles, and he saw sleepy villages grow into cities.

Walter B. Lownes grew to be tall and fair. He was as placid as he was big. In 1894, he married diminutive, energetic Anna Clark of Philadelphia. Walter joined his brother Charles (sixteen years older) in his hostely business. Charles also had a cider mill on the property which the mill is stil standing although abandon in Arcola, Pennslyvanis. Walter was not cut out to be in that kind of business. He moved his family to Gladwyne, Pennsylvania, where he became a well-known and respected builder.

When Walter B. Lownes Sr. and Anna were expecting Walter Jr., times were difficult. Anna helped provide for the family by baking home made pies, which Walter Sr. sold at the Pennsylvania Railroad Station in Philadelphia. Home-going commuters were happy to pay good prices for the fresh pastry. After a few years, Anna had a growing egg business, and little Walter Jr. helped deliver the orders.

Five roads lead up to beautiful Gladwyne, which sits on top of a hill. In all the towns she has visited throughout America and the world, none compares with the charm of wooded Gladwyne. The remodeled old stage coach inn still stands and operates in the center of town, serving its hungry patrons. The population of Gladwyne today is about 2500 (era 1978). Along Mill Creek, one can still see the ruins of the old mill used extensively during the Revolutionary War period. Before the Redcoats took over the area, the colonists ground glass into the flour which the unsuspecting British then served to their troops.

Gladwyne is about fifteen miles from Valley Forge, in the area now known as the suburban Main Line.

When Walter and Anna raised their young family, Gladwyne was only a hamlet. They had four boys and three girls: Walter, Myrtle, Thomas, Edna, Charles, Laura, and Irvin. Laura died at age one year and ten months. Most of their children were born in Kulpsville, Pennsylvania.

This is a picture of Walter B. Lownes and Anna Clark Lownes, Charlotte's and my grandparents.

When Walter's dear Annie died of a stroke in 1932, he was desolate. He remarried briefly and died of a broken heart three years later.

This is the grave stone for Walter B Lownes, Annie Lownes, and daughter Laura Lownes. They are buried in the Odd Fellows Cemetery in Gladwyne, Montgomery County, Pennsylvania.

Morris Lownes

Thomas Chapman Lownes and Sarah Frick's tenth child was Morris Lownes. No other information was available.

Children of James Roach Lownes and Euphemia Bisbing (G 7)

Sarah Lownes

James Roach Lownes and Euphemia Bisbing's first child was Sarah Lownes. No other information was available

Herbert Lownes

James Roach Lownes and Euphemia Bisbing's second child was Herbert Lownes. No other information was available.

Anna Lownes

James Roach Lownes and Euphemia Bisbing's third child was Anna Lownes. No other information was available.

James Oscar Lownes

James Roach Lownes and Euphemia Bisbing's fourth child was James Oscar Lownes, who married Hannah, no last name was avilable. James Oscar Lownes was bon in 1861 and died in 1930. No other information was available.

Milton Markley Lownes

James Roach Lownes and Euphemia Bisbing's fifth child was Milton Markley Lownes, who married Gladys Williams Dunlap. Gladys William Dunlap was a daughter of William A. Dunlap and Alice Dunlap. Gladys was the first licensed female funeral director in Philadelphia, serving more than forty years. Gladys was associated with her father, William A. Dunlap in Philadelphia and in 1955, became associated with her son, Richard D. Lownes of the funeral service in, Lafayette Hill.

Ella Lownes

James Roach Lownes and Euphemia Bisbing's sixth child was Ella Lownes, who married Scheetz (first name was not avilable). No other information was available.

Herbert E. Lownes

James Roach Lownes and Euphemia's seventh child was Herbert E. Lownes. No other information was available.

Children of Jane Eliza Lownes and John Eckel (G 7)

Benjamin Barker Echel

Jane Elliza Lownes and John Eckel's first child was Benjamin Barker Eckel. Benjamin Barker Eckel wrote the diray that is shown in Appendix XIV which discusses the fact that our Caleb Lownes (generation six) was killed at the Alamo in 1836. No other information was available.

Caroline Eckel

Jane Elliza Lownes and John Eckel's second child was Carolin Eckel. No other information was available.

Edwin Eckel

Jane Elliza Lownes and John Eckel's third child was Edwin Eckel. No other information was available.

Sarah Ellen Eckel

Jane Elliza Lownes and John Eckel's fourth child was Sarah Ellen Eckel. No other information was available.

Lilla Eckel

Jane Elliza Lownes and John Eckel's fifth child was Lilla Eckel. No other information was available.

Earl Eckel

Jane Elliza Lownes and John Eckel's sixth child was Earl Eckel. No other information was available.

Mary Eckel

Jane Elliza Lownes and John Eckel's seventh child was Mary Eckel. No other information was available.

John Eckel

Jane Elliza Lownes and John Eckel's eighth child was John Eckel. No other information was available.

Christina Eckel

Jane Elliza Lownes and John Eckel's ninth child was Christina Eckel. No other information was available.

Child of Mary Lowndes and Albert Sidney Johnson Owens (G 7)

Note the "d" has been reinstated.

Mary Lowndes Owens

Mary Lowndes and Albert Sidney Johnson Owens's child was Mary Lowndes Owens, who married John Collinson Jr. on February 21, 1917. They had one child, John Collinson III. Mary Lowndes was born on November 16, 1888; she died on April 15, 1975. No other information was available.

Children of Mary Ellen Lowndes and Lester Arrowsmith (G 7)

Lester Arrowsmith

Mary Ellen Lowndes and Lester Arrowsmith's first child was Lester Arrowsmith. Lester Arrowsmith was born on July 31, 1879. No other information was available.

Halstead Arrowsmith

Mary Ellen Lownes and Lester Arrowsmith's second child was Halstead Arrowsmith. Halstead Arrowsmith was born on February 10, 1882. No other information was available.

Jennie Arrowsmith.

Mary Ellen Lownes and Lester Arrowsmith's third child was Jennie Arrowsmith. Jennie Arrowsmith was born on September 17, 1886. No other information was available.

Children of Rueben Lowndes and Nellie Verbeck (G 7)

(note the "d" has been reinstated)

Raymond Gerald Lowndes

Rueben Lowndes and Nellie Verbeck's first child was Raymond Gerald Lowndes, who married Bridget Ruddy, who was born in 1903. They had two children: Raymond Gerald Lowndes Jr. and Donald Lowndes. Raymond Gerald Lowndes was born on March 19, 1897; he died on October 30, 1972. No other information was available.

Albert Lowndes

Rueben Lowndes and Nellie Verbeck's second child was Albert Lowdnes, who married Lillian O'Keefe; she was born in 1896. Albert Lowndes was born on March 16, 1899; he died on August 20, 1969. No other information was available.

George Lowndes

Rueben Lowndes and Nellie Verbeck's third child was George Lowndes, who married Sophia Rimminsland on June 6, 1923. They had one child: Dorothy Lowndes. George Lowndes was born on March 30, 1901; he died in 1989. Sophia Rimminsland was born in 1899; she died in 1989. No other information was available.

Children of Danison Lownes
and Nancy Catherine Gamble (G 7)

Robert Lownes

Danison Lownes and Nancy Catherine Gamble's first child was Robert Lownes. No other information was available.

Glynn Lownes

Danison Lownes and Nancy Catherine Gamble's second child was Glynn Lownes. No other information was available.

Chas Lownes

Danison Lownes and Nancy Catherine Gamble's third child was Chas Lownes. No other information was available.

Henry Grattan Lownes

Danison Lownes and Nancy Catherine Gamble's fourth child was Henry Grattan Lownes. No other information was available.

Edward Brackinridge Lownes

Danison Lownes and Nancy Catherine Gamble's fifth child was Edward Brackinridge Lownes. No other information was available.

Elise Gamble Lownes

Danison Lownes and Nancy Catherine Gamble's sixth child was Elise Gamble Lownes. No other information was available.

Cary Gamble Lownes

Danison Lownes and Nancy Catherine Gamble's seventh child was Cary Gamble Lownes. No other information was available.

Letitia Edwards Lownes

Danison Lownes and Nancy Catherine Gamble's eighth child was Letitia Edwards Lownes. No other information was available.

Children of Frank Lown and Nora Naden (G 7)

Note the "es" has been removed.

Frank Phillip Lown

Frank Lown and Nora Naden's first child was Frank Phillip Lown, who married Mary Rauterkus in 1944. Frank Phillip Lown was born in 1917; he died in 1993. No other information was available.

Wendall Naden Lown

Frank Lown and Nora Naden's second child was Wendall Naden Lown, who married Anita (no last name was avilable) in 1955. Wendall Naden Lown was born in 1921. No other information was available.

Children of Albert "Bert" Lown and Maud Eschleman (G 7)

Floyd Lown

Albert "Bert" Lown and Maud Eschleman's first child was Floyd Lown, who married Alma Lee (no last name was available). No other information was available.

Glenna Lown

Albert "Bert" Lown and Maud Eschleman's second child was Glenna Lown. Glenna Lown was born in 1897; she died in 1954. No other information was available.

Pauline Lown

Albert "Bert" Lown and Maud Eschleman's third child was Pauline Lown, who married Leo Schaller. Pauline Lown was born in 1905; she died in 1956. No other information was available.

Children of Sarah J. Lown and Wilson Brooks (G 7)

Oscar Brooks

Sarah J. Lown and Wilson Brooks's first child was Oscar Brooks, who married Amy (no last name was avilable). No other information was available.

Ernest Brooks

Sarah J. Lown and Wilson Brooks's second child was Ernest Brooks, who married Eliza (no last name was avilable). No other information was available.

Jay Brooks

Sarah J. Lown and Wilson Brooks's third child was Jay Brooks, who married Ruth (no last name was avilable). No other information was available.

Ralph Brooks

Sarah J. Lown and Wilson Brooks's fourth child was Ralph Brooks, who married Elizabeth (no last name was avilable). No other information was available.

Helen Brooks

Sarah J. Lown and Wilson Brooks's fifth child was Helen Brooks, who married Howard Saltzgaber. No other information was available.

Alice Brooks

Sarah J. Lown and Wilson Brooks's sixth child was Alice Brooks, who was unmarried. No other information was available.

Mary Brooks

Sarah J. Lown and Wilson Brooks's seventh child was Mary Brooks, who married Ward Cooper. No other information was available.

Harold Brooks

Sarah J. Lown and Wilson Brooks's eighth child was Harold Brooks, who married Juanita (no last name was avilable). No other information was available.

Children of Rees Rees Lown
and Olive Lanah Mason (G 7)

Bernie Colman Lown

Rees Rees Lown and Olive Lanah Mason's first child was Bernie Coleman Lown, who married LuLu Augusta Tippet in 1919. They had one child, Martha Ann Lown. Bernie Colman Lown was born in 1897; he died in 1986. No other information was available.

Emory Lester Lown

Rees Rees Lown and Olive Lanah Mason's second child was Emory Lester Lown, who married Lena Maud Baker in 1924; they had two children: Gordon L. Lown and Eldon Cyril Lown. Emory Lester Lown was born in 1901; she died in 1969. Lena Maud Baker was born in 1901; he died in 1985. No other information was available.

Ceetta Lown

Rees Rees Lown and Olive Lanah Mason's third child was Ceetta Lown, who married Owen James Cooper. Then Ceetta married Gerald Hall and then married James Pleasant. Ceetta Lown and Owen James Cooper had one child, James Reese Cooper. Ceetta Lown was born in 1905; she died in 1988. Owen James Cooper was born in 1902; he died in 1930. No other information was available.

This Second Group of Descendants is From the George Lownes and Mary Bowers's Branch of the Family

Child of William Maddock and M. Hannah (no first name available) (G 7)

Willie Maddock

William Maddock and M. Hannah's (no first name was available) only child was Willie Madock. He died in infancy. No other information was available.

Children of Phineas William Lownes and Eunice Stevens (G 7)

Edward Phineas Lownes

Phineas William Lownes and Eunice Stevens's first child was Edward Phineas Lownes. Edward Phineas Lownes was born on November 22, 1879; he died on January 6, 1896. No other information was available.

Edith B. Lownes

Phineas William Lownes and Eunice Stevens's second child was Edith B. Lownes. Edith B. Lownes was born on November 3, 1883. No other information was available.

Harry P. Lownes

Phineas William Lownes and Eunice Stevens's third child was Harry P. Lownes. No other information was available.

Children of Emily Lownes
and Dr. Walter Browning (G 7)

Walter Browning

Emily Lownes and Dr. Walter Browning's first child was Walter Browning. Walter Browning Jr. was born in October of 1882. No other information was available.

Eleanor Browning

Emily Lownes and Dr. Walter Browning's second child was Eleanor Browning. No other information was available.

Child of Israel Jackson and Joseph Taylor (G 7)

Joseph Taylor

Israel Jackson and Joseph Taylor's only child was Joseph Taylor. No other information was available.

Children of William Henry Lownes III and Florence Ida Thayer (G 7)

Nathan Thayer Lownes

William Henry Lownes III and Florence Ida Thayer's first child was Nathan Thayer Lownes, who married Breta Clara Dohan of Philadelphia on April 3, 1907. He was a professor at Temple University in Philadelphia, Pensylvania. He was a mechanical engineer, and did genealogy research and wrote historical papers. Nathan Thayer Lownes was born on May 16, 1883; he lived at 6719 N. 15th Street in Philadelphia when he died on May 16, 1950. No other information was available.

Rebecca Lownes

William Henry Lownes III and Florence Ida Thayer's second child was Rebecca Lownes. Rebecca Lownes was born on August 26, 1884 in Morton Delaware. No other information was available.

Emily Lownes

William Henry Lownes III and Florence Ida Thayer's third child was Emily Lownes. Emily Lownes was born on June 20, 1887. No other information was available.

Charlotte Lownes

William Henry Lownes III and Florence Ida Thayer's fourth child was Charlotte Lownes. Charlotte Lownes was born on September 1, 1895. No other information was available.

Children of George Bolton Lownes III and Mary Datterman (second marriage) (G 7)

Edward Datesman Lownes

George Bolton Lownes III andMary Daterman's first child was Edward Datesman Lownes. No other information was available.

George Bolton Lownes IV

George Bolton Lownes III and Mary Daterman's second child was George Bolton Lownes IV. No other information was available.

Children of Mary Moore Lownes and S. Edgar Levis (G7)

Florence Levis

Mary Moore Lownes and Edgar Levis's first child was Florence Levis, who married Trainer (first name was not available); they had two children: Banncroft Trainer and Mary L. Trainer. Florence Levis was born on October 11, 1881. No other information was available.

Ogborn Levis

Mary Moore Lownes and Edgar Levis's second child was Ogborn Levis. She was born on February 1, 1885. No other information was available.

George B. Levis

Mary Moore Lownes and Edgar Levis's third child was George B. Levis. He was born on October 23, 1890. No other information was available.

Hannah Darlington Levis

Mary Moore Lownes and Edgar Levis's fourth child was Hannah Darlington Levis, who married Elwood Garrett. They had two children: Florence Garrett and Mary Garrett. Hannah Darlington Levis was born on March 2, 1895. No other information was available.

Child of Edward Lownes and Viola Healy (G 7)

Viola Healy Lownes

Edward Lownes and Viola Healy's only child was Viola Healy Lownes, she was born on March 26, 1886. No other information was available.

Children of Frances "Frank" Lownes and Eliza Rogers (G 7)

John (Jack) Lownes (Quaker)

Frances "Frank" Lownes (Quaker) and Eliza Rogers's first child was John (Jack) Lownes (Quaker), who married Hannah Hannum. They had four children: Sarah Lownes, Margaret Lownes, John Roger Lownes, and Rebe Lownes. No other information was available.

Margaret Lownes (Quaker)

Frances "Frank" Lownes and Eliza Rogers's second child was Margaret Lownes (Quaker), who married Dagmar Conover. They had three children: Margaret Conover, Frank Conover, and Ann Conover. Margaret Lownes and Dagmar Conover were neighbors to Joe Lownes and Grace Lownes (more information to follow). Margaret Lownes was born on July 7. 1897. No other information was available.

Children of Jane Carpenter Lownes and John Webster (G 7)

Edward Webster

Jane Carpenter Lownes and John Webster's first child was Edward Webster. He was born on April 26, 1852. No other information was available.

Mary Rebecca Webster

Jane Carpenter Lownes and John Webster's second child was Mary Rebecca Webster. She was born on November 5, 1855; she died on November 7, 1895. No other information was available.

Harold Smedley Webster

Jane Carpenter Lownes and John Webster's third child was Harold Smedley Webster, who was born on March 29, 1897. No other information was available.

Lydia Smedley Webster

Jane Carpenter Lownes and John Webster's fourth child was Lydia Smedley Webster, who was born on October 5, 1900. No other information was available.

John Webster Jr.

Jane Carpenter Lownes and John Webster's fivth child was John Webster Jr. No other information was available.

Child of Joseph Lownes and Jennie Worrell Powell (G 7)

Joseph Lownes Jr.

Joseph Lownes and Jennie Worrell Powell's child was Joseph Lownes Jr., who married Grace Hamilton Custer on September 5, 1930. Joseph Jr.'s mother had joined the Baptist Church before she married Joseph's father. Joseph was raised in the Baptist Church of Media. Joseph Jr. enjoyed helping his parents on the farm, feeding the chickens, digging potatoes, et cetera.

In 1926, Joseph met Grace Hamilton Custer. Grace's father, Thomas John Custer, was a house painter. Her mother was Emma Jane Fisher, who was an orphan and the maid in the wealthy Custer household. Grace had been dating Henry Powell, son of Walter and Mabel Powell. Walter was Jennie Powell's brother. Henry introduced Grace to his cousin, Joe Lownes. This was the beginning of a long friendship. Grace had left high school to attend business school in Philadelphia. After dating for four years, the couple chose September 5, 1930, as their wedding date (the anniversary of their first date).

Joseph and Grace's first home was 144 S. Highland Road, Springfield, Pennsylvania, where their first son, Joseph Donald Lownes, was born. Joseph did landscaping for many town people. They moved to Powell Road, then to 255 E. Woodland Avenue where they lived from 1936 until they sold the property in 1986 and moved to West Chester. Joseph and Grace had five children: Joseph Donald Lownes, George Bolton Lownes, Kenneth Hugh Lownes, Jane Ann Lownes, and Bruce Thayer Lownes. Joseph Lownes Jr. was born on December 12, 1907.

There is an interesting story about the house at 255 E. Woodland Avenue. It was built by great-grandfather George Bolton Lownes (generation 6) in 1915 when he was ninety years old and retired from farming at his Thompson Road farm where he and his wife raised ten children. The stone used in building the house was from the Lownes Quarry that was at the corner behind Charley's Hamburger Stand (Woodland and Baltimore Pike). The house was rented for a few years until three of George Bolton Lownes' daughters moved in (Minerva and Hannah, both unmarried, and Mary Levis who was a widow).

While the three women lived in the house, Joseph Lownes Jr. built a greenhouse to grow vegetables and flowers. Shortly after that, Grandfather Joseph (generation 7), bought the property to settle the estate, providing a home for Joe and Grace. Grace had worked part-time in a flower shop, which inspired them to start their own retail florist business. Joe went to Baxter Floral Design School in Philadelphia, and Grace learned the hard way, already having a very creative talent for design. For over thirty years, these two worked together, creating beautiful floral arrangements for weddings, funerals, and many events in town, including many of the corsages received by high school girls for their proms. All of their children worked in the flower shop and greenhouse, potting, planting, delivering, and any other jobs that were needed. As a result of their experience, all of the children have been involved in some way in horticulture. They attended the Media and Springfield Baptist Churches, actively teaching Sunday school in addition to many other responsibilities.

Grace had a heart for missions and was involved with the many activities including a trip to Central America to present funds for the building of a health clinic. All their children married and lived within a twenty-five mile radius of the Springfield homestead (with the exception of Kenneth who lives in West End, North Carolina, with his wife, Judi). Grace and Joe retired in the 1970s from the retail florist business, but Joe still had an active interest in growing plants and was considered the best Christmas wreath maker in the county. Grace enjoyed her retirement, working with various activities at church, knitting, and craft work, and was voted Woman of the Year by the Business and Professional Women's Association, an organization that she had been actively involved in.

Joe worked for many years with the Gideons, who enjoy the responsibility of placing bibles in all the motels and distribute New Testaments to freshman college students each year.

The couple enjoyed a special celebration with family and friends on their fiftieth wedding anniversary (1980) and also visited the Holy Land that year. In 1986, Grace and Joe sold their property in Springfield (after three-hundred years of Lownes residing in the town) and moved to their new home in West Chester, Chester County, Pennsylvania, where they shared the property with their daughter, Jane and her husband, Marty.

DELAWARE COUNTY (PA.) DAILY TIMES
Monday, July 1, 1974

Lowneses make mark

SPRINGFIELD — Hugh Lownes of Coworth, Cheshire County, England, a baker, married Jane Straich, of Rands, same county, October, 1658. They had four children.

Joseph Lownes of Springfield, Delaware County, Pennsylvania, a landscaper, married Grace H. Carter of Media, same county, September, 1930. They had five children.

The road between Joseph Lownes, who now lives at 231 E. Woodland Ave. and his distant relative Hugh is long and intricate but it travels mainly throughout the township.

"I've spent my entire life here, except 10 years when my mother and father bought a farm in Marple Township between 1915-1925," Lownes said.

"There is a story my father always told about Jane Lownes. In fact there are two conflicting stories about her husband."

"Hugh Lownes may have died on the voyage over from England. However, the other story is that he died in prison for his religious beliefs."

A study of Negley K. Teeters, Department of Sociology at Temple University in 1937 on the Lownes background states:

"As a religion they professed the principles of truth held by the Society of Friends on which account he (Hugh) suffered much persecution, being often put in prison on account of fines for non-conformity. He there took cold and died, leaving a widow and four young children who came to Philadelphia in 1688."

One thing is certain is Jane Lownes came to this area: She patented 150 acres from William Penn on February 10, 1682.

"The cave she lived in was on the side of the hill where Tri-County Hospital now stands," Lownes said. "A way of identifying it was by an impression in the land and a was sign placed on the site that said: Jane Lownes. Cave Dwelling 1682.

"The piece of land where my house now stands is the last portion of any original land still owned by the Lownes. We have 2.79 acres.

"This house was built in 1821 but the building for Wick's Ski Shop, 321 Woodland Ave., is an original of the families," Lownes added, remembering romps through the woods and fishing with his cousins in the nearby stream.

Mrs. Lownes moved to Springfield when she was married but can remember minstrels and the carnival on Windsor Circle even before she was married.

"Springfield used to be a real nice place to live," she said. "Now with the times and the traffic, it's worse."

But, the Lownes family will always be remembered in Springfield, if only for Jane Lownes Park or Lownes Lane or Lownes Free Church.

"It's nice to recognize the older families that way," Joseph Lownes said.

"Of course, when my daughter Jade was in high school she hated her name," Mrs. Lownes laughed. "She used to come home and ask why she had to be named Jane. Especially in fourth grade when they studied the history of Springfield."

Springfield's history and growth can be traced very clearly by Joseph Lownes.

With a perennial flower business adjacent to the house Joseph Lownes constantly has his hands in the soil, which is his great love.

"I've been handling plant life and soil ever since I can remember," he said.

Stones from the old Lownes quarry were used in building his shop.

A beautiful grandfather's clock that has traveled with the family from Springfield to Marple and back again now stands in the Lownes' living room. framed embroidery work, now fraying, hangs on the walls. and sterling silver spoons made by an early Joseph Lownes also are displayed.

There are others in Springfield who have been here longer than I have," Joseph Lownes said with a grin. "I don't know who they are or where but I'm just a kid."

JOSEPH LOWNES is proud of grandfather clock.

CHAPTER NINE

Generation Nine

THIS FIRST GROUP OF DESCENDANTS IS FROM THE JAMES I. LOWNES AND SUSANNAH RICHARDS'S BRANCH OF THE FAMILY

Children of Alex Elmslio
Harvey and Rachel Wister (G 8)

Child (No Name)

Alex Elmsilo Harvey and Rachel Webster's first child's name was not available. No other information was available.

Esther Wister Harvey

Alex Elmslio and Rachel Wister's second child's was Esther Wister Harvey, who married Frank Tiers. They had lots of children, no names were avilable. No other information was available.

Child of William Maddock and M. Hannah (no first name was available) (G 8)

Willie Maddock

William Maddock and M. Hannah's only child was Willie Maddock, who died in infancy. No other information was available.

Children of Sarah Elizabeth Lownes and Charles B. Hellyer (G 8)

Rebecca Morris Hellyer

Sarah Elizabeth Lownes and Charles B. Hellyer's first child was Rebecca Morris Hellyer. She was born on April 1, 1890. No other information was available.

Marianna Hellyer

Sarah Elizabeth Lownes and Charles B. Hellyer's second child was Marianna Hellyer. She was born on September 30, 1891; she died on March 9, 1898. No other information was available.

Elizabeth Roach Hellyer

Sarah Elizabeth Lownes and Charles B. Hellyer's third child was Elizabeth Roach Hellyer, who married Thomas (no last name was avilable). Elizabeth Roach Hellyer was born on October 24, 1893. No other information was available.

Charles Henry Hellyer

Sarah Elizabeth Lownes and Charles B. Hellyer's fourth child was Charles Henry Hellyer. He was born on October 24, 1897. No other information was available.

Robert Conrad Hellyer

Sarah Elizabeth Lownes and Charles B. Hellyer's fifth child was Robert Conrad Heller. He was born on July 9, 1899. No other information was available.

Child of Samuel Cooper Lownes and Susan McDowell (first wife) (G 8)

Dorothy Lownes

Samuel Cooper Lownes and Susan McDowell's only child was Dorothy Lownes, who married Leo R. Gilroy. They had three children: Philip W. Gilroy, Robert Lownes Gilroy, and Peter O'Reilly Gilroy. After Leo died, Dorothy married David R. Rishell, and they had two children: Rebecca Lynn Rishell and Christine Louise Rishell. Dorothy Lownes was born on December 19, 1902. No other information was available.

Children of Samuel Cooper Lownes and Elizabeth (No Last Name was Listed) (Second Wife) (G 8)

Margaret Lownes

Samuel Cooper Lownes and Elizabeth's (no last name was avilable) (second wife) first child was Margaret Lownes, who married Charles Hiddeman. Margaret Lownes was born on October 16, 1906. No other information was available.

Elizabeth Lownes

Samuel Cooper Lownes and Elizabeth's (no last name was avilable) (second wife) second child was Elizabeth Lownes, who never married. Elizabeth was born in 1908. No other information was available.

Samuel Lownes Jr.

Samuel Cooper Lownes and Elizabeth's (no last name was available) (second wife) third child was Samuel Lownes Jr., who married; no name was avalable. He lived in Elverson, Pennsylvania. Samuel Lownes Jr. was born on February 26, 1911. No other information was available.

Robert Lownes

Samuel Cooper Lownes and Elizabeth's (no last name was available) (second wife) fourth child was Robert Lownes. He was widowed and lived in Philadelphia, Pennsylvania. Robert Lownes was born on December 23, 1912. No other information was available.

Donald Lownes

Samuel Cooper Lownes and Elizabeth's (no last name was avilable) (second wife) fidth child was Donald Lownes, who married Mary (no last name was available) in Barrington, New Jersey. Donald Lownes was born on September 28, 1913. No other information was available.

Frances Lownes

Samuel Cooper Lownes and Elizabeth's (no last name was available) (second wife) sixth child was Frances Lownes. Frances Lownes was born in 1916. No other information was available.

Child of John Scully Lownes and Cora German (G 8)

Harriet German Lownes

John Scully Lownes and Cora German's only child was Harriet German Lownes, who married Theodora Luff. They had two children: Clarence Luff and Dorothy Luff. Harriet German Lownes was born on May 17, 1901; she died in 1968. No other information was available.

Children of George Mahan Lownes
and Florence Worrell (G 8)

Alfred Russell Lownes

George Mahan Lownes and Florence Worrell's first child was Alfred Russell Lownes, who married Charlotte Eagle. They had five children: Charles D. Lownes, William Leslie Lownes, Harold Lownes, Margaret Elizabeth Lownes, and Doris Elaine Lownes. Alfred Russell Lownes was born on December 3, 1905; he died on October 12, 1957. No other information was available.

Wilmer Atkinson Lownes

George Mahan Lownes and Florence Worrell's second child was Wilmer Atkinson Lownes, who married Ruth Sickel of Doylestown, Pennsylvania; they had one child, Wilmer A. Lownes Jr. Wilmer Atkinson Lownes was born on November 16, 1907; he died on March 14, 1975. No other information was available.

Helen Eleanor Lownes

George Mahan Lownes and Florence Worrell's third child was Helen Eleanor Lownes, who married George E. Flack of Bethayres, Pennsylvania, on August 8, 1931, They had six children: Robert George Flack, Jane Eleanor Flack, Nora Jean Flack, Diane Joyce Flack, Carey Gene Flack, and Denise Lynn Flack. Helen Eleanor Lownes was born on January 17, 1911. No other information was available.

Child of Hannah Lownes and Husband (Name Uunknown) (G 8)

Margaret Elizabeth Lownes

Hannah Lownes and husband's (name unknown) second child was Margaret Elizabeth Lownes, who married Wesley Charles on November 13, 1954. They had three children: Allen WesleyCharles, Norman Glenn Charles, and Bruce Samuel Charles. Margaret Elizabeth Lownes was born on February 17, 1926. No other information was available.

Child of Helen Jones Lownes and Albert Cornell (G 8)

James Martin Cornell

Helen Jones and Albert Cornell's only child was James Martin Cornell. He lived in Churchville, Pennsylvania. Wife's name was not available, but he had two children: Margaret Elizabeth Cornell, and Doris Elaine Cornell. James Martin Cornell was born on June 25, 1917; he died on May 10, 1935. No other information was available.

Children of Joseph Ewell Lownes and Wife's (name was not avilable) (G 8)

Joseph Ewell Lownes and (wife's name was not available) first two daughter's names were not available. No other information was available.

Margaret Evelyn Lownes

Joseph Ewell Lownes and (wife's name was not available) third child was Margaret Evelyn Lownes, who married Ewing Mackey Carson, who lived in Ocean City, New Jersey. They had two children: Sandra Louise Carson and Susan Carson. Margaret Evelyn Lownes was born on May 28, 1929. No other information was available.

Children of Thomas Russell Lownes and Laura Lownes (G 8)

Thomas Russell Lownes and Laura Lownes's had two daughters' (their names were not available.) He was a twin to Joseph Ewell Lownes. No other information was available.

Child of Ruth Daniels and Art McCollion (G 8)

Jane Ellen McCollion

Ruth Daniels and Art McCollion's only child was Jane Ellen McCollion, who married David Martin; they had one child, Emily Jane Martin. Jane Ellen McCollion was born on January 14, 1948. No other information was available.

Child of Adaline Lownes and William J. Thompson (G 8)

William Thompson

Adaline Lownes and William J. Thompson's only child was William Thompson who was born in 1887 and died on January 2, 1925. No other information was available.

Children of Charles Thomas Lownes and Mary C. Heist (G 8)

Morris Lownes

Charles Thomas Lownes and Mary C. Heist's first child was Morris Lownes. He was born on April 5, 1884; he died on February 3, 1892. No other information was available.

John Barton Lownes

Charles Thomas Lownes and Mary C. Heist's second child was John Barton Lownes, who married Kathryn Weis. John Barton Lownes was a noted urologist. He was one of the founders of Philadelphia Urological Society. He was a writer of many valuable articles on urinary disease. He attended Brown Preparatory School and earned his medical degree at Jefferson Medical College in 1906. After receiving his degree, he served on the staff of the Ashland State Hospital and the Samaritan Hospital in Philadelphia. He was emeritus chief of urology of the Northern Division of the Albert Einstein Medical Center and was honored by the staff of that hospital in 1955. He was also director of urology at Montgomery Hospital in Norristown, consultant in Urology at the Sacred Heart Hospital in Norristown, and director and consultant of Germantown Hospital. As one of the founders of the Philadelphia Urological Society, he was also a member of the American Urological Society, Philadelphia County Medical Society, Meigs Society, Philadelphia Medical Club, Rotary International, Union League, Masons, LuLu Shrine, and Grace Episcopal Church. John Barton Lownes was born in 1887; he died on February 22, 1957.

Children of Anna Frick Lownes and Irvin Peltz Williams (G 8)

Bertha L. Wiliams

Anna Frick Lownes and Irvin Peltz Williams's first child was Bertha L. Williams, who married A. Wesley Poley on March 27, 19**. They had three children: Arlene G. Poley, Audrey Anna Poley, and Alma W. Poley. Bertha L. Williams was born on November 21, 1884. No other information was available.

Myrtle L. Williams

Anna Frick Lownes and Irvin Peltz Williams's second child was Myrtle L. Williams, who married John Charles Dyson on September 15, 1921. They had one child, John Douglas Dyson. Myrtle L. Williams was born on July 16, 1896. No other information was available.

Children of Samuel Lownes and Lillian Perch (G 8)

Florence Lownes

Samuel Lownes and Lillian Perch's first child was Florence Lownes. No other information was available.

Elmer Lownes

Samuel Lownes and Lillian Perch's second child was Elmer Lownes. He died in infancy. No other information was available.

Children of Robert C. Lownes and
Anna C. Bean (First Wife) (G 8)

Clarence Lownes

Robert C. Lownes and Anna C. Bean's first child was Clarence Lownes, who married Mamie Stover. Clarence Lownes was born on September 29, 1884; his death was unknown. No other information was available.

Harry Lownes

Robert C. Lownes and Anna C. Bean's second child was Harry Lownes who died in infancy. No other information was available.

Child of Robert C. Lownes and Susan Trumbower
Gotals (Second Wife) (G 8)

Ruth Lownes

Robert C. Lownes and Susan Trumbower Gotals's only child was Ruth Lownes, who married Frank W. Scholl. They had no children. No other information was available.

Children of Walter B. Lownes and Anna Clark (G 8)

Walter B. Lownes Jr.

Walter B. Lownes and Anna Clark's first child was Walter B. Lownes Jr., who married Florence Prinold on January 23, 1918. They had three children: Joyce Prinold Lownes, Charlotte Lownes, and Walter B. Lownes III. Walter B. Lownes was born on June 10, 1889; he died in September 1967.

Grave marker of Walter & Florence Lownes is located at
Valley Forge Gardens in King of Prussia, Pennsylvania.

Walter B. Lownes Jr. was often seen with a gavel in his hand, presiding over a civil matter in the Lower Merion Township Building. Charlotte's father was that justice of the peace, sometimes labeled the "battling judge" by the *Main Line Times* which faithfully recorded his speeches and press announcements. Frequently during his twelve years in office, he was in the headlines when he castigated the local police chief or other dignitaries in his crusades for fairness and justice. The righteous blood of Hugh Lowndes flowed hot in Charlotte's father upon occasion, although he knew nothing about his martyred Quaker ancestor. Charlotte's father is a ninth generation American Lownes.

There was a tiny bungalow with a fireplace, the first home, a labor of love that Walt B. Lownes Jr. built for his wife, Florence, a beauty born in Australia. (They met when he worked as a carpenter at the ship-building yards in Bristol, Pennsylvania, during the war). This was the first fireplace Charlotte's father ever built, but the draft drew beautifully from the very beginning.

There are many other homes built by Lownes and son in and around the Gladwyne area.

Walter and a Pennsylvania State Building Inspector checked out the construction of Independence Mall spread out before the grand old structure that houses our famous Liberty Bell. (This has since been replaced with a new structure). One could speculate that it is entirely possible that Walt's great-great-great-grandfather heard the original peel of that bell proclaiming the freedom for which Hugh Lowndes gave his life in Northgate Prison.

Family ties were strong cords binding Walter, Myrtle, Tom, Edna, Charles, and Irv, and it was fun being one of the cousins. We all looked forward to the family picnics, reunions, and gatherings which continued with great spontaneity for many years. Little did we realize that we were part of small- town America at its very best. At that time, we knew nothing of our dedicated ancestors, Hugh and Jane Lowndes. One wonders if it would have made any difference in our lives if the reality of their tragedies and triumphs had been unfolded to us earlier. What lessons should we learn from them? What made them so unique? They were certainly free thinkers.

Myrlte Lownes

Walter B. Lownes and Anna's second child was Myrtle Lownes who married James Halberstadt; they had one child, Rae Etta Halberstadt. Mrylte Lownes was born on September 7, 1895: she died in 1957.

Myrtle Lownes Halberstadt, a serene and gentle woman, second oldest child of Walter and Anna. She sits quietly with her hands folded in her lap. Her soft voice and measured speech are in keeping with her genteel personality.

Myrtle and her husband, James, built a lovely home in Gladwyne. It was set far back from the street with a well-kept front lawn. Charlotte remembers catching lightning bugs there with her sister, brother, and Cousin Rae, Myrtle and James's only child.

Uncle Jimmy Halberstadt owned a carpet mill in the nearby town of Conshohocken, just across the Schuylkill River. After a lengthy battle with cancer, Aunt Myrtle died in 1957 when Rae was fourteen years old. Aunt Myrtle's consistent prayer was that her gracious Lord permitted her to live long enough to raise her daughter, and she did. Mrytle Lownes was born on September 7, 1895; she died on November 17, 1944.

Thomas Lownes

Walter B. Lownes Sr. and Anna's third child was Thomas Lownes, who married Jean Barton in February 1921; they had one child, Thomas Lownes Jr. Thomas Lownes was born on January 10, 1897, he died on July 2, 1962.

Thomas was the top salesman for a local car dealership. He was drafted in the army during the First World War. On leave, he had attended one of the many family picnics. Tom was always smiling and proud in his United States Army uniform of World War I. Unfortunately, shortly after one of the event's, when Tom was home on leave, he fell off the back of Mr. Althouse's coal truck and broke his leg. By the time the bone healed, Armistice was declared, and all the doughboys were sent home.

At a picnic table at the Gladwyne playground, all the aunts, uncles and cousins and other assorted children are running and playing with happy abandon. The picnic was on the Fourth of July. As was the custom, most of the one thousand or so residents of Gladwyne congregated at the playground for speeches and festivities. Each family gathered together for a picnic. Everybody was there to see and to be seen. At the center of the gathering was Tom Lownes, the most fastidiously dressed man in the whole panorama. He is handing a set of car keys to his sixteen-year-old niece. Tom was top salesman for the Packard Motor Car Company and always drove the latest, flashiest model. The young girl, Charlotte, was ecstatic to be seen driving that gorgeous car, even though it was only one quick turn around the playground. Thomas Lownes and Jean had one son, Thomas Lownes Jr. Thomas Lownes was born January 10, 1897; he died July 2, 1962.

Edna Lownes

Walter B. Lownes Sr. and Anna Clark's fourth child was Edna Lownes, who married Charles Frederick Slaw in 1924; they had two children: Charles Slaw Jr. and Nancy Slaw. Edna Lownes was born on August 30, 1900; she died in 1975.

Edna had a ferocious looking bulldog. He had terrified the little Charlotte. When he sat in his usual place in Aunt Edna's living room, it seemed he was guarding the entrance to the dining room and kitchen. In order to avoid the dog, the little girl resolutely went out the front door, down the side yard, and in the back kitchen door. Other than the dog, visiting Charlotte's cousin's, Charlie and Nancy Slaw, was a real treat. They lived a few miles from Gladwyne.

Charles Lownes

Walter B. Lownes Sr. and Anna Clark's fifth child was Charles Lownes who never married. Charles Lownes was born on November 6, 1901; he died on November 6, 1954.

Charles was the third son of Walter and Annia. He left home at an early age and became a carpenter, real estate entrepreneur, and land developer. He was a bachelor but had a lady friend who lived near West Chester State Teachers College, Pennsylvania, where Charlotte was enrolled. Several times, they helped shake away the student cobwebs by taking her on long Sunday country drives. She was grateful.

Laura Lownes

Walter B. Lownes Sr. and Anna Clark's sixth child was Laura Lownes. She was born on October 8, 1904; she died on August 11, 1906. She is buried in the Odd Fellows Cemetery in Gladwyne next to her mother and father. No other information was available.

Irvin Sheldon Lownes

Walter B. Lownes Sr. and Anna Clark's seventh child was Irvin Sheldon Lownes who married Dorothy Deihm, and they had three children: Irvin Sheldon Lownes Jr., Howard G. Lownes, and John Brian Lownes.

Irvin and Dorothy met at a New Years Eve party and were married eleven days later on January 11, 1932. They struggled through those first few years, as many did in those times. Irvin drove a taxi cab for his brother Walter B. Lownes Jr. in Ardmore for a short time, then a bus for many years. He helped his brother Charles, build a warehouse in Bryn Mawr. He also helped his other brother, Walter; build several houses on Church Road in King of Prussia, as well as the home that was built for his brother Walter and Florence in Gladywne. Irvin built a new home in King of Prussia that his son Howard G. Lownes designed to live out their lives. Irvin and Dorothy made ceramics for a hobby for several years. They had their own molds, slip and kilns. Irvin and Dorothy shared a long life together, celebrating over fifty-one years of marriage.

This is the grave maker for Irvin and Dorothy Lownes at
Valley Forge Gardens in King of Prussia, Pennsylvania.

Irvin drove a bus and he was always pleasant. This was his demeanor, all his life. He was always pleasant and never seemed to be ruffled. For some years his bus route went through Gladwyne. Naturally Irv married a pleasant girl. Dorothy also had a congenial disposition. When Irv retired, they took up pottery as a hobby and mini business. They also greatly enjoyed traveling in their van, especially down South to visit their son, Brian, and grandchildren.

Irvin Sheldon Lownes was born on June 1, 1908; he died on February 14, 1983.

Children of Milton Markley Lownes and Gladys Williams Dunlap (G 8)

Dr. Milton Markley Lownes0

Milton Markley Lownes and Gladys Williams Dunlap's first child was Dr. Milton Markley Lownes wife's name was not available, but they had three children: Phillip Lownes, Joanne Lownes, and Mark Lownes. Dr. Milton Markley Lownes was born on February 26, 1925; he died on July 9, 2001. No other information was available.

Alice M. Lownes

Milton Markley Lownes and Gladys Williams Dunlap's second child was Alice M. Lownes who was unmarried. She was born in 1928. No other information was available.

Richard Dunlap Lownes Sr.

Milton Markley Lownes and Gladys Williams Dunlap's third child was Richard Dunlap Lownes Sr., who married Nancy Morrison; they had four children: Richard D. Lownes Jr., Ruthann M. Lownes, Robert S. Lownes, and Randall K. Lownes.

Richard Dunlap Lownes Sr. lived in Lafayette Hill, Pennsylvania, and was a third- generation funeral director (his mother and her father). He passed away on October 24, 2016 of lung cancer at Peter Becker Community in Harleysville, Pennsylvania, where he had lived for fifteen years.

For more than four decades, Richard Dunlap Lownes ran the Lownes Funeral Home, whose clients mainly came from Philadelphia and Montgomery County. "Blessed with the gift of making strangers feel at home almost from the minute he met them, he was a natural as a mortician," said son Randall. Mr. Richard Lownes's purpose was to serve clients regardless of their financial status and keep funeral's cost down. "He would help anyone at any time," Randall Lownes commented.

The Fairmont-based Dunlap-Lownes Funeral Home was founded in 1888 by William A. Dunlap, Richard Lownes's grandfather. In 1950, Gladys Dunlap Lownes, daughter of the founder and Richard Lownes's mother, moved the establishment to 659 Germantown Pike, Lafayette Hill.

Richard Lownes ran the business until retiring in 1992 when Randall Lownes took over. Randall changed the name of the business to its present form.

Born and reared in Roxborough, Richard Lownes graduated from Roxborough High School, where he received the Outstanding Athlete Award in 1946 and 1947 for performance in track and football.

Richard graduated from Muhlenberg College in Allentown, the Northwestern University School of Funeral Management near Chicago, and H.E. Dolan College of Mortuary Science in Philadelphia.

Because of his mortuary training, Richard Lownes served during the Korean War in Germany, processing casualties for the Army's Graves Registration Division. He became so adept at embalming that once he returned stateside, he became the go-to for other funeral directors who needed expert advice.

"Call Dick Lownes; he'll know what to do," his son repeated often. "He was proud of that skill."

Richard Lownes was a busy civic volunteer and church member. At St. Peter's Lutheran Church in Lafayette Hill, he was a leader and chairman of many turkey suppers over the years.

He was a member of the Whitemarsh Jaycees and the Kiwanis Club of Roxborough. As a board member of the Northern Institute of Psychiatry, Visiting Nurse Association of Greater Philadelphia, he also was involved with the Montgomery County Big Brother Association, which now includes Big Sisters.

He was a Masonic Home of Pennsylvania board member from 1974 to 1989. During that time, he was assigned to the institution's grounds, property, and admission committees.

A thirty-eight-year employee of the home, which became Masonic Village at Lafayette Hill in 2004, described Richard Lownes as a "total gentleman who was always looking out for someone else."

Starting in the early 1970s, he served as a Whitemarsh Township supervisor for eleven years. Under his guidance, the township created a police pension fund.

A true foodie, he loved to cook and go out to dinner, Randall remarked.

Richard Dunlap Lownes Sr. and Nancy Morrison's children: were Richard D. Lownes, Rutthann M. Lownes, Robert S. Lownes, and Randall K. Lownes,

Child of Mary Lowndes Owens and John Collinson Jr. (G 8)

(note the "d" has been restored).

John Collinson III

Mary Lowndes Owens and John Collinson Jr.'s only child was John Collinson III, who married Mary Clagett Magruder on August 28, 1943; they had one child, Mary Catherine Collinson. John Collinson III, was born May 24, 1918; he died on July 7, 1989. No other information was available.

Children of Raymond Gerald Lowndes and Bridget Ruddy (G 8)

(Note the "d" has been restored).

Raymond Gerald Lowndes Jr.

Raymond Gerald Lowndes and Bridget Ruddy's first child was Raymond Gerald Lowndes Jr., who married Rita Sears on June 25, 1955. They had four children: Patricia Lowndes, Margaret Lowndes, Jennie Lowndes, and Raymond Gerald Lowndes III. Raymond Gerald Lowndes Jr. was born on September 29, 1930; his death was unknown. Coincidentally I, Howard G. Lownes Sr. married my wife Verna M. Allebach five years later on June 25, 1960. No other information was available.

Donald Lowndes

Raymond Gerald Lowndes and Bridget Rubby's second child was Donald Lowndes, who married Josephine P. (no last name was available) on April 25, 1959. They had five children: Donna Lowndes, Debra Lowndes, Albert Lowndes, Marjorie Lowndes, and Dorothy Lowndes. Donald was born on September 22, 1936. No other information was available.

Child of George Lowndes and Sophia Rimminsland (G 8)

Dorothy Lowndes

George Lowndes and Sophia Rimminsland's only child was Dorothy Lowndes, her husband name was not available, but she had four children: Donald Lowndes, Susan Lowndes, William Lowndes, and Margaret Lowndes. Dorothy was born in 1934. No other information was available.

Child of Bernie Colman Lown
and LuLu Augusta Tippet (G 8)

Note the"es" has been removed

Martha Ann Lown

Bernie Colman Lown and LuLu Augusta Tippit's only child was Martha Ann Lown, who was unmarried. Martha Ann Lown was born in 1923; she died in 2008. No other information was available.

Children of Emory Lester Lown
and Lena M. Baker (G 8)

Gordon Leo Lown

Emory Lester Lown and Lena M. Baker's first child was Gordon Leo Lown, who married Patricia A. Leek in 1952. They had two children: Steven L. Lown and Barton Leo Lown. Gordon Leo Lown was born in 1930; and died in 1975. No other information was available.

Eldon Cyril Lown

Emory Lester Lown and Lena M. Baker's second child was Eldon Cyril Lown, who married Marilyn R. Woods in 1956; they had four children: Gary R. Lown, Jeff A. Lown, Susanne Kay Lown, and Mark Lown. Eldon Cyril Lown was born in 1934. No other information was available.

Child of Ceetta Lown and Owen James Cooper (G 8)

James Reese Cooper

Ceetta Lown and Owen James Cooper's only child was James Reese Cooper, who married Wilma Cave. They had two children: Linda Cooper and Teresa Cooper. James Reese Cooper was born in 1926; he died in 1988. No other information was available.

———◆———

THIS SECOND GROUP OF DESCENDANTS IS FROM THE GEORGE LOWNES AND MARY BOWERS'S BRANCH OF THE FAMILY

Children of Florence Levis and Trainer (no first name was avilable) (G 8)

Bancroft Trainer

Florence Levis and Trainer's (no first name was available) first child was Bancroft Trainer. No other information was available.

Mary L. Trainer

Florence Levis and Trainer's (no first name was available) second child was Mary L. Trainer. No other information was available.

Children of Hannah Darlington Levis
and Elwood Garrett (G 8)

Florence Garrett

Hannah Darlington Levis and Elwood Garrett's first child was Florence Garrett. No other information was available.

Mary Garrett

Hannah Darlington Levis and Elwood Garrett second's child was Mary Garrett. No other information was available.

Children of John (Jack) Lownes
and Hannah Hannum (G 8)

Sarah Lownes

John (Jack) Lownes and Hannah Hannum's first child was Sarah Lownes. No other information was available.

Margaret Lownes

John (Jack) Lownes and Hannah Hannum's second child was Margaret Lownes. No other information was available.

John Rodger Lownes

John (Jack) Lownes and Hannah Hannum's third child was John Rodger Lownes. He lived in Concordville, Pennsylvania. No other information was available.

Rebe Lownes

John (Jack) Lownes and Hannah Hannum's fourth child was Rebe Lownes. No other information was available.

Children of Margaret Lownes
and Dagmar Conover (G 8)

Margaret Conover

Margaret Lownes and Dagmar Conover's first child was Margaret Conover. No other information was available.

Frank Conover

Margaret Lownes and Dagmar Conover's second child was Frank Conover. Frank Conover went to school with Joseph Donald Lownes and Carol Ann Haworth (mentioned later). No other information was available.

Ann Conover

Margaret Lownes and Dagmar Conover's third child was Ann Conover. No other information was available.

Children of Joseph Lownes Jr.
and Grace Hamilton Custer (G 8)

Joseph Donald Lownes

Joseph Lownes Jr. and Grace Hamilton Custer's first child was Joseph Donald Lownes who married Carol Ann Haworth on September 12, 1953. They had three children: Bette Jane Lownes, Linda Lee Lownes, and Donna Mae Lownes. Joseph Donald Lownes was born on April 10, 1932. Joseph Donald Lownes graduated from Springfield High School in 1950 and worked with his parents in the flower business. After marring his wife Carol Ann he began an excavation business, established the Lownes Nursery and Landscape Design. His horticultural expertise and creative design became known throughout the region; and he later taught classes in the Chester County Night School. Another passion, in addition to horticulture, was music. From 1951 – 1963, Don and his wife Carol managed their dance band, The Sentimentalists. Don played trumpet and lead the band while Carol was the band's vocalist.,

Don was very proud of his service in the Naval Air Reserve. He signed up while still in his senior year of high school, and after a four-year term, signed up for another four years.

Carol Ann, Don's wife, was senior year class secretary, piano accompanist for the school choir, played drums in the marching band, and performed in the school play.

Both Joseph Donold Lownes and Carol Ann Haworth are buied at Birmingham Lafayette Cemetery.

George Bolton Lownes

Joseph Lownes Jr. and Grace Hamilton Custer's second child was George Bolton Lownes, who married Kay Kachel on May 17, 1958. They had four children: George Bolton Lownes Jr., Jeffery Steven Lownes, Gregory Douglas Lownes, and Gary Martin Lownes. George Bolton Lownes was born on April 12, 1937. No other information was available.

Kenneth Hugh Lownes

Joseph Lownes Jr. and Grace Hamilton Custer's third child was Kenneth Hugh Lownes, who married Judith Urian on August 7, 1965. They had no children. No other information was available.

Jane Ann Lownes

Joseph Lownes Jr. and Grace Hamilton Custer's fourth child was Jane Ann Lownes, who married Charles Gallagher on March 8, 1958. They had four children: Susanne Gallagher, Charles Kirk Gallagher, Sandra Lynn Gallagher, and Jennifer Jane Gallagher. They divorced. Her second marriage was to Martin Shea of Springfield on October 17, 1980.

They lived in West Chester, Pennsylvania and had a bed and breakfast cottage on their property. Jane Ann Lownes was born on January 31, 1941. No other information was available.

Bruce Thayer Lownes

Joseph Lownes Jr. and Grace Hamilton Custer's fifth child was Bruce Thayer Lownes, who married Paula Pastorius of West Grove, Pennsylvania. They had four children: Nathaniel Dean Lownes, Rebecca Jane Lownes, Joseph Jereny Lownes, and Sarah Grace Lownes. They had a Perennial business in Avondale, Pennsylvania. Bruce Thayer Lownes was born on November 22, 1948. No other information was available.

CHAPTER TEN

Generation Ten

THIS FIRST GROUP OF DESCENDANTS IS FROM THE JAMES I. LOWNES AND SUSANNAH RICHARDS'S BRANCH OF THE FAMILY

Childern of Esther Wister Harvey and Frank Tiers (G9)

Esther Wister Harvey and Frank Tiersx had lots of children no names were available. No other information or names were available.

Children of Dorothy Lownes and Leo R. Gilroy (First Husband) (G 9)

Philip W. Gilroy

Dorothy Lownes and Leo R. Gilroy's first child was Phillip W. Gilroy. He was born on October 25, 1924. No other information was available.

Robert Lownes Gilroy

Dorothy Lownes and Leo R. Gilroy's second child was Robert Lownes Gilroy. He was born on May 8, 1926. No other information was available.

Peter O'Reilly Gilroy

Dorothy Lownes and Leo R. Gilroy's third child was Peter O'Reilly Gilroy. He was born on May 21, 1932. No other information was available.

Children of Dorthoy Lownes and David R. Rishell (Second Husband) (G 9)

Rebecca Lynn Rishell

Dorothy Lownes and David R. Rishell's first child was Rebecca Lynn Rishell, who married Henry Carpenter; they divorced in 1976. Rebecca was born April 6, 1949. No other information was available.

Christine Louise Rishell

Dorothy Lownes and David R. Rishell's second child was Christine Louise Rishell. She was born on November 8, 1950. No other information was available.

Children of Harriet German Lownes and Theodore Luff (G 9)

Clarence Luff

Harriet German Lownes and Theodore Luff's first child was Clarence Luff, who married Evelyn Jackson and later married Arlene Tanner. Clarence Luff and Evelyn Jackson had two children: Bobby Luff and Diane Luff. Clarence Luff then married Arlene Tanner; they had four children: Sandra Luff, Brian Luff, Cheryl Luff, and Jeffery Luff. Clarence Luff was born on May 21, 1924. No other information was available.

Dorothy Luff

Harriet German Lownes and Theodore Luff's second child was Dorothy Luff, who married Frank Acuff on December 14, 1946. They had two children: Constance Acuff, and Frank Acuff. Dorothy Luff was born on December 21, 1927. No other information was available.

Children of Alfred Russell Lownes
and Charlotte Eagle (G 9)

Charles D. Lownes

Alfred Russell Lownes and Charlotte Eagle's first child was Charles D. Lownes, who married Esther Moyer. They had two children: Charles David Lownes Jr. and Robert William Lownes. Charles D. Lownes was born on September 14, 1924. No other information was available.

William Leslie Lownes

Alfred Russell Lownes and Charlotte Eagle's second child was William Leslie Lownes, who married Janice Dougherty. They had three children: Judith Ann Lownes, Susan Lee Lownes, and William Leslie Lownes Jr. William Leslie Lownes was born on May 7, 1926. No other information was available.

Harold Lownes

Alfred Russell Lownes and Charlotte Eagle's third child was Harold Lownes, who married Ethel Hammel Luff of Newtown, Pennsylvania, on August 10, 1946. They had five children: Virginia Lownes, Marian Elizabeth Lownes, Daniel Walter Lownes, Sally Edna Lownes, and Phyllis Edith Lownes. Harold Lownes was born on November 10, 1927. No other information was available.

Margaret Elizabeth Lownes

Alfred Russell Lownes and Charlotte Eagle's fourth child was Margaret Elizabeth Lownes, who married Wesley Charles on November 13, 1954. They had three children: Allen Wesley Charles, Norman Glenn Charles, and Bruce Samuel Charles. Margaret Elizabeth Lownes was born on February 17, 1929. No other information was available.

Doris Elaine Lownes

Alfred Russell Lownes and Charlotte Eagle's fifth child was Doris Elaine Lownes, who married Albert Harry Barthelmeh on April 10, 1947. They had three children: Albert Harry Barthelmeh, Thomas George Barthelmeh, and James Glenn Barthelmeh. Doris Elaine Lownes was born on June 18, 1930. No other information was available.

Child of Wilmer Atkinson Lownes and Ruth Sickel (G 9)

Wilmer Atkinson Lownes Jr.

Wilmer Atkinson Lownes and Ruth Sickel's only child was Wilmer Atkinson Lownes Jr., who married Ida Slack from Lambertville, New Jersey. They lived in Penndel, Pennsylvania. They had six children: Carol Lownes, Deborah Lownes, Steven Lownes, Lewis Lownes, Sandra Lownes, and Jeffery Lownes. No other information was available.

Children of Helen Eleanor Lownes and George E. Flack (G9)

Robert George Flack

Helen Eleanor Lownes and George E. Flack's first child was Robert George Flack, who married Wynne Layton. They had four children: Lane Flack, Terri Flack, Nerissa Flack, and Coral Flack. Robert George Flack was born on March 15, 1935. No other information was available.

Jane Eleanor Flack

Helen Eleanor Lownes and George E. Flack's second child was Jane Eleanor Flack, who married Bill Marlow of Alabama. Jane Eleanor Flack was born on May 4, 1936. No other information was available.

Nora Jean Flack

Helen Eleanor Lownes and George E. Flack's third child was Nora Jean Flack, who married Edward Montayne. Nora Jean Flack was born on October 31, 1940. No other information was available.

Diane Joyce Flack

Helen Eleanor Lownes and George E. Flack's fourth child was Diane Joyce Flack, who married Glenn Fahr. Diane Joyce Flack was born on May 12, 1944. No other information was available.

Cary Gene Flack

Helen Eleanor Lownes and George E. Flack's fifth child was Cary Gene Flack, who married Rose Banbridge. Cary Gene Flack was born on November 6, 1947. No other information was available.

Denise Lynn Flack

Helen Eleanor Lownes and George E. Flack's sixth child was Denise Lynn Flack. She was born April 2, 1951. No other information was available.

Children of George M. Lownes Jr. and Anna Somer Neil (G 9)

Ellen Louise Lownes

George M. Lownes Jr. and Anna Somer Neil's first child was Ellen Louise Lownes, who married Ed Gilmore. They had three children: Scott Gilmore and two others that were unnamed. Ellen Louise Lownes was born on October 1, 1948. No other information was available.

William George Lownes

George M. Lownes Jr. and Anna Somer Neil's second child was William George Lownes, who was married, but no name was available. William

George Lownes was born on January 9, 1952. No other information was available.

John Alfred Lownes

George M. Lownes Jr. and Anna Somer Neil's third child was John Alfred Lownes, who was married, but no name was available. John Alfred Lownes was born on May 20, 1955. No other information was available.

Cynthia Anna Lownes

George M. Lownes Jr. and Anna Somer Neil's fourth child was Cynthia Anna Lownes, who married Glen (no last name was available). Cynthia Anna Lownes was born on June 19, 1957. No other information was available

Children of Margaret Elizabeth Lownes and Wesley Charles (G 9)

Allen Wesley Charles

Margaret Elizabeth Lownes and Wesley Charles's first child was Allen Wesley Charles. He was born August 25, 1957. No other information was available.

Norman Glenn Charles

Margaret Elizabeth Lownes and Wesley Charles's second child was Norman Glenn Charles. He was born July 26, 1963. No other information was available.

Bruce Samuel Charles

Margaret Elizabeth Lownes and Wesley Charles's third child was Bruce Samuel Charles. He was born June 2, 1966. No other information was available.

Children of James Martin Cornell and Wife (name was not available) (G 9)

Margaret Elizabeth Cornell

James Martin Cornell and his wife's (name was not available) first child was Margaret Elizabeth Cornell. She was born on February 17, 1929. No other information was available.

Doris Elaine Cornell

James Martin Cornell and his wife's (name was not available) second child was Doris Elaine Cornell. She was born on May 18, 1930. No other information was available.

Children of Margaret Evelyn Lownes and Ewing Mackey Carson (G9)

Sandra Louise Carson

Margaret Evelyn Lownes and Ewing Mackey Carson's first child was Sandra Louise Carson. She was born on October 18, 1951. No othe information was available.

Susan Carson

Margaret Evelyn Lownes and Ewing Mackey Carson's second child was Susan Carson. She was born on August 16, 1954. No other information was available.

Child of Jane Ellen McCollian and David Martin (G 9)

Emily Jane Martin

Jane Ellen McCollian and David Martin's only child was Emily Jane Martin. She was born on January 5, 1977. No other information was available.

Children of Bertha L. Williams and A Wesley Poley (G 9)

Arlene G. Poley

Bertha L. Williams and A. Wesley Poley's first child was Arlene G. Poley, who married Raymond W. Kantner on June 7, 1942. They had one child, Bonnie Jill Kantner. Arlene G. Poley was born on July 10, No other information was available.

Audrey Anna Poley

Bertha L. Williams and A. Wesley Poley's second child was Audrey Anna Poley, who married Ivan F. Bennett M.D. on September 23, 1944. They had two children: Ivan Stanley Bennett and Judith Ann Bennett. Audrey Ann Poley was born on February 28, 1914. No other information was available.

Alma W. Poley

Bertha L. Williams and A. Wesley Poley's third child was Alma W. Poley, who married Robert L. Kendig on April 29, 1939. They had three children: Robert Kendig Jr., Kathleen Kendig, and Jon Thomas Kendig. Alma G. Poley was born September 15, 1915. No other information was available.

Child of Myrtle L. Williams and John Charles Dyson (G 9)

John Dyson

Myrtle Williams and John Charles Dyson's only child was John Dyson, who married Diane Cook on October 22, 1949. They had one child, James Douglas Dyson. John Dyson was born on February 21, 1923. No other information was available.

Children of Walter Bowen Lownes Jr. and Florence Prinold (G 9)

Joyce Prinold Lownes

Walter Bowen Lownes Jr. and Florence Prinold's first child wad Joyce Prinold Lownes, who married Henry (Hank) Augustus Hoyt II on May 11, 1949. They had four children: Joanne Linda Hoyt, Pamela Elizabeth Hoyt, James Warren Hoyt, and Henry Augustus Hoyt III. Joyce then married Hamilton Leftwich Robinson (11/13/1917-...) on May 20, 1972. Joyce Prinold Lownes was born on August 4, 1920; she died on May 28, 2018.

Joyce Lownes went to Ursinus College in Collegeville, Pennsylvania.

In an old album (no longer available) shows Joyce and her roommates in initiation outfits at Ursinus College. It was here Joyce joined the debating team and tasted the first delights of intellectual society. When she returned home for weekend visits, her conversations with her dad were controversial and varied, and they reflected the flow of speakers and subjects to which she was exposed in college. It was all to her advantage.

Joyce Prinold Lownes in her United States Women's Army Corp officers uniform was almost a contradiction of terms. The uniform was too mannish for her feminine figure, and her smile was too radiant for the texture of the cloth.

Joyce served as Army WAAC from November 7, 1942 to November 26, 1945. She worked at the Military Intelligence Office in Miami and the Pentagon. She was chosen to learn Japanese, and at the end of the Second World War, she served for a year under General Douglas MacArthur in Japan. Later she married Henry (Hank) Augustus Hoyt on May 11, 1949 in Asuncion, Paraguay, and later Hank become ambassador to Uruguay.

A picture (no longer avilable) showed the bride descending the stairs at the residence of the United States Ambassador in Asuncion, Paraguay. Joyce's versatility in three languages was invaluable at embassy dinner parties in Washington, Cuba, and South America. A few years after the death of Ambassador Hoyt, Joyce Prinold Lownes married Hamilton Leftwich Robinson, a manufacturer's, representative and was fortunate to have another happy marriage.

Hamilton Leftwich Robinson had one daughter, Margethal Clark Robinson who married George Edward Miller on June 5, 1971. They had two children: Alexander Miller and Nathan Miller.

Charlotte Lownes

Walter Bowen Lownes Jr. and Florence Prinold's second child was Charlotte Lownes, who married Grant Olewiler Jr. on March 13, 1942. Charlotte was born on November 14, 1921; she died on March 16, 2005. They had six children: Suzan Jill Olewiler, Megret Olewiler, Lora Olewiler, April Olewiler, Constance (Conny) Olewiler, and Grant Miller Olewiler III. Grant Olewiler Jr. was born on June 29, 1921; and he died on March 30, 2017.

Charlotte Lownes Olewiler did numerous researches into the family history in the 1970s. This book is dedicated to her for her do-diligence in all the research she did before the internet.

There is a little street in Gladwyne where two houses are special. They are four doors apart. Charlotte's husband, Grant M. Olewiler Jr.

was raised in one and her in the other from first grade together until they married in Southern California. They raised six children: five daughters and one son; they are Generation Eleven.

Walter Bowen Lownes III

Walter Bowen Lownes Jr. and Florence Prinold's third child was Walter Bowen Lownes III, who married Nancy Patricia Delaney on June 26, 1953. They had two children: Deborah (Debbie) Ann Lownes and Walter Craig Lownes. Walter Bowen Lownes III was born on November 27, 1926; he died on May 14, 1991.

Walter Bowen Lownes served in the army from January 16, 1945 to November 16, 1945 in Domestic Service and from November 17, 1945 to March 2, 1946 in Foreign Service in the Military Police. (Bud, as he was referred to on many occasions) was stationed in Germany during World War II. After graduating from University of Pennsylvania Warton School of Business, Bud worked for Del Monte Canned Foods for thirty-five years, moving frequently (Dallas, Texas to Toronto, Canada and eastward) before settling in Atlanta, Georgia, where he retired to work for an independent food broker. While Bud traveled, Nancy managed the household. After moving to Hilton Head, Island Bud passed away in 1991, with Nancy living on Hilton Head and enjoying the island life. They had two children: Deborah Lownes and Walter Craig Lownes.

To reminiscence, there was a picture in an old album (no longer exists) that shows a little boy about two years old pulling a wagon full of eggs on his delivery route, just as his father did before him. Bud (Walter B. Lownes III) is, of course, wearing his baseball cap. He was completely engrossed in the sport of each season. Later at the University of Pennsylvania, he not only became captain of the soccer team but also was named all American Captain. In later life, Bud and Nancy took up tennis. His son, Walter Craig, was a student at the University of Georgia.

Child of Myrtle Lownes and James Halberstadt (G 9)

Rae Etta Halberstadt

Myrtle Lownes and Ray Halberstadt's only child was Rae Etta Halberstadt, who married William Conley. They had three children: Dana Conley, James Conley, and Laura Conley. Ray Etta Halberstadt was born January 19, 1933. No other information was avaulable.

Child of Thomas Chapman Lownes Sr. and Jean Barton (G 9)

Thomas Chapman Lownes Jr.

Thomas Chapman Lownes Sr. and Jean Barton's only child was Thomas Chapman Lownes Jr., who married Anne Lampe on May 30, 1959; they had three children: Elizabeth Ann Lownes, Barbara Ann Lownes, and Thomas Chapman. Lownes III. Thomas Lownes Jr. was born October 3, 1936.

At one of the picnics there was a tow-headed boy about three or four years old. He was pointed to some cars on the street, accurately naming the make and model of each one as it drove by. This was Tommy Jr., only child of Tom and his jolly wife, Jean. Tommy became the vice-president of Wilcox, Walter and Furlong, a paper sales company. He was also a country gentleman and kept horses as a hobby at his farm in Malvern, Pennsylvania, where his three children were fine horsemen.

Children of Edna Lownes
and Charles Fredrick Slaw (G 9)

Charles Fredrick Slaw Jr.

Edna Lownes and Charles Fredrick Slaw's first child was Charles Fredrick Slaw Jr., who married Jean Roberts in 1947; they had two children: Fredrick Clayton Slaw and Edward Clayton law. Charles Fredrick Slaw Jr. was born in September 1924; and died in 2015.

Charles Fredrick Slaw Jr. always had a grin that covered his whole faces and never disappears. The grin belongs to Charles Fredrick Slaw Jr. His sister's grin looked exactly like his.

This persistent grin aided Charles later on to be a great parent to his two sons, Freddie and Eddie. Charles managed the Twilight Baseball Team and his wife kept score. Whenever the boys were playing any sport, Charles and Jean were faithful supporters. Inevitably, their sons turned out to be well adjusted, productive young men__"Imps," as Aunt Edna, their grandmother, used to call them. But they were a great delight to her, as were Nancy's who lived in the Wilmington, Delaware area.

Nancy Slaw

Edna Lownes and Charles Fredrick Slaw's second child was Nancy Slaw, who married R. Koelle, date is unknown. They had four children: no names have been available. Nancy Slaw's birth date is unknown. No other information was available.

Children of Irvin Sheldon Lownes Sr.
and Dorothy Deihm (G 9)

Irvin Sheldon Lownes Jr.

Irvin Sheldon Lownes Sr. and Dorothy Deihm's first child was Irvin Sheldon Lownes Jr., who married Eileen Becker (January 29, 1940; died on December 9, 2018) on June 7, 1958; they divorced in 1989. He then married Linda Rawson Pursell on September 23, 1989.

Irvin Sheldon Lownes Jr. was born October 14, 1932, in Gladwyn, Pennsylvania. According to his mother, he was born at home, not in a hospital (whether by a doctor or a mid-wife is not known). Irvin's father was the youngest of seven children of Walter B. Lownes, and his mother Dorothy Deihm was the middle child of five; her parents were Howard Louis Deihm (a railroad engineer) and Sarah Class.

Irvin graduated from Upper Merion School in Upper Merion, Pennsylvania. He attended a technical school to study radio and television repair. Irvin was drafted in February 1953. After basic training, he spent nine months at Fort Monmouth, New Jersey, to learn radar repair. Upon completion of radar training, he was deployed to the Panama Canal Zone for the remainder of his two-year service.

After he came home he found a job as a factory assembly technician with Univac Computer Company until the middle of December 1969.

Irvin Sheldon Lownes Jr. and Eileen Ruth Becker had four children: Nancy Jane Lownes, Sally Ann Lownes, Paul Thomas Lownes, and Bonnie Jean Lownes.

Irvin attended Drexel University for eight years, receiving a bachelor's degree in Engineering. He then enrolled at The University of Pennsylvania to earn a master's degree in Computer and Information Science.

In the mid-1960s, IBM developed a mid-sized computer system that used a smaller punch card for data entry. Several managers at Univac left the company to form a new company that would develop punch card equipment and compete with IBM. Irvin joined them as a digital logic designer. After spending nearly fifteen years at Univac, he spent about eighteen years with Decision Data Company where he had numerous positions.

When DDC could not keep up with market changes, Irvin was laid off along with many others. At age fifty-five, finding a new job in a technical field was not easy. Irvin received a call about an opening in Southern California for a temporary position, similar to what he had been doing at DDC. The company, Data Products Corporation, designed and built high speed printers for large computer systems. The temporary potion lasted for three years. Following his time at Data Products, Irvin moved to another Southern Capifornia printer company for a temporary potion, similar to what he had been doing at DDC.

Irvin Sheldon Lownes Jr. and Linda Rawson Pursell, his second wife, moved to the Sacramento area, and he retired.

Irvin met both of his wives in church. He sang in the choir.

Howard G. Lownes Sr.

Irvin Sheldon Lownes Sr. and Dorothy Deihm's second child was Howard G. Lownes Sr., who was born on July 6, 1935, and married Verna M. Allebach on June 25, 1960. Howard met his wife on a blind date on October 25, 1955. They lived in Audubon, Pennsylvania, for one year, and then moved to 78 W. Fifth Avenue, Trappe, Pennsylvania. Verna passed away on December 6, 2015. Howard still lives in the family home they bought in 1961. Howard and Verna had two children: Howard G. Lownes Jr. and April Lynn Lownes.

Howard G. Lownes Sr. learned the art of drafting at Lower Merion High School after graduating from Upper Merion High School. He had hoped to become a free lancing architect since he didn't have the license as an architect. Having designed three houses, the first home was for his parents and built by his father for both his mother and father to live in until they passed away.

This home served Mom and Dad for almost thirty
years and is in King of Prussia, Pennsylvania.

Two other homes were designed for his father-in-law, and he
helped build them. These two homes were bi-level homes with the
second one having a fireplace in the family room and another directly
over in the living room. This was a unique design since the chimneys
had to have their own path to get above the roof.

This home served his in-laws till they passed away
and is located in Eagleville, Pennsylvania.

After several positions in the drafting field, Howard was accepted as an engineer holding multiple positions as design engineer to his last position as Director of Technology, where he was responsible for every contract that was sold to the power industry for ten years. The company was the Allen-Sherman-Hoff Company. Howard worked for that company for thirty-three years. His job had him traveling all over the United States and to several countries overseas. In that span of time, he managed to get to forty-nine of the fifty states; after retirement, he took Verna to see all of those states. In 1993, he joined the ASTM organization and has received three awards for designing standards that are used world wide.

When their children were in grade school, Verna, was the Vice President of the Perkiomen Vally South Elementry Home and Schoo;l Association, volunteer tutor, and co-chairman of the school fund raising carnival.

Verna worked for Lansdale Tube in Lansdale, Pennslvania.and Philco Transister Division in Spring City, Pennsylvania, making transistors for radios for three years before she was with child. Back then when a woman was six months pregnant, she had to quit working. Verna became a housewife for the remainder of her life.

Verna was a graduate from the Famous Writers School in Westport, Connecticut, receiving a Certificate in Non-Fiction Writing on August 30, 1971. She also had two photographs that were published by the Workman Publishing, New York in their "The 1992 365 Dogs Calendar," which was selected as, "Winner of the Week" of April 27, 1992, which was April's twenty fifth birthday anniversary. See the picture below.

The caption reads "Cocker Two Step." Butterscotch and Cinnamon are in syc, standing guard at their porch in Trappe, Pennsylvania. The cockers were owned by their daughter, April Lownes.

The second picture was published in The International Library of photography, 2000 Edition of outstanding photography, and received a trophy for this effort. Verna was a remarkable woman with many talents.

The capion of the picture is "weight on my mind", that is Cinomon with her head on the scale.

228

Verna was also a volunteer baker for the Montgomery County SPCA for the winter Food Festivals, and the October Fest in Perkiomen Shelter of the SPCA fund raisers.

With all the responsibilities of being married and parents of two great children, starting in September of 1965, Verna and Howard had the first of eleven foster children that spanned a period of fourteen years. Four of these children were newborn babies, waiting to be adopted, so they were not able to keep them. One foster daughter wanted Howard and Verna to be part of her wedding as foster mother and father of the bride. Howard had the honor of walking her down the aisle to her husband.

During the 1970s, they also did ceramics, having their own kiln, molds, and, the slip to pour into the molds; they did it more as a hobby and gave some to the church for their annual bazaar.

Howard and Verna loved to travel all over this great United States and managed to see forty nine of the fifty states and enjoyed them all. One of their favorite places was a small town of Bennington, Vermont. It was about a six-hour drive from home, but it was the get-away place when they wanted a break. Howard and Verna called it their second home even though they didn't have a house there. It was a quiet small town, and they loved the area. It is at the bottom of the Green Mountains of Vermont.

John Brian Lownes

Irvin Sheldon Lownes Sr. and Dorothy Deihm's third child was John Brian Lownes, who married Marlene Murray on March 4, 1963. He served in the Army for several years. They had three daughters: Beverly Lynn Lownes, Kathlyn Edith Lownes, and Tobbie Lu Ann Lownes. They met in Alabama while Brian (The family used his middle name to avoid confusion with his Uncle John after whom he was named.) was stationed there in the Army. After he left the service, they lived in several states: Alabama, Texas, and Pennsylvania, settling in Alabama.

Brian was a long distance truck driver for many years. After he retired, he worked for another company that had him taking house trailers or boats from one location to another. John Brian Lownes was born on May 16, 1942, and died on May 31, 2004.

Children of Dr. Milton Markley Lownes Jr. (Wife name was not available) (G 9)

Phillip Lownes

Dr. Milton Markley Lownes and wife's (name was not available) first child was Phillip Lownes. No other information was available.

Joanne Lownes

Dr. Milton Markley Lownes and wife's (name was not available) second child was Joanne Lownes. No other information was available.

Mark Lownes

Dr. Milton Markley Lownes and wife's (name was not available) third child was Mark Lownes. No other information was available.

Children of Richard Dunlap Lownes Sr. and Nancy Mottison (G 9)

Richard Dunlap Lownes Jr.

Richard Dunlap Lownes Sr. and Nancy Morrison's first child was Richard Dunlap Lownes Jr., who married Catherine Amwake in 1988.

They had two children: Anna Lownes and Amanda Lownes. No other information was available.

Ruthann M. Lownes

Richard Dunlap Lownes Sr. and Nancy Morrison's second child was Ruthann Lownes. No other information was available.

Robert M. Lownes

Richard Dunlap Lownes Sr. and Nancy Morrison's third child was Robert M. Lownes. No other information was available.

Randall K. Lownes

Richard Dunlap Lownes Sr. and Nancy Morrison's fourth child was Randall K. Lownes, who married Margie (last name was not available). They had five children: Wesley Lownes, Ryan Lownes, Austin Lownes, Grant Lownes, and Harrison Lownes. Randall K. Lownes owns the Lownes Funneral Home in Laffette Hills, Pennsylvanis as a fourth generation funeral director. No other information was available.

Child of John Collinson III and
Mary Clagett Magruder (G 9)

Mary Catherine Collinson

John Collinson III and Mary Clagett Magruder's only child was Mary Catherine Collinson. Mary was born on July 14, 1944, in Baltimore, Maryland. No other information was available.

Children of Raymond Gerald Lowndes Jr. and Rita Sears (G 9)

(Note the "d" has been reinstaanted)

Patricia Lowndes

Raymond Gerald Lowndes Jr. and Rita Sears's first child was Patricia Lowndes, who married Ruben Arrieta on September 18, 1986. They had two children: Colton Arrieta and Kyle Arrieta. Patricia Lowndes was born on July 9, 1961. No other information was available.

Margaret Lowndes

Raymond Gerald Lowndes Jr. and Rita Sears's second child was Margaret Lowndes. She was born on October 2, 1962. No other information was available.

Jenne Lowndes

Raymond Gerald Lowndes Jr. and Rita Sears's third child was Jenne Lowndes. She was born on January 1, 1964. Jenne Lowndes had one child, Jennifer Lowndes; no husband's name was available. No other information was available.

Raymond Gerald Lowndes III

Raymond Gerald Lowndes Jr. and Rita Sears's fourth child was Raymond Gerald Lowndes III. He was born on September 1, 1969. No other information was available.

Children of Donald Lowndes and Josephine P. (no last name was available) (G 9)

Donna Lowndes

Donald Lowndes and Josephine P.'s (no last name was available) first child was Donna Lowndes, who married George Dombroski on May 10, 1986. They had one child, Daniel Dombroski. Donna Lownes was born on February 6, 1960. No other information was available.

Debra Lowndes

Donald Lowndes and Josephine P.'s (no last name was available) second child was Debra Lowndes, who married Glenn Barron on September 20, 1986. They had one child; Matthew Barrow. Debra Lowndes was born on February 26, 1961. No other information was available.

Albert Lowndes

Donald Lowndes and Josephine P.'s (no last name was available) third child was Albert Lowndes. He was born in 1963. No other information was available.

Marjorie Lowndes

Donald Lowndes and Josephine P.'s (no last name was available) fourth child was Marjorie Lowndes. She was born in 1964. No other information was available.

Dorothy Lowndes

Donald Lowndes and Josephine P.'s (no last name was available) fifth child was Dorothy Lowndes. She was born in 1970. No other information was available.

Children of Dorothy Lowndes (no husband's name was available) (G 9)

Donald Lowndes

Dorothy Lowndes and (no husband's name was available)'s first child was Donald Lowndes. No other information was available.

Susan Lowndes

Dorothy Lowndes and (no husband's name was available)'s second child was Susan Lowndes. No other information was available.

William Lowndes

Dorothy Lowndes and (no husband's name was available)'s third child was William Lowndes (no wifes name was available). He had one child, Kyle Lowndes. No other information was available.

Margaret Lowndes

Dorothy Lowndes and (her husband's name was not available)'s fourth child was Margaret Lowndes, who was born on October 2, 1962. No other information was available.

Children of Gordon Leo Lown and Patricia A. Leek (G 9)

(note the "es" was dropped)

Steven L. Lown

Gordon Leo Lown and Patricia A. Leek's first child was Steven L. Lown, who married Katherine L. Gatsch in 1984. They have three children: Patrick Logan Lown, Maxton Loren Lown, and Larissa "Lacey" Lauren Lown. Steven L. Lown was born in 1955. No other information was available.

Barton Leo Lown

Gordon Leo Lown and Patricia A. Leek's second child was Barton Leo Lown, who married Bethany L. Bean in 1989. They had two children: Laura Louise Lown and Lindsay Louise Lown. Barton Leo Lown was born in 1957. No other information was available.

Children of Eldon Cyril Lown
and Marilyn R. Woods (G 9)

Gary R. Lown

Eldon Cyril Lown and Marilyn R. Woods's first child was Gary R. Lown, who married Kim (no last name was available). They had two children: Justin R. Lown and Erin F. Lown. Gary R. Lown was born in 1957. No other information was available.

Jeff A. Lown

Eldon Cyril Lown and Marilyn R. Woods's second child was Jeff A. Lown, who married Melodie (no last name was available). They had one child, Michael Lown. Jeff A. Lown was born in 1959. No other information was available.

Susanne Kay Lown

Eldon Cyril Lown and Marilyn R. Woods's third child was Susanne Kay Lown, who married Russell L. Robson in 1989. They have two children: Michael Robson, and Thomas Robson. Susanne Kay Lown was born in 1960. No other information was available.

Mark Lown

Eldon Cyril Lown and Marilyn R. Woods's fourth child was Mark Lown, who never married. He was born in 1962. No other information was available.

Children of James Reese Cooper and Wilma Cave (G 9)

Linda Cooper

James Reese Cooper and Wilma Caves's first child was Linda Cooper, who married Chamblis (no first name was available). Linda was born in 1949. No other information was available.

Teresa Cooper

James Reese Cooper and Wilma Caves's second child was Teresa Cooper, who married M. Keith Ward in 1982. Teresa Cooper was born in 1965. No other information was available,

---

THIS SECOND GOUP OF DSCENDANTS IS FROM GEORGE LOWNES AND MARY BOWERS'S BANCH OF THE FAMILY

Children of Joseph Donald Lownes III and Carol Ann Haworth (G 9)

Bette Jane Lownes

Joseph Donald Lownes III. and Carol Ann Haworth's first child was Bette Jane Lownes, who married George A. Ferris of Elgin, Illinois on

October 9, 1982. They had one child, Mark Joseph Ferris. They lived in Williamsport, Pennsylvania. Bette Jane Lownes was born on August 16, 1957. Bette was a school teacher, vocalist, and home school mother. George worked at Vanguard. They are members of Good Samaritan Church in Paoli, Pennsylvania. They also lived at 903 Sconnelltown Road, West Chester, Pennsylvania.

Linda Lee Lownes

Joseph Donald Lownes III and Carol Ann Haworth's second child was Linda Lee Lownes, who married Gregory Thomas Hytha on July 2, 1983. They had four children: Robert Maxwell Hytha, Alexander Miles Hytha, Carrie Evangeline Hytrha, and Christopher Gregory Hytha. Linda Lee Lownes was born on December 16, 1959. Both Linda Lee and Gregory are musicians. They have been on staff at various churches and played music at church retreats and other activities. They also renovate and rent historic homes and live in Phoenixville, Pennsylvania.

Donna Mae Lownes

Joseph Donald Lownes III and Carol Ann Haworth's thid child was Donna Mae Lownes, who married Paul Andrew Brady on August 25, 1990. They had three children: Daniel Joseph Brady, Brian Robert Brady, and Steven Michael Brady. Donna Mae Lownes was born on May 13, 1965. Donna Mae Brady teaches dance and was employed as a secretary to the principal in her school district. Paul is department manager in his company in Chesterbrook. They are members of Church of Christ. They lived in Phoenixville, Elverson, and West Coventry Township, and on Geview Drive in Pottstown, Pennsylvania.

Children of George Bolton Lownes and Kay Kachel (G 9)

George Bolton Lownes Jr.

George Bolton Lownes.and Kay Kachel's first child was George Bolton Lownes Jr. He was born on February 19, 1959. No other information was available.

Jeffrey Steven Lownes

George Bolton Lownes and Kay Kachel's second child was Jeffrey Steven Lownes, who married Jennifer (no last name was available) (divorced). They had one child, Carly Grace Lownes. Jeffrey Steven Lownes was born on July 13, 1961. No other information was available.

Gregory Douglas Lownes

George Bolton Lownes and Kay Kachel's third child was Gregory Douglas Lownes. He was born on March 2, 1965. No other information was available.

Gary Martin Lownes

George Bolton Lownes and Kay Kachel's fourth child was Gary Martin Lownes. He was born on July 27, 1966. No other information was available.

Children of Jane Ann Lownes and Charles Gallagher (First Husband) (G 9)

Susanne Gallagher

Jane Ann Lownes and Charles Gallagher's first child was Susanne Gallagher, who married Robert Allen Murray on December 10, 1977. They had two children: Jill Murray and Robert Murray Jr. Susanne Gallagher was born on August 30, 1958. No other information was available.

Charles Kirk Gallagher

Jane Ann Lownes and Charles Gallagher's second child was Charles Kirk Gallagher, who married Marianne (no last name was available) then they divorced. Charles Kirk Gallagher was born on March 20, 1962. No other information was available.

Sandra Lynn Gallagher

Jane Ann Lownes and Charles Gallagher's third child was Sandra Lynn Gallagher, who married Christopher Mantin on April 30, 1988. They had two children: Brielle Mantin and Jamie Mantin. Sandra Lynn Gallagher was born on July 10, 1963. No other information was available.

Jennifer Jane Gallagher

Jane Ann Lownes and Charles Gallagher's fourth child was Jennifer Jane Gallagher, who married John Barnhart on December 19, 1992. Jennifer Jane Gallagher was born on March 24, 1969. No other information was available.

Jane Ann Lownes's second husband was Martin Shea on October 17, 1980. They have no children.

Children of Bruce Thayer Lownes and Paula Pastorius (G 9)

Nathaniel Dean Lownes

Bruce Thayer Lownes and Paula Pastorius's first child was Nathaniel Dean Lownes. He was born June 30, 1982. No other information was available.

Rebecca Jane Lownes

Bruce Thayer Lownes and Paula Pastorius's second child was Rebecca Jane Lownes who, married (name was not available). She was born on June 1, 1984. No other information was available.

Joseph Lownes

Bruce Thayer Lownes and Paula Pastorius's third child was Joseph Lownes. He was born on December 25, 1987. No other information was available.

Sarah Grace Lownes

Bruce Thayer Lownes and Paula Pastorius's fourth child was Sarah Grace Lownes. who married (name was not available). She was born on November 14, 1992. No other information was available.

CHAPTER ELEVEN

Generation Eleven

THIS FIRST GROUP OF DSCENDANTS IS FROM THE JAMES I. LOWNES AND SUSANNAH RICHARDS'S BRANCH OF THE FAMILY

Children of Clarence Luff and Evelyn Jackson (First Wfe) (G 10)

Bobby Luff

Clarence Luff and Evelyn Jackson's first child was Bobby Luff. He was adopted and was born on July 1, 1944. No other information was available.

Diane Luff

Clarence Luff and Evelyn Jackson's second child was Diane Luff. She was born on May 26, 1947. No other information was available.

Children of Clarence Luff and Arlene Tanner (Second Wfe) (G 10)

Sandra Luff

Clarence Luff and Arlene Tanner's first child was Sandra Luff. She was born on June 6, 1955. No other information was available.

Brian Luff

Clarence Luff and Arlene Tanner's second child was Brian Luff. He was born on July 13, 1957. No other information was available.

Cheryl Luff

Clarence Luff and Arlene Tanner's third child was Cheryl Luff. She was born on May 30, 1959. No other information was available.

Jeffrey Luff

Clarence Luff and Arlene Tanner's fourth child was Jeffrey Luff. He was born on April 24, 1963. No other information was available.

Children of Dorothy Luff and Frank Acuff (G 10)

Constance Acuff

Dorothy Luff and Frank Acuff's first child was Constance Acuff. She was born on April 27, 1948. She was married (husband's name was not available; they had two children, their names were not available). No other information was available.

Frank Acuff

Dorothy Luff and Frank Acuff's second child was Frank Acuff. He was married, (wife's name was not available). Frank Acuff was born on February 8, 1950. No other information was available.

Children of Charles D. Lownes and Esther Moyer (G 10)

Charles David Lownes Jr.

Charles D. Lownes and Esther Moyer's first child was Charles David Lownes Jr. Charles David Lownes Jr. was born on December 27, 1949. He was killed in action in Vietnam on May 4, 1970. No other information was available.

Robert William Lownes

Charles D. Lownes and Esther Moyer's second child was Robert William Lownes, who married Shirley Wheeler on February 24, 1973. Robert William Lownes was born on April 23, 1951. They had one child, Rita Jean Lownes. No other information was available.

Children of William Leslie Lownes and Janice Dougherty (G 10)

Judith Ann Lownes

William Leslie Lownes and Janice Dougherty's first child was Judith Ann Lownes, who married Lewis Conway on October 11, 1967. Judith Ann Lownes was born on August 11, 1949. No other information was available.

Susan Lee Lownes

William Leslie Lownes and Janice Dougherty's second child was Susan Lee Lownes. She was born on February 12, 1952, and died on May 1, 1956; after being hit by a truck.

William Leslie Lownes Jr.

William Leslie Lownes and Janice Dougherty's third child was William Leslie Lownes Jr., who married Linda (no last name was available) on February 7, 1977. Linda had a son from her first husband named Christofer Todd Fisher, who was born on April 27, 1956. William was her third husband. William Leslie Lownes Jr. was born on October 17, 1953. No other information was available.

Children of Harold Lownes and Ethel Hammel Luff (G 10)

Virginia Lownes

Harold Lownes and Ethel Hammel Luff's first child was Virginia Lownes, who married Frank Holmes on December 9, 1971. They have three children: Michael Lownes Holmes, Morgan Frank Holmes, and Kevin Matthew Holmes. Virginia Lownes was born on November 21, 1946. No other information was available.

Marian Elizabeth Lownes

Harold Lownes and Ethel Hammel Luff's second child was Marian Elizabeth Lownes. She was born on February 18, 1948. No other information was available.

Daniel Walter Lownes

Harold Lownes and Ethel Hammel Luff's third child was Daniel Walter Lownes. He was born on October 28, 1954. No other information was available.

Sally Edna Lownes

Harold Lownes and Ethel Hammel Luff's fourth child was Sally Edna Lownes. She was born on November 28, 1955. No other information was available.

Phyllis Edith Lownes

Harold Lownes and Ethel Hammel Luff's fifth child was Phyllis Edith Lownes. She was born on March 11, 1957. No other information was available.

Children of Margaret Elizabeth Lownes and Wesley Charles (G 10)

Allen Wesley Charles

Margaret Elizabeth Lownes and Wesley Charles's first child was Allen Wesley Charles. He was adopted and was born on August 25, 1957. No other information was available.

Norman Glenn Charles

Margaret Elizabeth Lownes and Wesley Charles's second child was Norman Glenn Charles. He was adopted and was born on July 26, 1963. No other information was available.

Bruce Samuel Charles

Margaret Elizabeth Lownes and Wesley Charles's third child was Bruce Samuel Charles. He was adopted and was born on June 2, 1966. No other information was available.

Children of Doris Elaine Lownes and Albert Harry Barthelmeh (G 10)

Albert Harry Barthelmeh Jr.

Doris Elaine Lownes and Albert Harry Barthelmeh's first child was Albert Harry Barthelmeh Jr. He was born on January 18, 1949. No other information was available.

Thomas George Barthelmeh

Doris Elaine Lownes and Albert Harry Barthelmeh's second child was Thomas George Barthelmeh, who married June Bryd on June 8, 1974. Thomas George Barthelmeh was born on December 10, 1951. No other information was available.

James Glenn Barthelmeh

Doris Elaine Lownes and Albert Harry Barthelmeh's third child was James Glenn Barthelmeh. He was born on August 27, 1954. No other information was available.

Children of Wilmer Atkinson Lownes Jr. and Ida Slack (G 10)

Carol Lownes

Wilmer Atkinson Lownes Jr. and Ida Slack's first child was Carol Lownes. She was married; no name was available. No other information was available.

Deborah Lownes

Wilmer Atkinson Lownes Jr. and Ida Slack's second child was Deborah Lownes. No other information was available

Steven Lownes

Wilmer Atkinson Lownes Jr. and Ida Slack's third child was Steven Lownes. He died about 1970. No other information was available.

Lewis Lownes

Wilmer Atkinson Lownes Jr. and Ida Slack's fourth child was Lewis Lownes. No other information was available.

Sandra Lownes

Wilmer Atkinson Lownes Jr. and Ida Slack's fifth child was Sandra Lownes. No other information was available.

Jeffery Lownes

Wilmer Atkinson Lownes Jr. and Ida Slack's sixth child was Jeffery Lownes. No other information was available.

Children of Robert George Flack and Wynne Layton (G 10)

Lane Flack

Robert George Flack and Wynne Layton's first child was Lane Flack, who married Beth Baker. They have one child, Rachel Flack. Lane Flack was born on October 25, 1955. No other information was available.

Terri Flack

Robert George Flack and Wynne Layton's second child was Terri Flack, who married Mark Okeson. They have one child, Joshua Okeson. Terri Flack was born on March 17, 1957. No other information was available..

Nerissa Flack

Robert George Flack and Wynne Layton's third child was Nerissa Flack, who married Mark Allen Nichols. They have seven children: Anna Nichols, Lane Nichols, Shea Nichols, Kyra Nichols, Aden Nichols, Iann Nichols, and Rhia Nichols. Nerissa Flack was born on March 16, 1971. No other information was available.

Coral Flack

Robert George Flack and Wynne Layton's fourth child was Coral Flack, who married Matthew Heyl on June 1, 1996. (Now divorced). They have five children: Corbin Andrew Heyl, Luke Justus Heyl, Mia Jo Heyl, Rebecca Annalee Heyl, and Emmanual Joseph Heyl. Coral Flack was born on October 10, 1974. No other information was available.

Children of Ellen Louise Lownes and Ed Gilmore (G 10)

Scott Gilmore

Ellen Louise Lownes and Ed Gilmore's first child was Scott Gilmore. No other information was available.

No information was available for two additional children..

Child of Arlene G. Poley and Raymond W. Kantner (G 10)

Bonnie Jill Kantner

Arlene G. Poley and Raymond W. Kantner's only child was Bonnie Jill Kantner, who married Samuel Kehrer on October 15, 1966. They have one child, Kristine Kehrer. Bonnie Jill Kantner was born on April 20, 1946. No other information was available.

Children of Audrey Anna Poley
and Ivan F. Bennett M.D. (G 10)

Ivan Stanley Bennett

Audrey Anna Poley and Ivan F Bennett's first child was Ivan Stanley Bennett. He was born on January 27, 1949. No other information was available.

Judith Ann Bennett

Audrey Anna Poley and Ivan F. Bennett's second child was Judith Ann Bennett. No other information was available.

Children of Alma W. Poley and Robert L. Kendig (G 10)

Robert Kendig Jr.

Alma W. Poley and Robert L. Kendig's first child was Robert Kendig Jr. He was born on August 24, 1944. No other information was available.

Kathleen Kendig

Alma W. Poley and Robert L. Kendig's second child was Kathleen Kendig, who married Donald A. Borden on August 28, 1971. Kathleen Kendig was born on February 6, 1946. No other information was available.

Jon Thomas Kendig

Alma W. Poley and Robert L. Kendig's third child was Jon Thomas Kendig, who married Janice Ellen Kroupa on August 26, 1972. Jon Thomas Kendig was born on March 2, 1949. No other information was available.

Child of John Dyson and Diane Cook (G 10)

James Douglas Dyson

John Dyson and Diane Cook's only child was James Douglas Dyson. He was born on March 2, 1955. No other information was available.

Children of Joyce Prinold Lownes and Henry Augustus Hoyt II (G10)

Joanne Linda Hoyt

Joyce Prinold Lownes and Henry Augustus Hoyt II's first child was Joanne Linda Hoyt, who married David Allen Young on December 31, 1983. They have two children; Brian David Young and Timothy Ryan Young. Joanne Linda Hoyt was born on February 19, 1950. David Allen Young was born on February 23, 1953. No other information was available.

Pamela Elizabeth Hoyt

Joyce Prinold Lownes and Henry Augustus Hoyt's second child was Pamela Elizabeth Hoyt, who married James Leon Schmutz on June 13, 1970. They have five children: Catherine Joy Schmutz, Christian James Schmutz, Jonathan David Schmutz, Carolyn Joanne Schmutz, and Jeremiah Wesley Schmutz. Pamela Elizabeth Hoyt was born on May 16, 1951, in Bryn Mawr, Pennsylvania. She graduated from Penn State University with a B.S. in Nutrition. She wrote articles on food and nutrition for a local newspaper and the Diet Manual for Pennsylvania State institutions. Jim received his doctorate in chemistry from Penn State University. After one and a half years in England for Jim's postdoctoral work, they moved to Central, South Carolina in 1977, where Jim taught chemistry at Southern Wesleyan University for thirty-two years. Pam worked for thirteen years in the area of food safety at Clemson University. Pam and Jim have been blessed with five children and twelve grandchildren.

James Warren Hoyt

Joyce Prinold Lownes and Henry Augustus Hoyt's third child was James Warren Hoyt, who married Amalia de los Angeles Beltran de Lopez on September 15, 1979. They have three children: James Warren Hoyt Jr., Jonathan Richard Hoyt, and Michael Justin Hoyt. James Warren Hoyt was born on July 23, 1956. No other information was available.

Henry Augustus Hoyt III

Joyce Prinold Lownes and Henry Augustus Hoyt's fourth child was Henry Augustus Hoyt III, who married Janice Allison Board. They have one child, Jacqueline Allison Hoyt. Henry Augustus Hoyt III was born on May 10, 1959. No other information was available.

Children of Charlotte Lownes
and Grant Miller Olewiler Jr. (G 10)

Suzan Jill Olewiler

Charlotte Lownes and Grant Olewiler's first child was Suzan Jill Olewiler, who married Walter Strader on June 20, 1964. They have three children: Vance Strader, Matthew Strader, and Chad Strader. Suzan's career was in the beauty salon industry and she is currently retired. She is a certified spiritual life coach. Suzan Jill Olewiler was born on February 11, 1944. No other information was available.

Megret Olewiler

Charlotte Lownes and Grant Olewiler's second child was Megret Olewiler, who married Reverend Dave Bransby on August 4, 1967. They have five children: Andrew David Bransby, Rebecca Bransby, Suzan Beth Bransby, Michael Bransby, and Anna Bransby. Mergret Olewiler then married Kenneth Westfall on February 7, 2004. Megret's stepson Adam Westfall and Tiffany Westfall have two daughters. Violet, and Adeline. Megret Olewiler was born on October 7, 1948. No other information was available.

Lora Olewiler

Charlotte Lownes and Grant Olewiler's third child was Lora Olewiler, who married James Stewart Moody on December 7, 1974. Lora Olewiler and James Stewart Moody have two children: Will Stewart Moody and Lora Leanne Moody. They divorced many years later; she then married Thomas J. Van Dixhorn on October 17, 1998. Lora Olewiler's step children of Thomas J. Van Dixhorn's: Jason Van Dickson, Joshua Van Dixhorn, and Tasha Van Dixhorn.

Lora's insurance career began as a teenager in the mail room of a large insurance company. She formed her own insurance brokerage firm years later, eventually becoming an expert for the bicycle industry, realizing an innate talent for sales. Her first husband, James Stewart Moody, worked for Universal Motion Pictures. Her second husband, Thomas J. Van Dixhorn, managed a Hawaiian water company and travels there often. Lora and Tom are followers of Jesus Christ, trusting Him with their lives. Lora Olewiler was born on September 3, 1952

April Olewiler

Charlotte Lownes and Grant Olewiler's fourth child was April Olewiler, who married Mark Brandes on March 10, 1979. They have one child, Kelly Brandes. April Olewiler graduated Cum Laude from Pepperdine University, Malibu, California in 1974. She was Director of Marketing and Art Director at Brandes Portraiture Westlake Village from 1980 to 2015. April helped to establish her husband's career as a portrait artist that would eventually bring him an international reputation for innovative portraits of dignitaries and families, spanning forty decades. Currently an established Real Estate Consultant, April represents clients all along the California Coast. An avid non-professional chef, April loves all facets of the culinary world and has a deep appreciation to her mother for encouraging those talents from a young age. April is actively involved in local church activities and worldwide missions. April and Mark have a daughter, Kelly, and two foster "daughters-in love" Katherine Braun Holstrom and Breanna Cuellar. April Olewiler was born April 17, 1954

Constance (Conny) Olewiler

Charlotte Lownes Olewiller and Grant Miller Olewiler's fifth child was Constance (Conny) Olewlier, who was born on June 2, 1957, and married Michael Bradley Crisalli on January 13. 1979. They have two children: Paul Michael Crisalli and Peter Joseph Crisalli.

After graduating college, Conny worked in the consumer electronics industry while her husband was a registered nurse on open heart and surgery teams at Valley Presbyterian Hospital in Southern California. In 1991, they moved to Salem, Oregon, where Mike worked for Kaiser Permanente in family practice and Conny had her own business, Maximum Office Management (M.O.M.), serving clients in several states and a few countries. Having volunteered with the elderly for years, Conny created The Write Word Game and sells it nationwide to retirement homes and independent/assisted living facilities. Both being born again Christians, Mike and Conny look forward to meeting in Heaven the Lownes ancestors who had a deep faith in the Lord.

Grant Miller Olewiler III

Charlotte Lownes Olewiller and Grant Miller Olewiler Jr.'s sixth child was Grant Miller Olewiler III, who married Catherine Ann Cashen on July 10, 1982. They have six children: James Miller Olewiler, Daniel Olewiler, Heather Olewiler, Emily Olewiler, Katy Olewiler and Christine Olewiler. Grant Olewiler was born on April 29, 1960. No other information was available.

Children of Walter Bowen Lownes III and Nancy Patricia Delaney (G 10)

Deborah (Debbie) Ann Lownes

Walter Bowen Lownes III and Nancy Patricia Delaney's first child was Deborah (Debbie) Ann Lownes, who married Rickey Eugene Robb on May 15, 1976, and divorced him in 1985. Debbie then married Stuart Kent Wise on October 7, 1989, and has enjoyed a loving adventurous relationship. Debbie has worked numerous jobs in the finance industry in the Metro Atlantic area, currently working for SunTrust Bank. Kent has worked in the technology industry for many years and recently retired. Debbie and Step-Dad, Stuart Kent Wise, have raised two daughters: Heather Elizabeth Robb and Patricia Jane Robb. Deborah Ann Lownes was born on March 11, 1955.

Walter Craig Lownes

Walter Bowen Lownes III and Nancy Patricia Delaney's second child was Walter Craig Lownes, who married Donna Elaine Michell on April 10, 1993, after a long friendship. They have two children: Loren Elaine Lownes and Catherine Anne Lownes. Craig has worked numerous jobs in the information technology industry in the Metro Atlanta area, and is currently working for US Bank. Donna worked in marking and retail positions before finding her passion in teaching. Walter Craig Lownes was born in Bryn Mahr, Pennsylvania, on April 29, 1958.

Children of Rae Etta Halberstadt
and William Conley (G 10)

Dana Conley

Rae Etta Halberstadt and William Conley's first child was Dana Conley. She was born on November 4, 1956. No other information was available.

James Conley

Rae Etta Halberstadt and William Conley's second child was James Conley. He was born on July 3, 1963. No other information was available.

Laura Conley

Rae Etta Halberstadt and William Conley's third child was Laura Conley. She was born on February 23, 1967. No other information was available.

Children of Thomas Chapman Lownes Jr.
and Anne Lampe (G 10)

Elizabeth Ann Lownes

Thomas Chapman Lownes Jr. and Anne Lampe's first child was Elizabeth Ann Lownes, who married Timothy R. Wolfers on September 14, 1991. They had one child, Robert Sawyer Wolfers. Elizabeth Ann Lownes was born on August 29, 1960. No other information was available.

Barbara Ann Lownes

Thomas Chapman Lownes Jr. and Anne Lampe's second child was Barbara Ann Lownes married Jeffery Lee Feldman on October 6, 1985, and then was divorced. She had two children: Morgan Feldman and

Max Feldman. Barbra Ann Lownes was born on April 5, 1962. No other information was available.

Thomas Chapma (Tucker) Lownes III

Thomas Chapman Lownes Jr. and Anne Lampe's third child was Thomas Chapman (Tucker) Lownes III, who married Kim E. Noonan. They had three children: Kari Lownes, Cooper Lownes, and Griffin Lownes. Thomas C. (Tucker) Lownes III was born on August 31, 1967. No other information was available.

Children of Charles Fredrick Slaw Jr. and Jean Roberts (G 10)

Fredrick Clayton Slaw

Charles Fredrick Slaw Jr. and Jean Roberts's first child was Fredrick Clayton Slaw, who married Paula Fredrick on December 12, 1970. They had one child, Bella Slaw. Fredrick Clayton Slaw was born on March 4, 1949. No other information was available.

Edward Clayton Slaw

Charles Fredrick Slaw Jr. and Jean Roberts's second child was Edward Clayton Slaw, who married Jeanette Forlano on October 3, 1975. They had one child, Jennifer Slaw. Edward Clayton Slaw was born on November 5, 1950. No other information was available.

Children of Nancy Slaw and R. Koelle (G 10)

Nancy Slaw and R. Koelle had four children: names were not available. No other information was available.

Children of Irvin Sheldon Lownes Jr.
and Eileen Becker (G 10)

Nancy Lownes

Irvin Sheldon Lownes Jr. and Eileen Becker's first child was Nancy Jane Lownes, who was born in Norristown, Pennsylvania; she attended schools in Plymouth Township, Montgomery County, Pennsylvania, and went to Bryant College in Rhode Island, graduating with a degree in Business Administration. She has three children: Richard Benjamin Lownes, Jennifer Marie Mathis, and Sean David McClure. Nancy Lownes was born on June 16, 1959. No other information was available.

Sally Ann Lownes

Irvin Sheldon Lownes Jr. and Eileen Becker's second child was Sally Ann Lownes, who was born in Norristown and married Arthur Karl Butcher on April 12, 1990. They had three children: Dean Michael Butcher, Courtney Lynn Butcher, and William Sheldon George Butcher. Sally Ann Lownes attended schools in Plymouth Township, Montgomery County, Pennsylvania, and went to the University of Colorado in Boulder for one year and then dropped out. Sally Ann Lownes was born on April 18, 1961. No other information was available.

Paul Thomas Lownes

Irvin Sheldon Lownes Jr. and Eileen Becker's third child was Paul Thomas Lownes, who was born in Norristown and married Lisa Marie O'Hara on June 15, 1991; they had three children: Joshua Paul Lownes, Austin Gregory Lownes, and Ean Patrick Lownes. Paul Thomas Lownes attended schools in Plymouth Township, Montgomery County, Pennsylvania. He went to Rochester Institute of Technology in Rochester, New York, and graduated with a degree in Electrical

Engineering. Paul was born on May 4, 1963. The family resides in Dresher, Pennsylvania. No other information was available.

Bonnie Jean Lownes

Irvin Sheldon Lownes Jr. and Eileen Becker's fourth child was Bonnie Jean Lownes, who was born in Norristown and married James Joseph Cameron (Jace) on October 7, 1989. They had two children: James Giles Cameron (transitioned to Amanda Cameron) and Dorothea Marie Cameron. Bonnie Jean Lownes attended schools in Plymouth Township, Montgomery County, Pennsylvania, and took a few courses at Montgomery County Community College. Bonnie Jean Lownes was born on October 3, 1964. No other information was available.

Children of Howard G. Lownes Sr. and Verna M. Allebach (G 10)_

Howard G. Lownes Jr.

Howard G. Lownes Sr. and Verna M. Allebach's first child was Howard G. Lownes Jr., who married Linda Schmidt on May 12, 1990. Howard Jr. enlisted in the US Air Force on January 10, 1980, and was assigned to inactive duty as a reserved until being enlisted full time directly out of high school. He served in the Air Force for four years and was stationed at Shepard AFB, Texas, for nine weeks for award of AFSC (computer operator); he also served as a card tape converter operator, then console operator, tape typist, central clerk, data processing I, and high speed printer operator. On February 12, 1981, he was assigned to ACd10 then briefed on security. On February 17, 1981, he was upgraded to Level 5. On February 17, 1981, he completed his upgraded training for his Level 5 mandatory requirements, having fulfilled a 2096 and was recommended for award of full

Level 5 effective November 1, 1981. Howard received a promotion to airman, and was assigned new supervisor effective on July 12, 1982, as a highly qualified competent computer operator separated from the service. He was stationed for three years at Hickam Air Base Oahu, Hawaii (obtaining AIC on June 6, 1983 then on August 19, 1983, obtaining Senior Airman). On July 3, 1984, then on July 6, 1984, and was separated from active, duty on January 9, 1986 as a SRA (E 4) from San Antonio Kelly Air Force Base. He was a computer operator in the intelligence department. He worked in computers until his "military career was over." Afterward, he maintained a position in the computer field, working for several drug companies as well at SEI, a firm that handled banking information until retirement. Howard G. Lownes Jr. was born January 20, 1962. and passed away on November 16, 2018, due to pancreatic cancer.

April Lynn Lownes

Howard G. Lownes Sr. and Verna M. Allebach's second child was April Lynn Lownes, who married William Hostler on May 27, 2000, and they have no children. April Lynn Lownes worked in banking for ten years at different institutions due to company mergers, starting with positions from being a teller and moving up to senior teller before leaving for a better position. She went to work for Fox and Roach Realtors, the fifth largest real estate company in the United States. She worked in the accounting department at F & R, paying the real estate agents their commissions. When not working, April was involved with several volunteer organizations. April joined the Board of Directors' of the Montgomery County SPCA in March 2004 and served as secretary for twelve years before becoming a vice president at the time of this writing; she helped run fund-raising events for the SPCA. April was a charities representative for Fox and Roach Charities beginning in May 2000. She volunteered at the Cannon Shop at Gettysburg National Military Park for six years, painting cannons that were repaired and returned to the battlefield. In January 2018, both April and her husband Bill became caregivers buddies at Thomas Jefferson University Hospitals Buddy Program as well as running several events for the Otolaryngology (Ear, Nose and Throat) Department at TJU due to her husband's oral cancer. In October 2018, April was awarded the Excellence in Service Award for her work as secretary for the MCSPCA. April Lynn Lownes was born on April 27, 1967. In August of 2019, April resigned her postion at Fox and Roach to attend college at the Mongomery County community college. In late 2022 when she graduates from college, she will seek employment as a surgens assistamnt in the operating room.

April with her award from the MCSPCA for outstanding achievement

Children of John Brian Lownes
and Marlene Murray (G 10)

Beverly Lownes

John Brian Lownes and Marlene Murray's first child was Beverly Lynn Lownes, who married Carl Lynn Carter on March 29, 1980. Beverly was a successful real-estate sales woman. She was kidnapped and murdered while showing a house on September 30, 2014. They had three children: Carl Lynn Carter Jr., Christopher Brian Carter, and Chad Carter. Beverly Lynn Lownes was born on December 20, 1963. No other information was available.

Kathlyn Edith Lownes

John Brian Lownes and Marlene Murray's second child was Kathlyn Edith Lownes, who married James Seigler on July 17, 1983; they have three children: James Dean Seigler, Krystal Seigler, and Joshua Dewayne Seigler. Kathlyn Edith Lownes was born on August 26, 1965. No other information was available.

Tobbie LuAnn Lownes

John Brian Lownes and Marlene Murray's third child was Tobbie LuAnn Lownes; she married Kenneth (last name was not available). Tobbie Lownes was born on July 25, 1970. No other information was available.

Children of Richard Dunlap Lownes Jr. and Catherine Amwake (G 10)

Anna Lownes

Richard Dunlap Lownes Jr. and Catherine Amwake's first child was Anna Lownes. No other information was available.

Amanda Lownes

Richard Dunlap Lownes Jr. and Catherine Amwake's second child was Amanda Lownes. No other information was available.

Children of Randall K. Lownes and Margie (last name was not available) (G 10)

Wesley James Lownes

Randall K. Lownes and Margie's (last name was not available) first child was Wesley James Lownes. Wesley attended local parch elementary school, Saint Phillip Neri in Lafayetrte Hill, and graduated from a Roman Catholic High School in Philadelphia. He received a degree from Saint Joseph's University, then graduated from the American Academy McAllister Institute in New York (Mortuary Science College), and became a licensed funeral director in December of 2016. Wesley is a fifth generation funeral director.

Ryan Lownes

Randall K. Lownes and Margie's (last name was not available) second child was Ryan Lownes. No other information was available.

Austin Lownes

Randall K. Lownes and Margie's (last name was not available) third child was Austin Lownes. No other information was available.

Grant Lownes

Randall K. Lownes and Margie's (last name was not available) forth child was Grant Lownes. No other information was available.

Harrison Lownes

Randall K. Lownes and Margie's (last name was not available) fifth child was Harrison Lownes. No other information was available.

Children of Patricia Lownes and Ruben Arrieta (G 10)

Colton Arrieta

Patricia Lownes and Ruben Arrieta's first child was Colton Arrieta. He was born on February 22, 1985. No other information was available.

Kyle Arrieta

Patricia Lownes and Ruben Arrieta's second child was Kyle Arrieta. He was born in 1986. No other information was available.

Child of Jenne Lownes (Husband's Name was not avilable) (G 10)

Jennifer Lownes

Jenne Lownes's (husband's name was not avilable) only child was Jennifer Lownes, who was born in 1986. No other information was available.

Child of Donna Lowndes and George Dombroski (G 10)

(note that the "d" has been reinstated)

Daniel Dombroski

Donna Lowndes and George Dombroski's only child was Daniel Dombroski, who was born in 1989. No other information was available.

Child of Debra Lowndes and Glenn Barron (G 10)

(note that the "d" has been reinstated)

Matthew Barron

Debra Lowndes and Glenn Barron's only child was Matthew Barron, who was born in 1989. No other information was available.

Child of William Lowndes (wife's name was not available) (G 10)

(note that the "d" has been reinstated)

Kyle Lowndes

William Lowndes's (wife's name was not available)'s only child was Kyle Lowndes born on December 11, 1966. No other information was available.

Children of Steven L. Lown
and Katherine L. Gatsch (G 10)

(note the "es" has been removed)

Patrick Logan Lown

Steven L. Lown and Katherine L. Gatsch's first child was Patrick Logan Lown, who married Raynee Gutting in 2017. Patrick Logan Lown was born in 1987. No other information was available.

Larissa "Lacey" Lauren Lown

Steven L. Lown and Katherine L. Gatsch's third child was Larissa "Lacey" Lauren Lown, who married Matthew Lawrence Harnford in 2014. Larissa "Lacey" Lauren Lown was born in 1989. No other information was available.

Maxton Loren Lown

Steven L. Lown and Katherine L. Gatsch's second child was Maxton Loren Lown. Maxton Loren Lown was born in 1990. No other information was available.

Children of Barton Leo Lown
and Bethany L. Bean (G 10)

Laura Louise Lown

Barton Leo Lown and Bethany L. Bean's first child was Laura Louise Lown. She was born in 1991. No other information was available.

Lindsay Louise Lown

Barton Leo Lown and Bethany L. Bean's second child was Lindsay Louise Lown, who married Nathan Baker in 2017. Lindsay Louise Lown was born in 1994. No other information was available.

Children of Gary R. Lown and Kim (last name was not available) (G 10)

Justin R. Lown

Gary R. Lown and Kim's (last name was not available) first child was Justin R. Lown. No other information was available.

Erin F. Lown

Gary R. Lown and Kim's (last name was not available) second child was Erin F. Lown. No other information was available.

Child of Jeff A. Lown and Melodie (last name was not available) (G 10)

Michael Lown

Jeff A. Lown and Melodie's (last name was not available)'s only child was Michael Lown. No other information was available.

Chilren of Susanna Kay Lown and Russell L. Robson (G 10)

Michael Robson

Susanna Kay Lown and Russell Robson's frst child was Michael Robson. No other information was available.

Thomas Robson

Sussanna Kay Lown and Russell Robson's scond child was Thomas Lown. No other information was available.

━━━◆◆◆━━━

THIS SECOND GROUP OF DESCENDANTS IS FROM THE GEORGE LOWNES AND MARY BOWERS'S BRANCH OF THE FAMILY

Child of Bette Jane Lownes and George A Ferris (G 10)

Mark Joseph Ferris

Bette Jane Lownes and George A. Ferris's only child was Mark Joseph Ferris who married Alexandria Morgan on March 10, 2018. He was born on January 31, 1994. No other information was available.

Children of Linda Lee Lownes and Gregory Thomas Hytha (G 10)

Robert Maxwell Hytha

Linda Lee Lownes and Gregory Thomas Hytha's first child was Robert Maxwell Hytha who married Kathanne Marris on October 6, 2018. He was born June 29, 1990. No other information was available.

Alexander Miles Hytha

Linda Lee Lownes and Gregory Thomas Hytha's second child was Alexander Miles Hytha. He was born on November 9, 1992. No other information was available.

Carrie Evangeline Hytha

Linda Lee Lownes and Gregory Thomas Hytha's third child was Carrie Evangeline Hytha who married Noah Morgan on June 9, 2018. She was born on April 25, 1995. No other information was available.

Christopher Gregory Hytha

Linda Lee Lownes and Gregory Thomas Hytha's fourth child was Christopher Gregory Hytha. He was born on June 28, 1997. No other information was available.

Children of Donna Mae Lownes and Paul Andrew Brady (G 10)

Daniel Joseph Brady

Donna Mae Lownes and Paul Andrew Brady's first child was Daniel Joseph Brady. He was born on April 25, 1994. No other information available.

Brian Robert Brady

Donna Mae Lownes and Paul Andrew Brady's second child was Brian Robert Brady. He was born on October 23, 1996. No other information was available.

Steven Michael Brady

Donna Mae Lownes and Paul Andrew Brady's third child was Steven Michael Brady. He was born on May 17, 1998. No other information was available.

Chil of Jeffery Steven Lownes and Jennifer (last name was not available) (G 10)

Carly Grace Lownes

Jeffery Steven Lownes and Jenniffer (last name was not available) only child was Carly Grace Lownes. She was born on June 25, 2000. No other information was available.

Children of Susanne Gallagher and Robert Allen Murray (G 10)

Jill Murray

Susanne Gallagher and Robert Allen Murray's first child was Jill Murray. She was born on September 17, 1993. No other information was available.

Robert Murray Jr.

Susanne Gallagher and Robert Allen Murray's second child was Robert Murry Jr. He was born on September 9, 1995. No other information was available.

Children of Sandra Lynn Gallagher and Christopher Mantin (G 10)

Brielle Mantin

Sandra Lynn Gallagher and Christopher Mantin's first child was Brielle Mantin. She was born on February 13, 1991, No other information was available.

Jamie Mantin

Sandra Lynn Gallagher and Christopher Mantin's second child was Jamie Mantin. He was born on September 6, 1994. No other information was available.

CHAPTER TWELVE

Generation Twelve

THIS GROUP OF DESCENDANTS IS FROM THE JAMES I. LOWNES AND SUSANNAH RICHARDS'S BRANCH OF THE FAMILY

Children of Constance Acuff (husband's name was not available) (G 11)

Constance Acuff (husband's name was not available) had two children: no names of the children or other information was available.

Child of Robert William Lownes and Shirley Wheeler (G 11)

Rita Jean Lownes

Robert William Lownes and Shirley Wheeler's only child was Rita Jean Lownes. Rita was born on April 22, 1974. No other information was available.

Children of Virginia Lownes and Frank Holmes (G 11)

Michael Lownes Holmes

Virginia Lownes and Frank Holmes's first child was Michael Lownes Holmes. He was born on September 23, 1970. No other information was available.

Morgan Frank Holmes

Virginia Lownes and Frank Holmes's second child was Morgan Frank Holmes. He was born on July 27, 1972. No other information was available.

Kevin Matthew Holmes

Virginia Lownes and Frank Holmes's third child was Kevin Matthew Holmes. He was born on December 22, 1973. No other information was available.

Child of Lane Flack and Beth Baker G 11)

Rachel Flack

Lane Flack and Beth Baker's only child was Rachel Flack, who married Jonathan Bottom. They had five children: Audrey Bottom, Caroline Bottom, Naomi Bottom, Caleb Flack Bottom, and Miriam Flack Bottom. No other information was available.

Child of Terri Flack and Mark Okeson (G 11)

Joshua Okeson

Terri Flack and Mark Okeson's only child was Joshua Okeson, who married April (last name was not available). They had four children:

Lily Okeson, Natalie Okeson, Emily Okeson, and Aimee Lynn Okeson. No other information was available.

Children of Nerissa Flack and Mark Allen Nichols (G 11)

Anna Nichols

Nerissa Flack and Mark Allen Nichols's first child was Anna Nichols. No other information was available.

Lane Nichols

Nerissa Flack and Mark Allen Nichols's second child was Lane Nichols. No other information was available.

Shea Nichols

Nerissa Flack and Mark Allen Nichols's third child was Shea Nichols. No other information was available.

Kyra Nichols

Nerissa Flack and Mark Allen Nichols's fourth child was Kyra Nichols. No other information was available.

Aden Nichols

Nerissa Flack and Mark Allen Nichols's fifth child was Aden Nichols. No other information was available.

Iann Nichols

Nerissa Flack and Mark Allen Nichols's sixth child was Ian Nichols. No other information was available.

Rhia Nichols

Nerissa Flack and Mark Allen Nichols's seventh child was Rhia Nichols. No other information was available.

Children of Coral Flack and Matthew Heyl (G 11)

Corbin Andrew Heyl

Coral Flack and Matthew Heyl's first child was Corbin Andrew Heyl. He was born on March 27, 2000. No other information was available.

Luke Justus Heyl

Coral Flack and Matthew Heyl's second child was Luke Justus Heyl. He was born on July 12, 2002. No other information was available.

Mia Jo Heyl

Coral Flack and Matthew Heyl's third child was Mia Jo Heyl. She was born on December 20, 2005, in Eksjo, Sweden. No other information was available.

Rebecca Annalee Heyl

Coral Flack and Matthew Heyl's fourth child was Rebecca Annalee Heyl. She was born on October 20, 2007, in Eksjo, Sweden. No other information was available.

Emmanual Joseph Heyl

Coral Flack and Matthew Heyl's fifth child was Emmanuel Joseph Heyl. He was born on January 11, 2011. No other information was available.

Child of Bonnie Jill Kantner and Samuel Kehrer (G 11)

Kristine Kehrer

Bonnie Jill Kantner and Samuel Kehrer's only child was Kristine Kehrer. She was born on June 28, 1970. No other information was available.

Children of Joanne Linda Hoyt and David Allen Young (G 11)

Brian David Young

Joanne Linda Hoyt and David Allen Young's first child was Brian David Young, who married Dorothy Kangah Gyeni on August 9, 2014. Brian David Young was born on August 9, 1985. No other information was available.

Timothy Ryan Young

Joanne Linda Hoyt and David Allen Young's second child was Timothy Ryan Young, who married Christine Noel Glendening on September 17, 2016. Timothy Ryan Young was born on May 18, 1989. No other information was available.

Children of Pamela Elizabeth Hoyt and James Leon Schmutz (G 11)

Catherine Joy Schmutz

Pamela Elizabeth Hoyt and James Leon Schmutz's first child was Catherine Joy Schmutz, who married Peter Andrew Sutton on August 21, 2004. They have two children: Julia Kathleen Sutton and Nina

Elizabeth Sutton. Catherine Joy Schmutz was born on November 10, 1976. No other information was available.

Christian James Schmutz

Pamela Elizabeth Hoyt and James Leon Schmutz's second child was Christian James Schmutz, who married Caryn Elizabeth Herzog on July 12, 2002. They have four children: Ezekiel Christian Schmutz, Nehemiah Christian Schmutz, Malachi Christian Schmutz, and Amariah Faith Schmutz. Christian James Schmutz was born on May 14, 1978. No other information was available.

Jonathan David Schmutz

Pamela Elizabeth Hoyt and James Leon Schmutz's third child was Jonathan David Schmutz, who married Cheryl Elizabeth Lucas on January 5, 2008. They have three children: Lucas James Schmutz, Jude Thomas Schmutz, and Annabeth Florence Schmutz. Jonathan David Schmutz was born on December 25, 1982. No other information was available.

Carolyn Joanne Schmutz

Pamela Elizabeth Hoyt and James Leon Schmutz's fourth child was Carolyn Joanne Schmutz, who married Matthew Keith Lenard on September 8, 2018. She was born on March 27, 1985. No other information was available.

Jeremiah Wesley Schmutz

Pamela Elizabeth Hoyt and James Leon Schmutz's fifth child was Jeremiah Wesley Schmutz, who married Ashley Rose Couch on June 23, 2012. They have three children: Titus James Schmutz, Francis David Schmutz, and Winry Rose Schmutz. Jeremiah Wesley Schmutz was born on December 31, 1988. No other information was available.

Children of James Warren Hoyt and Amalia de los Angeles Beltran de Lopez (G 11)

James Warren Hoyt Jr.

James Warren Hoyt and Amalia de los Angeles Beltran de Lopez's, first child was James Warren Hoyt Jr., who married Julia Lindsey Ragan on January 28, 2012. They have one child, Jenna Rose Hoyt. James Warren Hoyt Jr. was born on December 1, 1981. No other information was available.

Jonathan Richard Hoyt

James Warren Hoyt and Amalia de los Angeles Beltran de Lopez's second child was Jonathan Richard Hoyt. He was born on December 28, 1982. No other information was available.

Michael Justin Hoyt

James Warren Hoyt and Amalia de los Angeles Beltran de Lopez's third child was Michael Justin Hoyt. He was born on November 29, 1987 and passed away on November 27, 2017. No other information was available.

Child of Henry Augustus Hoyt III and Janice Allison Board (G 11)

Jacqueline Allison Hoyt

Henry Augustus Hoyt III and Janice Allison Board's only child was Jacqueline Hoyt, who married Ross Pallansch on August 31, 2019. She was born on August 20, 1992. No other information was available.

Children of Suzan Jill Olewiler
and Walter Strader (G 11)

Vance Strader

Suzan Jill Olewiler and Walter Strader's first child was Vance Strader, who married Annie (last name was not available). Vance Strader and Annie had three children: Hannah Strader, Jack Strader, and Alex Strader. He then married Cathy (last name was not available), then Debbie (last name was not available). Vance Strader and Debbie were married on January 25, 2014. Vance Strader was born on February 21, 1967. No other information was available.

Matthew Strader

Suzan Jill Olewiler and Walter Strader's second child was Matthew Strader, who married Rebecca (last name was not available). They had two children: Tobias Strader and Samuel Strader. Matthew Strader was born on July 23, 1969. No other information was available.

Chad Strader

Suzan Jill Olewiler and Walter Strader's third child was Chad Strader, who was married Kristina (last name was not available) on April 1, 2019. Chad Strader and Kristina have one child; Ethan Strader Chad Strader was born on December 27, 1971. No other information was available.

Children of Megret Olewiler and
Rev. David Ransome Bransby (G 11)

Andrew Bransby

Megret Olewiler and Rev. David Ransome Bransby's first child was Andrew David Bransby. He was born August 2, 1969, in Van Nuys,

California. Andrew David Bransby married Frances Marie Bilhorn Sullivan on April 4, 1998. After graduating with a General Art degree from California State University Long Beach, Andrew worked in digital marketing and sales while Frances returned to college while raising four children in Bakersfield, California. She received an additional degree from UCLA to become a special education teacher. They started a small honey business to employ the children as they grew. They volunteered for local Down syndrome groups. They have four children: Caitlyn Ruth Bransby, Naomi Bilhorn Bransby, Dawn Bransby, and Andrew Luke Bransby. Being born-again Christians, Andrew and Frances trust in the grace of the Lord Jesus for all things.

Rebecca Bransby

Megret Olewiler and Rev. David Ransome Bransby's second child was Rebecca Bransby, who married Jay Forbes on December 7, 1998. They had two children: Tuck Forbes and Jorie Forbes. Rebecca Bransby was born on January 19, 1972. No other information was available.

Suzan Beth Bransby

Megret Olewiler and Rev. David Ransome Bransby's third child was Suzan Beth Bransby, who married C.J. Rebstock on December 7, 1998, and later married Peter Morrison. Suzan Beth Bransby and C.J. Rebstock have two children: Kasey Rebstock and Nora Rebstock. Suzan Bransby was born on February 26, 1975. No other information was available.

Michael Bransby

Megret Olewiler and Rev. David Ransome Bransby's fourth child was Michael Bransby, who married Priscilla Payan. They had four children: Evangeline Bransby, Jack Bransby, Isabeau Bransby, and Michael Finn Bransby. Michael Bransby was born on December 8, 1976. No other information was available.

Anna Bransby

Megret Olewiler and Rev. David Ransome Bransby's fifth child was Anna Bransby, who married Ronald Merrell on April 17, 2004. They had three children: Braddock Merrell, Brody Merrell, and Leilani Merrell. Anna Bransby was born on January 11, 1983. No other information was available.

Megret Bransby and Kenneth Westfall (Third Husband) (G 11)

Megret Bransby's stepchild of Kenneth Westfall was Adam Westfall, who married Tiffany (last name was not available); they had two children: Violet Westfall and Adeline Westfall. No other information was available.

Children of Lora Olewiler
and James Stewart Moody (First Husband) (G 11)

Will Stewart Moody

Lora Olewiler and James Stewart Moody's first child was Will Stewart Moody. He was born on September 4, 1983. No other information was available.

Lora Leanne Moody

Lora Olewiler and James Stewart Moody's second child was Lora Leanne Moody, who married Ed Cannon IV on October 17, 1998. They had one child; Ed Cannon V. Lora Leanne Moody was born on August 4, 1985. No other information was available.

Stepchildren of Lora Olewiler and Thomas J. Van Dixhorn (Second Husband) (G 11)

Lora Olewiler's step children of Thomas J. Van Dixhorn, were Jason Van Dixkson, Joshua Van Dixhorn, and Tasha Van Dixhorn. No other information was available.

Jason Van Dixhorn

Stepchild of Lora Olewiler and Tom Van Dixhorn (second husband)'s first child was Jason Van Dixhorn. He was born on November 30, 1979. Jason had one child Bryn Van Dixhorn (mother's name was Kimberly). No other information was available.

Joshua Van Dixhornn

Stepchild of Lora Olewiler and Tom Van Dixhorn (second husband)'s second child was Joshua Van Dixhorn, who married Kathryn (last name was not available). They had three children: Genevieve Van Dixhorn, James Van Dixhornn, and Felicity Van Dixhornn. Joshua Van Dixhorn was born on October 6, 1981. No other information was available.

Tasha Van Dixkson

Stepchild of Lora Olewiler and Tom Van Dixkson (second husband)'s third child was Tasha Van Dixkson, who married Ted Leon. Tasha Van Dixkson was born on August 2, 1986. No other information was available.

Child of April Olewiler and Mark Brandes (G 11)

Kelly Brandes

Lora Olewiler and Mark Brandes's only child was Kelly Brandes, who married Andrew Hartman. They had two children: Emma Hartman and Luke Hartman. April Olewiler and Mark Brandes have two foster "daughters in love": Katherine Brown Holstrom and Breanna Cuellar. Kelly Brandes was born on November 15, 1980. No other information was available.

Children of Constance (Conny) Olewiler and Michael Crisalli (G 11)

Paul Crisalli

Constance (Conny) Olewiler and Michael Crisalli's first child was Paul Michael Crisalli, who married Shannon Lawless on May 17, 2006, the same day he graduated from the University of Oregon Law School. Paul Crisalli was born on December 21, 1982. Paul Crisalli is an assistant attorney general for the State of Washington, and Shannon is a law partner at a Seattle law firm. They had two children: Jamie Lawless Crisalli and Lucia Lawless Crisalli. No other information was available.

Peter Joseph Crisalli

Constance (Conny) Olewiler and Michael Crisalli's second child was Peter Joseph Crisalli, who was born on March 31, 1986, in Van Nuys, California. Having met

Meredith Anne Roberts at college, they married on September 17, 2011. Peter graduated from Stanford University's Pds. graduate program inorganic Chemistry where he published multiple papers, a patent, and a book chapter on his research. When Meredith was working on her Pds in Inorganic chemistry at the University of California Santa Barbara, Peter did his post-doctoral research there and generated multiple publications and patents. They moved to Sunnyvale, California, where Pete works for Roche Sequencing Solutions and has his name on four issued patents while Meredith works for Evans Analytical Group, focusing in the semiconductor industry. Peter Joseph Crisalli and Meredith Ann Roberts' have two children: Lucas Alexander Crisalli, and Rachel Sofia Crsalli.

Children of Grant Miller Olewiler III and Catherine Ann Cashen (G 11)

James Miller Olewiler

Grant Miller Olewiler and Catherine Ann Cashen's first child was James Miller Olewiler who was born June 10, 1984, in Glendale, California. James married Amy Elizabeth Summers on November 3, 2006. James obtained a bachelor's degree in computer science at Biola University in 2006, and works at Wonderful Orchards in Bakersfield, California, as a database analyst. James serves regularly in his church, leading the audio-visual ministry and in his spare time manages several ministry and local business websites. Amy cares for their household, teaching their children at home and serving in the music and children's ministry of their church. Both James and Amy enjoy raising and spending time with four children: Isaac Miller Olewiler, Evelyn Faith Olewiler, adopted son Jacob Russell Olewiler, and Levi James Olewiler.

Daniel Olewiler

Grant Miller Olewiler and Catherine Ann Cashen's second child was Daniel Olewiler, who married Karen Rader. They had three children: Jonathan Olewiler, Alaina Olewiler, and Haddon Thomas Olewiler.

Daniel Olewlier was born on March 7, 1986. No other information was available.

Heather Olewiler

Grant Miller Olewiler and Catherine Ann Cashen's third child was Heather Olewiler. Heather Olewiler was born on October 16, 1987. No other information was available.

Emily Olewiler

Grant Miller Olewiler and Catherine Ann Cashen's fourth child was Emily Olewiler, who married Joshua Moore. Emily Olewiler and Joshua Moore have one child. Nathan Moore. No other information was available.

Katy Olewiler

Grant Miller Olewiler and Catherine Ann Cashen's sixth child was Katy Olewiler, was born on January 20, 1993. No other information was available.

Christine Olewlier

Grant Miller Olewiler and Catherine Ann Cashen's fifth child was Christine Olewiler, who married Jarid Johnson on May 13, 2017. Christine Olewiler was born on October 11, 1999. No other information was available.

Children of Deborah (Debbie) Ann Lownes and Rickey Eugene Robb (G 11)

Heather Elizabeth Robb

Deborah Ann Lownes and Rickey Eugene Robb's first daughter was Heather Elizabeth Robb, who was born in Hapeville, Georgia, on

February 2, 1981. Heather graduated from the University of Georgia in 2004, with a master's deegree in accounting. Heather Elizabeth Robb married Garrett Matthew Vonk on July 10, 2004. Heather has worked for Price Waterhouse in the tax department since she graduated from college. Heather and Garrett have resided in Atlanta for many years and moved to Portland, Oregon in 2017. Heather and Garrett have two children: Madeline Anne Vonk and Zackary Ryan Vonk.

Patricia Jane Robb

Deborah Ann Lownes and Rickey Eugene Robb's second child was Pateicia Jane Robb, who was born in Hapeville, Georgia, on February 7, 1984. Patricia graduated from Georgia Institute of Technology with a bachelor of science in business management in 2016 and a master's degree in Education from Georgia State University in 2017. Patricia currently teaches at Strong Rock Christian School in Locust Grove, Georgia. Patricia Jane Robb married Jacob Robert Pitman on July 10, 2010. Patricia and Jacob reside in Fayetteville, Georgia. Patricia and Jacob have two children: Elizabeth Marie Pitman and Ethan Robert Pitman. Patricia Jane Robb was born on February 7, 1984.

Children of Walter Craig Lownes and Donna Elaine Mitchell (G 11)

Loren Elaine Lownes

Walter Craig Lownes and Donna Elaine Mitchell's first child was Loren Elaine Lownes, who was born in Lawrenceville, Georgia, on October 17, 1995. Loren graduated from Georgia State College and University in Milledgeville, Georgia, in May 2017, with a degree in outdoor education. Loren has a passion and commitment to the outdoors and has been employed by several schools to teach outdoor and worldly skills to children.

Catherine Anne Lownes

Walter Craig Lownes and Donna Elaine Mitchell's second child was Catherine Anne Lownes, who was born in Lawrenceville, Georgia, on May 17, 1997. Anne is attending the University of North Georgia graduated in May 2019 with a degree in management. Anne has not yet decided how she will impact the world.

Child of Elizabeth Ann Lownes and Timothy R. Wolfers (G 11)

Robert Sawyer Wolfers

Elizabeth Ann Lownes and Timothy R. Wolfers's only child was Robert Sawyer Wolfers. He was born on July 8, 1996. No other information was available.

Children of Barbara Ann Lownes (Divorced) (G 11)

Morgan Feldman

Barbara Ann Lownes's first child was Morgan Feldman, who married Josh Merkel on May 24, 2014. They had one child, Mason Merkel. Morgan Feldman was born on October 22, 1986. No other information was available.

Max Feldman

Barbara Ann Lownes's second child was Max Feldman, who married Stacey Belcher on March 20, 2019. Max Feldman was born on June 17, 1993. No other information was available.

Children of Thomas Chapman Lownes III (Tucker) and Kim E.Noonan (G 11)

Kari Lownes

Thomas Chapman Lownes III (Tucker) and Kim E. Noonan's first child was Kari Lownes. Kaei Lownes was born on Febraury 22, 1997. No other information was available.

Cooper Lownes

Thomas Chapman Lownes III (Tucker) and Kim E. Noonan's second child was Cooper Lownes. Cooper Lownes was born on December 3, 1998. No other information was available.

Griffin Lownes

Thomas Chapman Lownes III (Tucker) and Kim E. Noonan's third child was Griffin Lownes. Griffin Lownes was born on November 30, 2000. No other information was available.

Child of Fredrick Clayton Slaw and Paula Fredrick (G 11)

Bella Slaw

Fredrick Clayton Slaw and Paula Fredrick's only child was Bella Slaw. She was born on October 1, 1971. No other information was available.

Child of Edward Clayton Slaw and Jeanette Forlano (G 11)

Jennifer Slaw

Edward Clayton Slaw and Jeanette Forlano's only child was Jennifer Slaw. She was born on February 16, 1978. No other information was available.

Children of Nancy Lownes (G 11)

Richard Benjamin Lownes

Nancy Lownes's first child was Richard Benjamin Lownes. He was born on July 24, 1982. No other information was available.

Jennifer Marie Mathis

Nancy Lownes's second child was Jennifer Marie Mathis, who married Edwin Victor Berg III on October 15, 2011. They have two children: Taylor Rosemary Berg and Riley Alexander Berg. Jennifer Marie Mathis was born on November 24, 1984. No other information was available.

Sean David McClure

Nancy Lownes's third child was Sean David McClure. He was born on September 12, 1992. No other information was available.

Children of Sally Ann Lownes and Authur Karl Butcher (G11)

Dean Michael Butcher

Sally Ann Lownes and Arthur Karl Butcher's first child was Dean Michael Butcher, who married Leeann Frances Carl. Dean enlisted in the Army and has been employed as a motor pool mechanic. He has achieved the rank of Sergeant First Class and expects to retire after twenty or more years of service. Dean married Leeann Frances Carl in a civil ceremony on July 6, 2010 before a deployment to Afghanistan. They had a chapel cermemony at Fort Campbell on November 12, 2011.. They have three children: Isabella Rose Butcher (still born), Anabelle Lynn Butcher, and Issac Garrett Butcher. Dean Michael Butcher was born on June 16, 1985.

Courtney Lynn Butcher

Sally Ann Lownes and Arthur Butcher's second child was Courtney Lynn Butcher. She was born on April 26, 1991. Courtney Lynn Butcher married Clayton Park on May 17, 2013. They divorced. She will marry Michael Moulton on August 1, 2020. No other information was available.

William Sheldon George Butcher.

Sally Ann Butcher's third child was William Sheldon George Butcher. He was born on September 4, 1993. No other information was available.

Children of Paul Thomas Lownes and Lisa Marie O'Hara (G 11)

Joshua Paul Lownes

Paul Thomas Lownes and Lisa Marie O'Hara's first child was Joshua Paul Lownes. He was born on January 8, 1996. No other information was available.

Austin Gregory Lownes

Paul Thomas Lownes and Lisa Marie O'Hara's second child was Austin Gregory Lownes. He was born on March 15, 1998. No other information was available.

Ean Patrick Lownes

Paul Thomas Lownes and Lisa Marie O'Hara's third child was Ean Patrick Lownes. He was born on March 30, 2000. No other information was available.

Children of Bonnie Jean Lownes and James Joseph Cameron (G 11)

James Giles Cameron (transitioned to Amanda Cameron)

Bonnie Jean Lownes and James Joseph Cameron's first child was James Giles Cameron Transitioned to Amanda Cameron). He was born on March 7, 1991. No other information was available.

Dorothea Marie Lownes

Bonnie Jean Lownes and James Joseph Cameron's second child was Dorothea Marie Lownes. She was born on April 28, 1995. No other information was available.

Children of Beverly Lynn Lownes and Carl Lynn Carter Sr. (G 11)

Carl Lynn Carter Jr.

Beverly Lynn Lownes and Carl Lynn Carter Sr.'s first child was Carl Lynn Carter Jr., who married Alicia Susanne Clark on June 16, 2001; they had two children: Luke Jordan Carter and Chloe Christian Carter. Then he married Kimberly Michelle Duval on October 28, 2011; they had one child, Collin Reese Carter. Carl Lynn Carter Jr. was born on September 13, 1980. No other information was available.

Christopher Brian Carter

Beverly Lynn Lownes and Carl Lynn Carter Sr.'s second child was Christopher Brian Carter. He had one child, Bailey Briann Carter (Christopher never married). Christopher Brian Carter was born on March 8, 1984. He was killed in an automobile accident on August 29, 2003.

Chad Carter

Beverly Lynn Lownes and Carl Carter Sr.'s third child was Chad Carter, who married Carrie Carthy McCatrhy; they had two children: Sawyer Brooks Carter and Raley Lynn Carter. Chad Carter was born on October 17, 1987. No other information was available.

Children of Kathlyn Edith Lownes
and James Seigler (G 11)

James Dean Seigler

Kathlyn Edith Lownes and James Seigler's, first child was James Dean Seigler, who married Hannah Walker; they had two children: Madison Marie Seigler and James Seigler. James Dean Seigler was born on June 16, 1984. No other information was available.

Krystal Lynette Seigler

Kathlyn Edith Lownes and James Seigler's, second child was Krystal Lynette Seigler, who married Robert Jenkins, they had one child, Haylee Danielle Jenkins. Krystal Lynette Seigler was born on August 11, 1986. No other information was available.

Joshua Dewayne Seigler

Kathlyn Edith Lownes and James Seigler's third child was Joshua Dewayne Seigler; who married Sheivena (last name was not available). Joshua Dewayne Seigler was born on January 4, 1990. No other information was available.

CHAPTER THIRTEEN

Generation Thirteen

THIS FIRST GROUP OF DESCENDANTS IS FROM THE JAMES I. LOWNES AND SUSANNAH RICHARDS'S BRANCH OF THE FAMILY

Children of Rachel Flack and Jonathan Bottom (G 12)

Audrey Bottom

Rachel Flack and Jonathan Bottom's first child was Audrey Bottom. No other information was available.

Caroline Bottom

Rachel Flack and Jonathan Bottom's second child was Caroline Bottom. No other information was available.

Naomi Bottom

Rachel Flack and Jonathan Bottom's third child was Naomi Bottom, who married Kevin Nollmeyer. No other information was available.

Caleb Flack Bottom

Rachel Flack and Jonathan Bottom's fourth child was Caleb Flack Bottom, who married Jana Hallmark. No other information was available.

Miriam Flack Bottom

Rachel Flack and Jonathan Bottom's fifth child was Miriam Flack Bottom. No other information was available.

Children of Joshua Okeson and April (last name was not available) (G 12)

Lily Okeson

Joshua Okeson and April's (last name was not available) first child was Lily Okeson. No other information was available.

Natalie Okeson

Joshua Okeson and April's (last name was not available) second child was Natalie Okeson. No other information was available.

Emily Okeson

Joshua Okeson and April's (last name was not available) third child was Emily Okeson. No other information was available.

Aimee Lynn Okeson

Joshua Okeson and April's (last name was not available) fourth child was Aimee Lynn Okeson, who married Byron Freund. They had two children: Oden Freund and Monica Eleanor Fruend. No other information was available.

Children of Catherine Joy Schmutz and Peter Andrew Sutton (G 12)

Julia Kathleen Sutton

Catherine Joy Schmutz and Peter Andrew Sutton's first child was Julia Kathleen Sutton. She was born on April 16, 2009. No other information was available.

Nina Elizabeth Sutton

Catherine Joy Schmutz and Peter Andrew Sutton's second child was Nina Elizabeth Sutton. She was born on July 6, 2011. No other information was available.

Children of Christian James Schmutz and Caryn Elizabeth Herzog (G 12)

Ezekiel Christian Schmutz

Christian James Schmutz and Caryn Elizabeth Herzog's first child was Ezekiel Christian Schmutz. He was born on August 7, 2007. No other information was available.

Nehemiah Christian Schmutz

Christian James Schmutz and Caryn Elizabeth Herzog's second child was Nehemiah Christian Schmutz. He was born on March 28, 2010. No other information was available.

Malachi Christian Schmutz

Christian James Schmutz and Caryn Elizabeth Herzog's third child was Malachi Christian Schmutz. He was born on June 11, 2012. No other information was available.

Amariah Faith Herzog

Christian James Schmutz and Caryn Elizabeth Herzog's fourth child was Amariah Faith Herzog. She was born on March 30, 2017. No other information was available.

Children of Jonathan David Schmutz and Cheryl Elizabeth Lucas (G12)

Lucas James Schmutz

Jonathan David Schmutz and Cheryl Elizabeth Lucas's first child was Lucas James Schmutz. He was born on September 13, 2008. No other information was available.

Jude Thomas Schmutz

Jonathan David Schmutz and Cheryl Elizabeth Lucas's second child was Jude Thomas Schmutz. He was born on April 15, 2014. No other information was available.

Annabeth Florence Schmutz

Jonathan David Schmutz and Cheryl Elizabeth Lucas's third child was Annabeth Florence was born on July 27, 2018. No other information was available.

Children of Jeremiah Wesley Schmutz
and Ashley Rose Couch (G 12)

Titus James Schmutz

Jeremiah Wesley Schmutz and Ashley Rose Couch's first child was Titus James Schmutz. He was born on June 14, 2014. No other information was available.

Francis David Schmutz

Jeremiah Wesley Schmutz and Ashley Rose Couch's second child was Francis David Schmutz. He was born on July 22, 2016. No other information was available.

Winry Rose Schmutz

Jeremiah Wesley Schmutz and Ashley Rose Couch's third child was Winry Rose Schmutz, who was born on July 30, 2019. No other information was available.

Child of James Warren Hoyt Jr.
and Julia Lindsey Ragan (G 12)

Jenna Rose Hoyt

James Warren Hoyt Jr. and Julia Linsey Ragan's only child was Jenna Rose Hoyt. She was born January 12, 2015. No other information was available.

Children of Vance Strader and Annie (last name was not available) (First Wife) (G 12

Hannah Strader

Vance Strader and Annie's (last name was not available) first child was Hannah Strader. She was born on September 16, 1991. No other information was available.

Jack Strader

Vance Strader and Annie's (last name was not available) second child was Jack Strader. He was born on May 22, 1994. No other information was available.

Alex Strader

Vance Strader and Annie's (last name was not available) third child was Alex Strader. He was born on April 4, 1996. No other information was available.

Children of Matthew Strader and Rebecca (No Last Name Available) (G 12)

Tobias Strader

Matthew Strader and Rebecca's (no last name was available)'s first child was Tobias Strader. He was born on August 13, 2002. No other information was available.

Samuel Strader

Matthew Strader and Rebecca's (no last name was available) second child was Samuel Strader. He was born onApril 17, 2004. No other information was available.

Child of Chad Strader and Kristina (last name was not available) (G 12)

Ethan Strader

Chad Strader and Kistina (wife's last name was not available) only child was Ethan Strader. No other information was available.

Children of Andrew David Bransby and Frances Bilhorn Sullivan (G 12)

Caitlyn Ruth Bransby

Andrew David Bransby and Frances Bilhorn Sulliivan's first child was Caitln Ruth Bransby. Andrew David Bransby adopted Frances Bilhorn's daughter Caitlyn Ruth. She was born on March 11, 1995, in San Mateo, California and is engaged to Joseph Andrew Spinelli. She works in online marketing. No other information was available.

Naomi Bransby

Andrew David Bransby and Frances Bilhorn Sullivan's second child was Naomi Bransby. She was born on March 5, 1999, in Newport Beach, California. Having special needs, she enjoys the movie industry. No other information was available.

Dawn Bransby

Andrew David Bransby and Frances Bilhorn Sullivan's third child was Dawn Bransby. She was born on March 10, 2000, in Newport Beach, California. She attends Arizona State University as a pre-med student. No other information was available.

Andrew Luke Bransby

Andrew David Bransby and Frances Bilhorn Sullivan's fourth child was Andrew Luke Bransby. He was born on March 13, 2002. He is in high school and enjoys math and engineering. No other information was available.

Children of Rebecca Bransby and Jay Forbes (G 12)

Tuck Forbes

Rebecca Bransby and Jay Forbes's first child was Tuck Forbes. He was born on January 11, 2003. No other information was available.

Jorie Forbes

Rebecca Bransby and Jay Forbes's second child was Jorie Forbes. She was born on June 24, 2004. No other information was available.

Children of Suzan Beth Bransby and C. J. Rebstock (G 12)

Kasey Rebstock

Suzan Beth Bransby and C. J. Rebstock's first child was Kasey Restock. She was born on January 5, 2004. No other information was available.

Nora Rebstock

Suzan Beth Bransby and C. J. Rebstock's second child was Nora Rebstock. She was born on September 7, 2007. No other information was available.

Children of Michael Bransby and Priscilla Payan (G 12)

Evangeline Bransby

Michael Bransby and Priscilla Payan's first child was Evangeline Bransby. She was born on March 21, 2009. No other information was available.

Jack Bransby

Michael Bransby and Priscilla Payan's second child was Jack Bransby. He was born on November 15, 2010. No other information was available.

Isabeau Bransby

Michael Bransby and Priscilla Payan's third child was Isabeau Bransby. She was born on November 19, 2013. No other information was available.

Michael Finn Bransby

Michael Bransby and Priscilla Payan's fourth child was Michael Finn Bransby. He was born on January 7, 2017. No other information was available.

Children of Anna Bransby and Ronald Merrell (G 12)

Braddock Merrell

Anna Bransby and Ronald Merrell's first child was Braddock Merrell. He was born on May 9, 2006. No other information was available.

Brody Merrell

Anna Bransby and Ronald Merrell's second child was Brody Merrell. He was born on September 14, 2007. No other information was available.

Leilani Merrell

Anna Bransby and Ronald Merrell's third child was Leilani Merrell. She was born on January 9, 2014. No other information was available.

Child of Lora Leanne Moody and Ed Cannon IV (G 12)

Ed Cannon V

Lora Leanne Moody and Ed Cannon IV's only child was Ed Cannon V. He was born on April 20, 2015. No other information was available.

Children of Joshua Van Dickson and Kathern (last name was not available) (G 12)

Genevieve Van Dickson

Joshua Van Dickson and Kathern (last name was not available)'s first child was Genevieve Van Diclson. She was born on April 19, 2008. No other information was available.

James Van Dickson

Joshua Van Dickson and Kathern (last name was not available)'s second chil was James Van Dickson. He was born on April 3, 2011. He is a twin to his siter Felisity. No other information was available.

Felicity Van Dickson

Joshua Van Dickson and Kathern (last name was not available)'s thid child was Felisity Van Dickson. She was born on April 3, 2011. She is a twin to her brother James. No other information was available.

Children of Kelly Brandes and Andrew Hartman (G 12)

Emma Hartman

Kelly Brandes and Andrew Hartman's first child was Emma Hartman. She was born on February 25, 2008. No other information was available.

Luke Hartman

Kelly Brandes and Andrew Hartman's second child was Luke Hartman. He was born on August 11, 2010. No other information was available.

Kelly Brandes and Andrew Hartman also have two foster daughters In Love: Katherine Brown Holstrom and Breanna Cuellar.

Children of Paul Crisalli and Shannon Lawless (G 12)

Jamie Lawless Crisalli

Paul Crisalli and Shannon Lawless's first child was Jamie Lawless Crisalli. She was born on August 24, 2013. No other information was available.

Lucia Lawless Crisalli

Paul Crisalli and Shannon Lawless's second child was Lucia Lawless Crisalli. She was born on August 25, 2016. No other information was available.

Children of Peter Joseph Crisalli and Meredith Ann Roberts (G 12)

Lucas Crisalli

Peter Joseph Crisalli and Meredith Ann Roberts's first child was Lucas Alexander Crisalli. He was born on October 18, 2016. No other information was available.

Rachel Sofia Crialli

Peter Joseph Crisalli and Meredith Ann Roberts's second child was Rachel Sofia Crisalli. She was born on September 10, 2019. No other information was available.

Children of James Miller Olewiler and Amy Elizabeth Summers (G 12)

Isaac Miller Olewiler

James Miller Olewiler and Amy Elizabeth Summer's first child was Isaac Miller Olewiler. He was born on August 31, 2009, and loves reading and building/creating. No other information was available.

Evelyn Faith Olewiler

James Miller Olewiler and Amy Elizabeth Summer's second child was Evelyn Faith Olewiler. She was born July 23, 2011, and loves art and reading. No other information was available.

Jacob Russell Olewiler

James Miller Olewiler and Amy Elizabeth Summer's adopted son was Jacob Russell Olewiler who was born August 4, 2013. Jacob was adopted. He loves swimming and swimming with animals. No other information was available.

Levi James Olewiler

James Miller Olewiler and Amy Elizabeth Summer's fourth child was Levi James Olewiler. He was born on May 13, 2019. No other information was available.

Children of Daniel Olewiier and Karen Rader (G 12)

Jonathan Olewiler

Daniel Olewiler and Karen Rader's first child was Jonathan Olewiler. He was born on November 15, 2014. No other information was available.

Alaina Olewlier

Daniel Olewiler and Karen Rader's second child was Alaina Olewiler. She was born on September 28, 2016. No other information was available.

Haddon Thomas Olewiler

Daniel Olewiler and Karen Rader's third child was Haddon Thomas Olewiler. He was born on February 18, 2019. No other information was available.

Child of Emily Olewiler and Joshua Moore (G 12)

Nathan Moore

Emily Olewiler and Joshua Moore's only child was Nathan Moore. No other information was available.

Children of Heather Elizabeth Robb and Garrett Matthew Vonk (G 12)

Madeline Ann Vonk

Heather Elizabeth Robb and Garrett Matthew Vonk's first child was Madeline Ann Vonk, who was born in Northside Hospital in Atlanta, Georgia, on April 17, 2009. Maddie enjoys reading, playing the piano, being outside, and reading Harry Potter books. No other information was available.

Zackary Ryan Vonk

Heather Elizabeth Robb and Garrett Matthew Vonk's second child was Zachary Ryan Vonk, who was born in Northside Hospital in Atlanta, Georgia, on November 13, 2011. Zach enjoys playing the piano, soccer, being outside, and Pokemon. No other information was available.

Children of Patricia Jane Robb and Jake Robert Pitman (G 12)

Elizabeth Marie Pitman

Patricia Jane Robb and Jake Robert Pittman's first child was Elizabeth Marie Pitman, who was born in Northside Hospital in Atlanta, Georgia, on November 5, 2011. Lizzie enjoys church activities, dancing, and playing with her dolls. No other information was available.

Ethan Robert Pitman

Patricia Jane Robb and Jake Robert Pittman's second child was Ethan Robert Pitman, who was born in Piedmont Fayette Hospital on September 29, 2015. Ethan enjoys church activities, football, and playing with his cars. No other information was available.

Child of Morgan Felman and Josh Merkel (G 12)

Mason Merkel

Morgan Felman and Josh Merkel's only child was Mason Merkel. He was born on November 29, 2015. No other information was available.

Children of Jennifer Marie Mathis and Edwin Victor Berg III (G 12)

Taylor Rosemary Berg

Jennifer Marie Mathis and Edwin Berg III's first child was Taylor Rosemary Berg. She was born on October 27, 2009. No other information was available.

Riley Alexander Berg

Jennifer Marie Mathis and Edwin Berg's second child was Riley Alexander Berg. He was born on April 17, 2012. No other information was available.

Children of Dean Michael Bucher and Leeann Frances Carl (G 12)

Isabella Rose Butcher

Dean Michael Butcher and Leeann Frances Carl's first child was Isabella Rose Butcher. She was still born on August 2, 2012. No other information was available.

Anabelle Lynn Butcher

Dean Michael Butcher and Leeann Frances Carl's second child was Anabelle Lynn Butcher. She was born on September 13, 2014. No other information was available.

Isaac Garrett Butcher

Dean Michael Butcher and Leeann Frances Carl's third child was Isaac Garret Butcher. He was born on February 8, 2017 in Germany. No other information was available.

Children of Carl Lynn Carter Jr. and Alicia Susanne Clark (First Wife) (G 12)

Luke Jordan Carter

Carl Lynn Carter Jr. and Alicia Susanne Clark's first child was Luke Jordan Carter. He was born on September 26, 2002. No other information was available.

Chloe Christian Carter

Carl Lynn Carter Jr. and Alicia Susanne Clark's second child was Chloe Christian Carter. She was born on January 13, 2004. No other information was available.

Child of Carl Lynn Carter Jr. and Kimberly Michelle Duval (Ssecond Wife) (G 12)

Collin Reese Carter

Carl Lynn Carter Jr. and Kimberly Michelle Duval's only child was Collin Reese Carter. He was born on March 21, 2014. No other information was available.

Child of Christopher Brian Carter (G 12)

Bailey Briann Carter

Christopher Brian Carter's only child was Bailey Briann Carter. She was born February 24, 2003. No other information was available.

Children of Chad Carter and Carrie McCarthy (G 12)

Sawyer Brooks Carter

Chad Carter and Carrie McCarthhy's first child was Sawyer Brooks Carter. He was born on March 31, 2015. No other information was available.

Raley Lynn Carter

Chad Carter and Carrie McCarthy's second child was Raley Lynn Carter. He was born on April 4, 2016. No other information was available.

Children of James Dean Seigler and Hannah Walker (G 12)

Madison Marie Seigler

James Dean Seigler and Hannah Walker's first child was Madison Marie Seigler. She was born on July 30, 2017. Madison Marie Seigler is a twin to James Siegler. No other information was available.

James Siegler

James Dean Seigler and Hannah Walker's second child was James Siegler. He was born on July 30, 2017. James Siegler is a twin to Madison Marie Siegler. No other information was available.

Children of Krystal Lynette Siegler
and Robert Jenkins (G 12)

Haylee Danielle Jenkins

Krystal Lynette Siegler and Robert Jenkins's only child was Haylee Danielle Jenkins. She was born on September 22, 2010. No other information was available.

CHAPTER FOURTEEN

Generation Fourteen

THIS GROUP OF DESCENDANTS IS FROM THE JAMES I. LOWNES AND SUSANNAH RICHARDS'S BRANCH OF THE FAMILY

Children of Aimee Lynn Okeson and Byron Freund (G 13)

Oden Freund

Aimee Lynn Okeson and Byron Freund's first child was Oden. No other information was available.

Monica Eleanor Freund

Aimee Lynn Okeson and Byron Freund's second child was Monica Eleanor Freund, who married Vilmar Alves. They had two children: Mac Alves and Eli Alves. No other information was available.

CHAPTER FIFTEEN

Generation Fifteen

THIS GROUP OF DESCENDANTS IS FROM THE JAMES I LOWNES AND SUSANNAH RICHARDS'S BRANCH OF THE FAMILY

Children of Monica Eleanor Freund and Vilmar Alves (G 14)

Mac Alves

Monica Eleanor Freund and Vilmar Alves's first child was Mac Alves. No other information was available.

Eli Alves

Monica Eleanor Freund and Vilmar Alves's second child was Eli Alves. No other information was available.

CHAPTER SIXTEEN

A final thought

Lest pride rear its ugly head, it is good to reflect, as did the early Quakers, that God is not a respect or of persons. These children, precious as they are to us are loved by God because they are His children. What can a photograph album tell of the personality and character of an individual, or of his hopes and dreams and convictions? Man looks on the outward appearance, but God looks on the heart. Each one of them has accepted the beautiful free love gift from God ... the sacrifice of His dear Son to pay the penalty for sin in their stead.

Today, men everywhere are asking the question, what do you mean "born again"?

In the preface to "The Blood of Christ" written in 1863 by Rev. William Read of England, this question is answered.

> "Give your heart to Christ", is rather law than gospel. It is most proper that it should be done, for God himself demands it; but mearly the urging the doing of it is far short of the gospel. The true gospel is, Accept the free gift of salvation from wrath and sin by receiving Jesus himself, and all benefits. He purchased with "His own Blood" (Acts 20: 28) and your heart will be His in a moment, being given to Him, not as a matter of law, but of love; for, if you have the love of His heart poured into yours by his blessed spirit, you will feel yourself under the constraining influence of a spontaneous spiritual impulse to give Him in return your heart,

and all that you possess. It is right to give Him your heart, but unless you first receive His you will never give Him yours".

Our ancestors were unique. They were thinkers for their day. Their religious beliefs were shaped and molded strongly by the Reformation. They had their convictions and persistence even in the face of the most violent anthoritative opposition. They had a personal conviction and were willing to suffer for their faith. Our ancestors were lifelong examples of perservering for light and truth regardless of the consequences. Joshua's charge to the faithless Isaelities resounds today as a challenge worth pondering. "And if it seems evil unto you, to serve the Lord, choose you this day whom ye will serve;... but for me and my house, we will serve the Lord." (Joshua 24:15)

This then is our heritage. Their blood is yours. Will the knowledge of their persecurion and their faithfulness and obedience to God Almighty be an exhorting and molding influence on the lives of the next generations? Only as the Holy Spirit draws them, and hearts remain tender and open to His Holy persuasion. If indeed the return of the Lord for His own is imminent, the most precious heritage that we can give to our children and children's children is a love and delight in the open Word of God, the Holy Bible, and the knowledge of His love for each of us.

May God bless all my readers, especially the descendants of Hugh and Jane Lowndes of Gawsworth, England.

CHAPTER SEVENTEEN

The Connection to William Penn

The famous William Penn, (October 14, 1644 – July 30, 1718) at age fifteen and about the same age as our Hugh, met in prison when William Penn was acquainted with a Thomas Loe, a Quaker missionary, who was a courtier in the court of King Charles II at that time. Loe was convicted by the Holy Spirit at age twenty-three by the verse, "There is a faith that is overcome by the world and a faith that overcomes the world." Despite the dangers, Penn began to attend Quaker meetings near Cork. A chance re-meeting with Thomas Loe confirmed Penn's rising attraction to Quakerism. Soon Penn was arrested for attending Quaker meetings. Rather than state that he was not a Quaker and thereby dodges any charges, he publicly declared himself a member and finally joined the Quakers (the Religious Society of Friends) at the age of twenty-two. In pleading his case, Penn stated that since the Quakers had no political agenda (unlike the Puritans), they should not be subject to laws that restricted political action by minority religions and other groups. Sprung from jail because of his father's rank rather than his argument, Penn was immediately recalled to London by his father. The admiral was severely distressed by his son's actions and took the conversation as a personal affront. In the end, young Penn was more determined than ever, and the admiral felt he had no option but to order him out of the house and to withhold his inheritance.

As Penn became homeless, he began to live with Quaker families. Quakers were relatively strict Christians in the seventeenth century.

They refused to bow or take off their hats to social superiors, believing all men equal under God, a belief antithetical to an absolute monarchy which believed the monarch divinely appointed by God. Therefore, Quakers were treated as heretics because of their principles and their failure to pay tithes. They also refused to swear oaths of loyalty to the king. Quakers followed the command of Jesus not to swear. The basic ceremony of Quakerism is silent medication in a meeting house, conducted in a group. There was no ritual and no professional clergy, and many Quakers disavowed the concept of original sin. God's communication comes to each individual directly, and if so moved, the individual shares their relations, thoughts, or opinions with the group. Penn found all these tenets to sit well with his conscience and his heart.

Penn became a close friend of George Fox, the founder of the Quakers, whose movement started in 1650s during the tumult of the Cromwellian revolution. The times spouted many new sects besides Quakers, including Seekers, Ranters, Antinomians, Seventh Day Baptists, Soul Sleepers, Adamites, Diggers, Levellers, Anabaptists (such as Swiss and German Mennonites, et cetera.), and many others. Following Oliver Cromwell's death, however, the crown was reestablished, and the King responded with harassment and persecution of all religions and sects other than Anglicanism. Fox risked his life, wandering from town to town, and he attracted followers who likewise believed that "God who made the world did not dwell in temples made with hands."

Penn and other Quakers believed that everyone had to seek God in his or her own way. Penn also thought that religious tolerance or "liberty of conscience" would create stronger governments and wealthier societies. Other English thinkers in the 1600s shared these ideas. But Penn had the opportunity to act on his beliefs in Pennsylvania; religious tolerance was the law.

He said of his conversion: "Being ready to faint concerning my hope of the restitution of all things, it was at that time that the Lord visited me with a certain sound and testimony of his eternal word."

The qualities of the Quakers that fascinated Penn were their ability to judge lucidly and to make forthright decisions, their integrity, their capacity for self approval, and their absolute convincement.

He was attracted to George Fox, a founder of the Religious Society of Friends, because of the power of his message that there was direct dealing between God and man. He came to know that "Without a cross of suffering, there can be no crown of fulfillment." Penn also said, "Ministers needed to be changed men themselves before they went about to change others." He was also a great believer in discourse and communication. Most likely, he kept abreast of the steady stream of pamphlets and tracts printed by the Quakers. Most of them were arguments in defense of their faith or bitter denunciation of their detractors.

Penn himself was an eloquent writer and pamphleteer. Possibly his most famous is "No Cross, No Crown," which he wrote when he was in the Tower of London in 1669 for his Anti-Trinitarianism doctrine. He was accused of elevating the Holy Spirit above the other members of the Trinity. Ordered to recant, he said, "My prison shall be my grave before I shall budge a jot, for I owe my conscience to no mortal man." After his conversation, Penn wrote that the main point of the Quaker belief was "the light of Christ within as God's gift for man's salvation."

This is followed by repentance from dead works to serving the living God, repent from the sight of sin, from the sorrow of sin, and make amendment for time to come. Following this, there is perfection from sin and finally eternal rewards and punishment.

Later he wrote that Quakers observe the following doctrine:

I	Communion and loving one another
II	To love one's enemies

II	Speak the truth with Yea and Nay, without swearing
IV	Not fighting
V	No title to a national church
VI	Not to respect persons (no flattering titles)
VII	Plain language (thee and thou)
VIII	Silence or few words
IX	Forbade drinking to people (no toasting)
X	That God alone can join two in marriage (no heathenish wedding ring but a simple self-wedding ceremony)
XI	No burial ceremony and no morning dress (but a time to exhort the living)

The climax of all the persecution came in 1670. William Penn and William Meade were arrested for attending a meeting for worship in Gracechurch Street, London, in defiance of the Conventicle Act. An unknown writer with a knowledge of shorthand took down the proceedings of the trial verbatim and published them immediately afterward.

Meade and Penn were charged with causing a riot. Actually, they were preaching inside the locked doors of Gracechurch Street Meeting House. But the noise outside the place was so great, those people could not have known if the men were preaching or not. At the onset of the trial, Meade and Penn were trying to stay out of jail while defending the right of the Quakers to preach in public. But on September 1, 1670, by his skill, Penn set a precedent which established the independence of the jury systems forever.

John Sykes wrote a brief review of the matter in "The Quakers." William Penn and William Meade pleaded "Not Guilty," and Penn spoke to such effect that he and Meade were ushered out of court, and the jury instructed in their absence. Next it was the jury's turn to offend. They returned, from the crown's point of view, an unsatisfactory verdict. "Gentlemen," cried the recorder, "you have not given in your verdict and you had as good say nothing. Therefore go and consider it once more. They did so, but again returned a verdict that would acquit Penn. "Gentlemen," pursued the recorder, now beside himself with rage, "You shall not be dismissed "til we have a verdict the court will accept."

Penn back at the bar called out to fortify them. "You are Englishmen; mind your privilege, give not away your right."

"Nor will we ever do it," sturdily replied the jury foreman.

Nor did they, shut up all night, bullied next day, finally thrown into Newgate Prison, and fined for their pains, Penn and Meade stood firm. Released on a writ of habeas corpus, they promptly sued the recorder for illegal imprisonment and won the case before a bench of twelve judges headed by the lord chief justice, and so established in English and American courts the right of independence of the jury. Bushel, the foreman, had nerved his colleagues, but the inspiration for the whole spirited stand had come from William Penn.

In 1681, King Charles II handed over a large piece of his American land holdings to William Penn to satisfy a debt the king owed to Penn's father. This land included present-day Pennsylvania and Delaware. Penn immediately set sail on the *Welcome* and took his first step on American soil in New Castle in 1682. On this occasion, the colonist pledged allegiance to Penn as their new proprietor, and the first general assembly was held in the colony. Afterwards Penn journeyed up-river and founded Philadelphia. However, Penn's Quaker government was not viewed favorably by the Dutch, Swedish, and English settlers in what is now Delaware. They had no "historical allegiance to Pennsylvania," so they almost immediately began petitioning for their own assembly. In 1704, they achieved their goal when the three southernmost counties of Pennsylvania were permitted to split off and became the new semi-autonomous colony of Lower Delaware. As the most prominent, prosperous, and influential city in the new colony, New Castle became the capital.

As one of the earlier supporters of colonial unification, Penn wrote and urged for a union of all the English colonies in what was to become the United States of America. The democratic principles that he set forth in the Pennsylvania Frame of Government served as an inspiration for the United States Constitution. As a pacifist Quaker, Penn considered the problems of war and peace deeply. He developed a forward-looking project for a United States of Europe through the creation of a European Assembly, made of deputies that could discuss and adjudicate controversies peacefully. He is therefore considered the first thinker to suggest the creation of a European Parliament.

Penn first called the area New Wales and then Sylvania (Latin for forest or woods), which King Charles II changed to Pennsylvania in honor of the elder Penn. On 4 March 1681, the king signed the charter, and the following day, Penn wrote, "It is a clear and just thing, and my God who has given it to America."

Meanwhile in 1681, after years of planning and frustration, William Penn signed the final documents, establishing the territory known as Pennsylvania. He spent two years at his beloved Pennsbury estate (which is open to the public today), and while there, he negotiated Pennsylvania's first land-purchase survey with the Lenape Indian tribe. Penn purchased the first tract of land under a white oak tree at Graystones on July 15, 1682. Penn drafted a charter of liberties for the settlement, creating a political utopia guaranteeing free and fair trial by jury, freedom of religion, freedom from unjust imprisonment, and free elections.

Having proved himself an influential scholar and theoretician, Penn had to demonstrate the practical skills of a real estate promoter, city planner, and governor for his Holy Experiment: the province of Pennsylvania.

During this time, Mr. Penn made a point of visiting every Quaker Meeting House in Pennsylvania at least once. He may have been present at the First Day Meeting when young James Lownes announced his intent to marry Susannah Richards (whose father, Joseph was a "Doctor of fissicke." Perhaps Penn was present also when the simple wedding ceremony took place.

Jane must have renewed her acquaintance with Mr. Penn at one of these meetings because on February 10, 1685, she "patented 150 acres from William Penn." no doubt the beautiful acreage surrounding her warm cave.

Quaker Men of the Eearly Movement

In the seventeenth century, there were a number of men that believed in Christ as their personal Savior.

George Fox

George Fox (July 1624 – November 13, 1690) was an English dissenter and founder of the Religious Society of Friends, commonly know as the Quakers or Friends.

George Fox

Early Rendering of George Fox

The son of a Leicestershire weaver, Fox lived in a time of great social upheaval and war. He rebelled against the religious and political authorities by proposing an unusual and uncompromising approach to the Christian faith. He traveled throughout Britain as a dissenting preacher, for which he was often persecuted by the authorities who disapproved of his beliefs.

While his movement disdain from some, others such as William Penn and Oliver Cromwell viewed Fox with respect. George Fox was born in the strongly Puritan village of Drayton-in the Clay, Leicestershire, England (now known as Fenny Drayton), and 15 miles (24 km) west-south-west of Leicester. He was the eldest of four children of Christopher Fox, a successful weaver, called "Righteous Christer" by his neighbors, and his wife, Mary Nee Lago. Christopher Fox was a churchwarden and was relatively wealthy; when he died in the late 1650s, he left his son a substantial legacy. From childhood, Fox was of a serious, religious disposition.

There is no record of any formal schooling, but he learned to read and write. "When I came to eleven years of age," he said, "I knew pureness and righteousness; for while I was a child, I was taught how to walk to be kept pure. The Lord taught me to be faithful, in all things, and to act faithfully two ways; viz., inwardly to God, and outwardly to man." Known as an honest person, he also proclaimed, "The Lord taught me to be faithful in all things... and to keep to Yea and Nay in all things."

George Fox knew people who were professors (followers of the standard religion), but by the age of nineteen, he had begun to look down on their behavior, in particular, drinking alcohol. He recorded that in prayer one night after leaving two acquaintances at a drinking session, he heard an inner voice saying, "Thou seest how young people go together into vanity and the earth, thou must forsake all, young and old, keep out all, and be as a stranger unto all."

Driven by his inner voice, George Fox left Drayton-in-the-Clay in September 1643, moving toward London in a state of mental torment and confusion. The English Civil War had begun, and troops were stationed in many towns through which he passed. In Barnet, he was torn by depression (perhaps from the temptation of the resort town near London). He alternately shut himself in his room for days at a time or went out alone into the countryside. After almost a year, he returned to Drayton, where he engaged Nathaniel Stephens, the clergyman of his hometown, in long discussions on religious matters. Stephens considered Fox a gifted young man, but the two disagreed on so many issues that he called Fox mad and spoke against him.

Fox complained to judges about decisions he considered morally wrong, as in his letter on the case of a women due to be executed. He campaigned against the paying of tithes, which funded the established church and often went into the pockets of absentee landlords or religious colleges far away from the paying parishioners. In his view, as God was everywhere and anyone could preach, the established church was unnecessary and a university qualification irrelevant for a preacher. Conflict with civil authority was inevitable. Fox was imprisoned several times, the first at Nottingham in 1649. At Derby in 1650, he was imprisoned for blasphemy; a judge mocked Fox's exhortation to "tremble at the word of the Lord," calling him and his followers "Quakers." Following his refusal to fight against the return of the monarchy (or to take up arms for any reason), his sentence was doubled. The refusal to swear oaths or to take up arms came to be a much more important part of his public statements. Refusal to take oaths meant that Quakers could be prosecuted under laws compelling subject to pledge allegiance, as well as making testifying in court problematic. In a letter of 1652 (that which is set up by the sword), he urged Friends not to use "carnal weapons" but "spiritual weapons," saying, "let the waves [the power of nations] break over your heads."

The 1650s when the Friends were most confrontational was one of the most creative periods of their history. During the Commonwealth, Fox had hoped that the movement would become the major church in

England. Disagreements, persecution, and increasing social turmoil, however, led Fox to suffer from a severe depression, which left him deeply troubled at Reading, Berkshire, for ten weeks in 1658 or 1659. In 1659, he sent parliament his most politically radical pamphlet, "Fifty nine Particulars Laid Down for the Regulating Things," but the year was chaotic so it never considered them; the document was not reprinted until the twenty-first century.

George Fox preached extensively in the north of England in 1652.

On reaching Sedbergh on June thirteenth of that year, he visited an isolated chapel on Firbank Fell, located a few miles from town. From the nearby outcrop of rocks, he preached to a congregation of more than a thousand people for three hours. The place has become known as Fox's Pulpit.

Fox described the event in his journal: "While others were gone to dinner, I went to a brook, got a little water, and then came and sat down on the top of a rock hard by the chapel. In the afternoon, the people gathered about me, with several of their preachers. It was judged there were above a thousand people, to whom I declared God's everlasting truth and Word of life freely and largely for about the space of three hours."

Plaque where Fox's Pulpit was in Sedbergh in 1652

In 1952, the tercentenary year of the founding of the Quaker movement, a plaque was erected to commemorate Fox's historic visit.

Next to Fox's pulpit stands a disused burial ground enclosed by drystone walls. Quakers were forbidden burial in consecrated ground or in churchyards. They buried their dead on private land. The chapel which once occupied the site ruined during a storm of the winter 1839-1840 and later rebuilt on the other side of the fell.

In 1652, Fox preached for several hours under a walnut tree at Bally, where his disciple, Thomas Aldham, was instrumental in setting up the first meeting in the Doncaster area. In June that year, Fox felt that God led him to ascend Pendle Hill, where he had a vision of many souls coming to Christ. From there, he traveled to Sedbergh in Westmorland, where he had heard a group of seekers were meeting, and over a thousand people on Firbank Fell, convincing many, including Francis Howgill, to accept that Christ might speak to people directly. At the end of the month, he stayed at Swathmoor Hall, near Ulverston, the home of Thomas Fell, vice-chancellor of the Duchy of Lancaster, and his wife, Margaret.

At around this time, the *ad hoc* meetings of Friends began to be formalized, and a monthly meeting was set up in County Durham. Margaret became a Quaker, and although Thomas did not convert, his familiarity with the Friends proved influential when Fox was arrested for blasphemy in October. Fell was one of three presiding judges and had the charges dismissed on a technicality.

Fox remained at Swarthmoor until the summer 1653 then left for Carlisle where he was arrested again for blasphemy. It was proposed to put him to death, but Parliament requested his release rather than have "a young man die for religion." Further imprisonments came at London in 1654, Launceston in 1656, Lancaster in 1660, Leicester in 1662, Lancaster again, Scarborough in 1664-1666, and Worcester in 1673-75. Charges usually included causing a disturbance and traveling without a pass. Quakers fell foul of irregularly enforced laws acknowledgeing titles, taking hats off in court, or bowing to those who considered themselves socially superior; all were seen as disrespectful. While imprisoned at Launceston, Fox wrote, "Christ our Lord and master saith, "Swear not at all, but let your communication be yea, yea, and nay, nay, for whatsoever is more than these cometh of evil'. The Apostle James saith, "My brethren, above all things swear not, neither by heaven, nor by earth, nor by any other oath. Lest ye fall into condemnation.'"

In prison, George Fox continued writing and preaching, feeling that imprisonment brought him into contact with people who needed his help: the jailers as well as his fellow prisoners. In his journal, he told his magistrate, "God dwells not in temples made with hands." He also sought to set an example by his actions there, turning the other cheek when being beaten and refusing to show his captors any dejected feelings.

The persecutions of these years with about a thousand Friends in prison by 1657 hardened George Fox's opinions of traditional religions and social practices. In his preaching, he often emphasized the Quaker's rejection of baptism by water; this was a useful way of highlighting how the focus of Friends on inward transformation differed from what he saw as the superstition of outward ritual. It was also deliberately provocative of those practices, providing opportunities for Fox to argue with them on matters of Scripture. This pattern was also found in his court appearances when a judge challenged him to remove his hat. Fox reposted by asking where in the Bible such an injunction could be found.

At least on one point, King Charles II listened to Fox. The seven-hundred Quakers who had been imprisoned under Richard Cromwell were released, though the government remained uncertain about the group's links with other, more violent, movements. A revolt by the Fifth Monarchists in January 1661 led to the suppression of that sect and the repression of other nonconformists, including Quakers. In the aftermath of this attempted coup, Fox and even other Quakers issued a broadside proclaiming what became known among Friends in the twentieth century as the "peace testimony." They committed themselves to oppose all outward wars and strife as contrary to the will of God.

In 1669, Fox married Margaret Fell, the widow of one of his wealthier supporters; she was a leading Friend. His ministry expanded, and he undertook tours of North America and the Low Countries. Between these tours, he was imprisoned for more than a year. He spent the final decade of his life working in London to organize the expanding Quaker movement.

Margaret Fell of Swarthmoor Hall was a lady of high social position and one of his early converts. Fox and Fell married on 27 October 1669 at a meeting in Bristol. She was ten years his senior and had eight children (all but one of them Quakers) by her first husband, Thomas Fell, who had died in 1658. She was herself active in the movement and had campaigned for equality and the acceptance of women as preachers. As there were no priests at Quaker weddings to perform the ceremony, the union took the form of a civil marriage approved by the principals and the witnesses at a meeting. Ten days after the marriage, Margaret returned to Swarthmoor to continue her work there while George went back to London. They shared religious work at the heart of their life together, and they later collaborated on a great deal of the administration the Society required. Shortly after the marriage, Margaret was imprisoned at Lancaster. George remained in the south east of England, becoming so ill and depressed that for a time he lost his sight.

Over the next few years, Fox continued to travel around the country as his particular religious beliefs took shape. At times, he actively sought the company of clergy but received no comfort from them as they seemed unable to help with the matters troubling him. One in Warwickshire advised him to take tobacco (which Fox disliked) and sing psalms; another in Coventry lost his temper when Fox accidentally stood on a flower in his garden; a third suggested bloodletting. Fox became fascinated by the Bible, which he studied assiduously. He hoped to find among the "English Dissenters" a spiritual understanding absent from the established church but fell out with one group, for example, because he maintained that women had souls.

As I had forsaken the priests, so I left the separate preachers also, and those esteemed the most experienced people; for I saw there was none among them all that could speak to my condition. And when all my hopes in them and in all men were gone, so that I had nothing outwardly to help me, nor could tell what to do, then oh, then, I heard a voice which said, "There is one, even Christ Jesus, that can speak to thy condition," and when I heard it my heart did leap for joy. Then the Lord let me see why there was none upon the earth that could speak to my condition namely, that I might give Him all the glory; for all are concluded under sin and shut up in unbelief as I had been, that Jesus Christ might have the pre-eminence who enlightens, and gives grace, and faith, and power. This when God doth work shall let (i.e. prevent) it? And this I knew experimentally.

By 1671, Fox had recovered and Margaret had been released by order of the king. Fox resolved to visit the English settlements in America and the West Indies, remaining there for two years, possibly to counter any remnants of Perrot's teaching. After a voyage of seven weeks, during which dolphins were caught and eaten, the party arrived in Barbados on 3 October 1671. From there, Fox sent an epistle to the Friends, spelling out the role of women's meetings in the Quaker marriage ceremony, a point of controversy when he returned home. One of his proposals suggested that the prospective couple should be interviewed by an all-female meeting prior to the marriage to determine whether there were any financial or other impediments. Though women's meetings had been held in London for the last ten years, this was an innovation in Bristol and the north west of England, which many there felt went too far.

The Society of Friends became increasingly organized toward the end of the decade. Large meetings were held, including a three day event in Bedfordshire, the precursor of the present Britain Yearly Meeting system. Fox commissioned two Friends to travel around the country, collecting the testimonies of imprisoned Quakers, as evidence of their persecution; this led to the establishment in 1675 of Meeting for Sufferings, which has continued to the present day.

With the restoration of the monarchy, Fox's dreams of establishing the Friends as the dominant religion seemed at an end. He was again accused of conspiracy, this time against Charles II, and fanaticism, a charge he resented. He was imprisoned in Lancaster for five months, during which he wrote to the king, offering advice on governance: Charles should refrain from war and domestic religious persecution and discourage oath-taking, plays, and maypole games. These last suggestions reveal Fox's Puritan leanings, which continued to influence Quakers for centuries after his death. Once again, Fox was released after demonstrating that he had no military ambitions.

Not all his followers accepted this statement; Isaac Penington, for example, dissented for a time, arguing that the state had a duty to protect the innocent from evil, if necessary, by using military force. Despite the testimony, persecution against Quakers and other dissenters continued.

Penington and others, such as John Perrot and John Pennyman, were uneasy at Fox's increasing power within the movement. Like Nayler before them, they saw no reason why men should remove their hats for prayer, arguing that men and women should be treated as equals, and if, as according to the apostle Paul, women should cover their heads, then so could men. Perrot and Penington lost the argument. Perrot emigrated to the New World, and Fox retained leadership of the movement.

Fox wrote a letter to the governor and assembly of the island in which he refuted charges that Quakers were stirring up the slaves to revolt and tried to affirm the orthodoxy of Quaker beliefs. After a stay in Jamaica, Fox's first landfall on the North American continent was at Maryland, where he participated in a four-day meeting of local Quakers. He remained there while various of his English companions traveled to the other colonies, because he wished to meet some Native Americans who were interested in Quaker ways, though he relate that they had "a great dispute" among themselves about whether to participate in the meeting. Fox was impressed by their general demeanor, which he said was "courteous and loving." He resented the suggestion (from a man in North Carolina) that "the Light and Spirit of God... was not in the Indians," proposition which Fox refuted. Fox left no record of encountering slaves on the mainland.

19th-century engraving of
George Fox, based on a
painting of unknown date

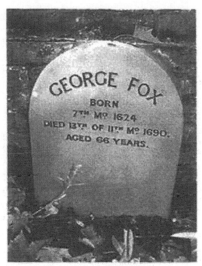

George Fox's marker in Bunhill
Fields, next to the Meeting House[61]

Encounters with Oliver Cromwell

Parliamentarians grew suspicious of monarchist plots and fearful that the group traveling with Fox aimed to overthrow the government. By this time, his meetings were regularly attracting crowds of over a thousand. In early 1655, he was arrested at Whetstone, Leicestershire, and taken to London under armed guard. In March, he was brought before the Lord Protector Oliver Cromwell. After affirming that he had no intention of taking up arms, Fox was able to speak with Cromwell for most of the morning about the Friends and advised him to listen to God's voice and obey it so that, as Fox left, Cromwell with tears in his eyes said, "Come again to my house; for if thou and I were but an hour of a day together, we should be nearer one to the other," adding that he wished Fox no more ill than he did to his own soul.

This episode was later recalled as an example of "speaking truth to power," a preaching technique by which subsequent Quakers hoped to influence the powerful. Although not used until the twentieth century, the phase is related to the ideas of plain speech and simplicity, which

Fox practiced but motivated by the more worldly goal of eradicating war, injustice, and oppression.

Fox petitioned Cromwell over the course of 1656, asking him to alleviate the persecution of Quakers. Later that year, they met for a second time at Whitehall. On a personal level, the meeting went well; despite disagreements between the two men, they had a certain rapport. Fox invited Cromwell to "lay down his crown at the feet of Jesus,"which Cromwell declined to do. Fox met Cromwell again twice in March 1657. Their last meeting was in 1658 at Hampton Court though they could not speak for long again because of the Protector's worsening illness. Fox wrote that "he looked like a dead man." Cromwell died in September of that year.

James Nayler

James Nayler (1616-1660) was an English Quaker leader. He was among the members of the Valant sixty, a group of early Quaker preachers and missionaries. At the peak of his career, he preached against enclosure and the slave trade.

James Nayler, with a "B" ("blasphemy") branded on his forehead.

He was born in the town of Ardsley in Yorkshire. In 1643, he joined the Parliamentarian army and served as quartermaster under John Lambert until 1650.

After experiencing what he described as the voice of God calling him from work in the fields, Nayler gave up his possessions and began seeking a spiritual direction, which he found in Quakerism after meeting the leader of the Quaker Friends movement, George Fox, in 1652. Nayler became the most prominent of the traveling Quaker evangelists known as the "Valiant Sixty;" he attacted many converts and was considered a skilled theological debater.

Beginning in 1656, Fox expressed his concerns to Nayler that both Nayler's ministry and that of his associate, Martha Simmonds, were becoming over-enthusiastic and erratic. Fox's concerns apparently centered specifically on Nayler's having allowed a group of his followers consider that Nayler himself might in some sense be a great profit or a messiah figure. They were soon hardly on speaking terms. On 23 September 1656, Fox visited Nayler in his prison at Exeter; when the prisoner refused to kiss the hand, Fox pushed his foot toward him, "It is my foot," clearly displaying his extreme displeasure with Nayler. The two men soon parted ways; their differences remaining sharp and unresolved.

Nayler tried to make a show of love and would have kissed Fox, but the latter would receive no sham hisses from one whose spirit was plainly wrong, "James," he said, "it will be harder for thee to get down thy rude company [of followers] than it was for thee to set them up."

In October 1656, Nayler and his friends, including Simmonds, staged a demonstration which proved disastrous: Nayler re-enacted the Palm Sunday arrival of Christ in Jerusalem by entering Bristol on a horse. He was imprisoned and charged with blasphemy.

Following Nayler's Palm Sunday Re-enactment, Nayler and some of his followers were apprehended and subsequently examined before

Parliament. The examination found that many of Nayler's followers, then referred to Nayler by such titles as Lord, Prince of Peace, et cetera, apparently believing that Nayler was in some manner representing the return of Jesus Christ. On 16 December 1656, he was convicted of blasphemy in a highly publicized trial before the Second Protectorate Parliament. Narrowly escaping execution, instead he was sentenced to be branded with the letter B for Blasphemer for two years of hard labor.

The Nayler case was part of a broader political attack against the Quakers. Initially, it was discussed under the Blasphemy Ordinance of 1648 with the hope of imposing an authoritative Presbyterian religious settlement upon the Commonwealth (the Presbyterians had also attempted to use the Ordinance against John Bibble in the previous parliament). But ultimately, the prosecution did not rely on any staute. Many of the speeches in the debates were about MPs to quash vice and heresy. After the verdict, Cromwell rejected representations on behalf of Nayler, but at the same time, he wanted to make sure the case did not provide a precedent for action against the people of God.

George Fox was horrified by the Bristol event, recounting in his journal that "James ran out into imaginations, and a company with him, and they raised up a great darkness in the nation," despite Nayler's belief that his actions were consitant with Quaker theology, and despite Fox's own having occasionally acted in some certain ways as if he himself might have been somehow similar to the Biblical prophets. Nevertheless, Fox and the movement in general denounced Nayler publicly, though this did not stop anti-Quaker critics using the incident to paint Quakers as heretics or to equate them with Ranters.

Nayler left prison in 1659 a physically ruined man. He soon went to pay a visit to George Fox, before whom he then knelt and asked for forgiveness, repenting of his earlier actions. Afterwards he was formally (but reluctantly) forgiven by Fox.

After having been accepted again by Fox, Nayler joined other Quaker critics of the Cromwellian regime, condemning the nation's rulers. In October 1660 while traveling to rejoin his family in Yorkshire, Naylor was robbed and left near death in a field then brought to the home of a Quaker doctor in Kings Ripton, Huntingdonshire. A day later and two hours before he died on 21 October, aged forty-two, he made a moving statemen which many Quakers since have come to value deeply:

There is a spirit which I feel that delights to do no evil, nor to revenge any wrong, but delights to endure all things, in hope to enjoy its own in the end. Its hope is to outlive all wrath and contention, and to weary out all exaltation and cruelty, or whatever is of a nature contrary to itself. It sees to the end of all temptations. As it bears no evil in itself, so it conceives none in thoughts to any other. If it be betrayed, it bears it, for its ground and spring is the mercies and forgiveness of God. Its crown is meekness, its life is everlasting, love unfeigned; it takes its kingdom with entreaty and not with contention, and keeps it by lowliness of mind.

In God alone it can rejoice none else regard it, or can own its life. It is conceived in sorrow, and brought forth without any to pity it, nor doth it murmur at grief and oppression. It never rejoiceth but through sufferings; for with the world's joy it is murdered. I found it alone, being forsaken. I have fellowship therein with them who lived in dens and desolate places in the earth, who through death obtained this resurrection and eternal holy life.

James Nayler was buried on 21 October 1660 in Thomas Parnell's burying ground at Kings Ripton. According to the villager's website, "There is also a Quakers Burial ground to the rear of "Quaker Rest" on Ramsey Road."

Edward Burrough

Edward Burrough (1634 – 1663) was an early English Quaker leader and controversialist. He is regarded as one of the Valiant Sixty, early Quaker preachers and missionaries.

Burrough was born in Underbarrow, Westmorland, and educated in the Church of England, but became a Presbyterian before converting to Quakerism. During his late teens, he heard George Fox preach in 1652 and immediately converted to what later came to be known as the Religious Society of Friends. He was consequently rejected by his parents. Burrough began itinerant preaching throughout England, traveling with another Friend, Francis Howgill. Among those converted by their preaching was Hester Bibble, probably in 1654.

During the years 1656-1657, Burrough and John Bunyan were engaged in a pamphlet debate, began by Buyan, who published "Some Gospel Truths Opened," in which he attacked Quaker beliefs. Burrough responded with "The True Faith of the Gospel of Peace." Buyan countered with "A Vindication of Some Gospel Truths Opened," which Burrough answered with "Truth (the Strongest of All) Witnessed Forth." Later the Quaker leader, George Fox entered the fray by publishing a refutation of Bunyan's essay in his "The Great Mystery of the Great Whore Unfolded."

Upon the Restoration in 1660, Burrough approached King Charles II, requesting protection and relief of Quakers in New England, who were being persecuted by Purtains there. Charles granted him an audience in 1661 and was persuaded to issue a wit stopping (temporarily) the corporal and capitol punishment of the Quakers in Massachusetts.

Burrough arranged for the writ to be delivered by Samuel Shattuck, himself a Quaker under a ban from Massachusetts. Charles's writ commanded the Massachusetts authorities to send the imprisoned Quakers to England for trial, but they chose instead to release them. The king's order effectively stopped the hangings, but imprisonments and floggings were resumed the next year.

In 1662, Burrough was arrested for holding a meeting, which was illegal under the terms of the Quaker Act. He was sent to Newgate Prison, London.

An order for his release signed by Charles II was ignored by the local authorities, and Burrough remained in Newgate until his death on February 14, 1663, aged twenty-nine. He was buried in the Quaker Burying Ground, Bunhill Fields.

James Parnell

Parnell was born at East Retford, Nottinghamshire, the son of Thomas and Sarah Parnell, and was apprenticed to his father. As a teenager, he became a nonconformist, visited George Fox in prison in 1653, and joined the Society of Friends.

Parnell is said to have been "young, small of stature, and poor in appearance," but thousands in England were made to confess that "he spoke as one having authority, and not as the scribes." He was convinced of the Truth when only fourteen years of age, and became a mighty preacher and promoter of the gospel by sixteen. Following a debate with a prominent priest, Parnell was arrested on spurious charges of being an "idle and disorderly person" and imprisoned at Colchester Castle. There he was confined to a small hole in the thick castle well, twelve feet above ground. He died from sickness and ill-treatment at the young age of nineteen. According to historian William Sewel, "So great was the malice and envy of his persecutors, that to cover their guilt and shame, they spread among the people, that by immoderate fasting, and afterwards with too greedy eating, he had shortened his days. But this was a wicked lie."

Other Quaker Leaders in the 1600's

Thomas Adian

Hester Bibble

John Bunyan

Sam Fisher

Francis Howgill
William Meade
William Penn
John Pennyman
John Perrot
Samel Shattock
Martha Simonds
Andrew Sowels
John Stubbs
John Sykes

The Lownes Tree

(G-1) Hugh Lowndes (5/3/1635 -7/11/1680, buried 9-1680) married Jane Stretch (4/3/1636 -2/ 1694) on 10/2/1658

(G 2) Joseph Lowndes (11/10/1660 - 1690

(G 2) Hannah Lowndes (10/23/1662 – 1756) married Thomas Collier (1660 – 1720) on 12/31/1688

    (G 3) Isaac Collier (11/20/1690 – 1757)

        (G 4) Hannah Collier (3/26/1739 – unk)

        (G 4) Rebecca Collier

        (G 4) Isaac Collier

        (G 4) Elizabeth Collier

        (G 4) James Collier

    (G 3) Hannah Collier (11/10/1693 – unk) married Mordecai Thompson On 9/28/1741

    (G 3) Joseph Collier (1696 – 1748)

    (G 3) John Collier (1703 – 1755)

(G-2) James I. Lownes (9/7/1665 – 6/18/1759) married Susannah Richards (1669 – 5/12/1739) on 10/9/1692

    (G 3) JoAseph Lownes (1/30/1693 – 10/12/1762) married Sarah Tidmarch (1700 – 8/1/1781) on 4/30/1725

        (G 4) Ann Lownes (12/25/1721 - 1791) married John Page on 3/24/1744, John Page died, second marriage Thomas James

        (G 4) John Lownes (12/15/1723- 4/8/1807) (buried 8/15/1807) married Agnes Cowpland (8/4/1727 – 5/3/1775) on 8/24/1753

(G 5) Caleb Lownes (8/17/1754 – 8/1828) married Margaret
Robeson (10/23/1761 – 3/28/1800) on 12/31/1790

  (G 6) Edward F. Lownes (1792 – 9/9/1834) married Hannah
Pancoast Byrnes (unk – 6/4/1820) on 10/2/1816.
Married second wife Elizabeth Richlo on 2/26/1829

    (G 7) Hannah Ann Lownes (5/12/1820 – unk) married
William Ellis Philadelphia, PA

      (G 8) Catherine Ellis

      (G 8) Edward Ellis

      (G 8) Rebecca Ellis

Edward F. Lownes and second wife Elizabeth Richlo's child

    (G 7) William Edward Lownes

  (G 6) George Bolton Lownes (1796 – 8/16/1825) married
Mary Paul of Valley Forge, PA

    (G 7) Margaret R. Lownes died 9/26/1825 at the age of
six months

  (G 6) John Lownes (unk – 7/24/1827) Louisville, KY

    (G 7) George Lownes

  (G 6) Catherine Lownes (unk – 8/9/1799) died at six months

(G 5) Sarah Lownes (6/18/1756 – 9/17/1757)

(G 5) Joseph Lownes (4/23/1758 – 12/16/1820) married Esther
Middelton (1766 – 5/25/1799) on 1/12/1786

  (G 6) Agnes Lownes (11/18/1786 – unk) married Isaac
Harvey on 12/7/1814

    (G 7) Josiah Harvey married; wife's name was not
avilable

      (G 8) Alex Elmslio Harvey married Rachel Wister

        (G 9) Child (name was not available)

        (G 9) Esther Wister Harvey married Frank Tiers

          (G 10) They had lots of children (names were not
available)

(G 6) Josiah Hewes Lownes (12/8/1791 – 10/4/1823)

(G 6) Esther Lownes (9/3/1795 – unk) married Michael Newbold on 1/31/1821

    (G 7) Martha Newbold married Thomas Mummy

    (G 7) Alexander Newbold

    (G 7) Josiah Newbold unmarried

    (G 7) Helen Newbold unmarried

(G 6) Martha Powell Lownes (1/7/1798 – unk)

(G 5) David Lownes (1/16/1760 – 10/28/1810) allegedly unmarried yet had three children.

(G 6) Rebecca Lownes (1799 – 4/19/1829)

(G 6) Edmond Lownes (4/21/1801 – 6/21/1805)

(G 6) Hannah Lownes (1805 – 6/8/1829)

(G 5) Grace Lownes (1/26/1762 – 10/31/1813) married her cousin Curtis Lownes (1759 – 10/23/1810) on 12/21/1794

(G 6) John Lownes (3/10/1796 – 7/8/1829) married Rebecca Crosby on 1/13/1820

    (G 7) Curtis Lownes (7/18/1829 – 1831) died at age 3

    (G 7) Sarah Crosby Lownes married Crosby P. Morton on 9/19/1839

        (G 8) Susannah Crosby Morton married Frank Black on 2/16/1865

    (G 7) Hannah Lane Lownes married William J. Maddock on 3/10/1843

        (G 8) Lownes Maddock married Elizabeth Worrall on 1/22/1872

        (G 8) William Maddock married M. Hannah (first name was not available)

        (G 9) Willie Maddock died in infancy

(G 6) Agnes Lownes (5/13/1797 – 5/28/1871) married Edward Levis (1775 – 1850) in 6/1817

(G 7) Elizabeth Levis (8/5/1819 – 4/24/1886) married
Philip Brooke (1821-1903)

    (G 8) Agnes Levis Brooke (7/23/1844 – 1914)

(G 5) John Lownes (12/20/1763 – 8/11/1765)

(G 5) Agnes Lownes (8/21/1766 – 7/27/1788)

(G 5) Agnes Lownes (No. 2) (8/21/1773 – 9/22/1793)

(G 5) Elizabeth Lownes (12/19/1798 – unk) married Samuel
Huggins on 5/4/1820

    (G 6) Curtis Huggins (9/19/1803 – 4/2/1821) Twin

    (G 6) Emily Huggins (9/19/1803 – Jan 1804) Twin

    (G 6) Margaret Huggins (2/17/1805 – 10/21/1821)

    (G 6) Esther Huggins (10/12/1810 – unk)

(G 5) Hannah Lownes (2/21/1799) died two days old

(G 5) Susannah Lownes (5/9/1726 – 10/6/1812) married James.
Lindley on 7/12/1745

(G 4) Joseph Lownes (8/25/1728 – 11/12/1781) married Hannah
Robinson (unk – 12/1757) on 12/15/1757

    (G 5) James Lownes (unk – 12/16/1743)

(G 4) Sarah Lownes (3/17/1731 – 1825) married Jonathan
Shoemaker on 10/20/1757

    (G 5) Joseph Shoemaker (wife's name was not available)

        (G 6) Elizabeth Shoemaker married Richard Paxon

        (G 7) Richard Paxon

        (G 7) Lashbrook Paxon

        (G 7) Anna Paxon married Joshua Pancoast

           (G 8) Richard Pancoast

           (G 8) Henry Pancoast

        (G 7) Sarah Paxon married Allen (last name was not
available)

        (G 7) Elizabeth Paxon married Chas Pickering

(G 4) Hannah Lownes (6/15/1733 – 11/16/1815) married Joshua Pancoast on 5/7/1761

   (G 5) Ann Pancoast married Luke Morris

      (G 6) Hannah Morris married Effingham Buckley

         (G 7) Ann Buckley married Israel W. Morris

            (G 8) Effingham Morris married Ellen Burroughs

   (G 5) Hannah Pancoast married Buckley (first name was not available)

(G 4) William Lownes (10/17/1735 – 11/18/1814) married Rebecca Elwell on 5/6/1762, then married Rachel Fell on 5/13/1784, she (died 9/1/1784) then married Mary Whitson on 12/16/1790, she (died 8/23/1807).

Children of William and Rebecca Elwell

   (G 5) Joseph Lownes (4/25/1765 – unk)

   (G 5) Mary Lownes (11/10/1768 – unk) married Robert Knowles

   (G 5) Daniel Lownes (5/28/1771 – unk)

   (G 5) William Lownes Jr. (9/4/1776 – 9/22/1852) married Mary (last name was not available) then married Susanna Stokes in 1795, and then married Sarah Canby in 1800. Sarah died (5/16/1834)

Children of William Lownes and Sarah Canby

   (G 6) Mary Lownes (10/9/1800 – 10/4/1831)

   (G 6) Thomas Lownes (1/29/1804 – 5/10/1864)

   (G 6) Samuel Lownes (3/11/1806 – 6/24/1806)

   (G 6) Beulah Lownes (3/13/1807 – 5/15/1888)

   (G 6) Rebecca Lownes (2/2/1809 – 7/24/1891)

   (G 6) Joseph Lownes (4/18/1810 – 4/2/1847) married Sarah Ann Ely (unk – 6/18/1867) on 3/14/1832 After Joseph died, Sarah married Samuel Cooper

(G 7) Henry Ely Lownes (2/23/1833 – 4/4/1884) married
 Sarah Jane Walton on 1/10/ 1855

  (G 8) Marianna Lownes (7/1/1857 – 12/4/1899) married
 J. Russell Lownes in 1876

  (G 8) Sarah Elizabeth Lownes (8/14/1859 – 7/28/1941)
 married Charles B. Hellyer on 12/1/1888 (he
 died on 1/10/1942)

    (G 9) Rebecca Morris Hellyer (4/1/1890 - unk)

    (G 9) Marianna Hellyer (9/30/1891 – 3/9/1898)

    (G 9) Elizabeth Roach Hellyer (10/24/1893 – unk)
 married Thomas (last name was not available).

    (G 9) Charles Henry Hellyer (10/24/1897 – unk)

    (G 9) Robert Conrad Hellyer (7/9/1899 – unk)

(G 7) Mary Lownes (4/3/1837 – 12/4/1899)

  (G 8) Marianna Lownes (4/2/1857 – 12/4/1899)

(G 7) Elias Paxsen Lownes (4/22/1842 – 2/10/1926)
 married Margaret Norcross on 12/23/1898 (she
 died on 4/17/1934)

  (G 8) Martha Conrad Lownes (9/5/1860 – 5/11/1959)

  (G 8) Beulah Lownes (12/13/1873 – 6/30/1875)

  (G 8) William Elias Lownes (1/11/1876 – 4/12/1968)

(G 7) Joseph Lownes (11/4/1847 – 4/4/1919) married
 Margaret Ann Scully (1856 – 1/10/1933) on 3/26/1874

  (G 8) Samuel Cooper Lownes (3/6/1875 – 9/8/1948)
 married Susan McDowell, then married Elizabeth
 (last name was not available)

    (G 9) Dorothy Lownes (12/19/1902 – unk) married
 Leo R. Gilroy died, then married David R.
 Rishell

    (G 10) Philip W. Gilroy (10/25/1924 – ...)

    (G 10) Robert Lownes Gilroy (5/8/1926 – ...)

(G 10) Peter O'Reilly Gilroy (5/21/1932 – ...)

Dorothy Lownes then married David R. Rishell

(G10) Rebecca Lynn Rishell (4/6/1949 -...) married Henry Carpenter.(divorced in 1976)

(G 10) Christine Louise Rishell (11/8/1950-...)

Children of Samuel Cooper Lownes (G 8) and Elizabeth (last name was not available)

(G 9) Margaret Lownes (10/16/1906 – unk) married Charles Hiddeman

(G 9) Elizabeth Lownes (1908 - unk) never married

(G 9) Samuel Lownes, Jr. (2/26/1911 - unk) married (name was not available)

(G 9) Robert Lownes (12/23/1912 - unk) widowed

(G 9) Donald Lownes (9/28/1913 - unk) married Mary (last name was not available)

(G 9) Frances Lownes (1916 – unk)

(G 8) John Scully Lownes (10/8/1877 – 2/19/1948) married Cora German

(G 9) Harriet German Lownes (5/17/1901 – 1968) married Theodore Luff

(G 10) Clarence Luff (5/21/1924 -...) married Evelyn Jackson, then married Arlene Tanner

(G 11) Bobby Luff (7/1/1944-...) adopted

(G 11) Diane Luff (5/26/1947-...)

Children of Clarence Luff and Arlene Tanner

(G 11) Sandra Luff (6/6/1955-...)

(G 11) Brian Luff (7/13/1957-...)

(G 11) Cheryl Luff (5/30/1959-...)

(G 11) Jeffrey Luff (4/24/1963-...)

(G 10) Dorothy Luff (12/21/1927-...) married Frank Acuff on 12/14/1946

(G 11) Constance Acuff (4/27/1948-...)

    (G 12) Child number 1 (name was nor available)

    (G 12) Child number 2 (name was not available)

(G 11) Frank Acuff (2/8/1950-...) married (wife's name was not available)

(G 8) Fanny Edith Lownes (9/5/1880 – died of walking typhoid)

(G 8) Sarah Ann Lownes (7/17/1882 –7/7/1892)

(G 8) George Mahan Lownes (11/8/1884 – 2/14/1959) married Florence Worrell (unk – 1973)

    (G 9) Alfred Russell Lownes (12/3/1905 – 10/12/1957) married Charlotte Eagle (unk – 2/4/1974)

    (G 10) Charles D. Lownes (9/14/1924 – unk) married Esther Moyer (2/1/1947 – unk)

    (G 11) Charles David Lownes Jr. (12/27/1949 – 5/4/1970) killed in action in Vietnam

    (G 11) Robert William Lownes (4/23/1951-...) married Shirley Wheeler on 2/24/1973

    (G 12) Rita Jean Lownes (4/22/1974-...)

    (G 10) William Leslie Lownes (5/7/1926 – unk) married Janice Dougherlty (6/17/1930-...)

    (G 11) Judith Ann Lownes (8/11/1949 - ...) married Lewis Conway on 10/11/1967

    (G 11) Susan Lee Lownes (2/12/1952 – 5/1/1956) hit by a truck

    (G 11) William Leslie Lownes Jr. (10/17/1953-...) married Linda (last name was not available) on 2/7/1977

(G 10) Harold Lownes (11/10/1927 – ...) married Ethel Hammel Luff on 8/10/1946

(G 11) Virginia Lownes (11/ 21/1946-...) married Frank Holmes on 12/9/1971

(G 12) MichaelLownesHolmes(9/23/1970-...)

(G 12) Morgan Frank Holmes (7/27/1972-...)

(G 12) KevinMatthewHolmes(12/22/1973-...)

(G 11) Marian Elizabeth Lownes (2/18/1948-...)

(G 11) Daniel Walter Lownes (10/28/1954-...)

(G 11) Sally Edna Lownes (11/28/1955-...)

(G 11) Phylis Edith Lownes (3/11/1957-...)

(G 10) Margaret Elizabeth Lownes (2/17/1929 – ...) married Wesley Charles on 11/13/1954

(G 11) Allen Wesley Charles (8/25/1957-...) adopted

(G 11) Norman Glenn Charles (7/26/1963-...) adopted

(G 11) Bruce Samuel Charles (6/2/1966-...) adopted

(G 10) Doris Elaine Lownes (6/18/1930-...) married Albert Harry Barthelmeh (4/10/1927-...) on 4/10/1947

(G 11) AlbertHarryBarthelmehJr.(1/18/1949-...)

(G 11) ThomasGeorgeBarthelmeh(12/10/1951-...) married June Bryd (3/1/1952-...) on 6/8/1974

(G 11) James Glenn Barthelmeh (8/27/1954-...)

(G 9) Wilmer Atkinson Lownes (11/16/1907 – 3/14/1975) married Ruth Sickel

(G 10) Wilmer Atkinson Lownes, Jr. married Ida Slack

(G 11) Carol Lownes married

(G 11) Deborah Lownes

(G 11) Steven Lownes died about 1970

(G 11) Lewis Lownes

(G 11) Sandra Lownes

(G 11) Jeffery Lownes

(G 9) Helen Eleanor Lownes (1/17/1911 – unk) married George E. Flack on 8/8/1931

    (G 10) Robert George Flack (3/15/1935-...) married Wynne Layton

        (G 11) Lane Flack (10/25/1955-...) married Beth Baker

            (G 12) Rachel Flack married Jonathan Bottom

                (G 13) Audrey Bottom

                (G 13) Caroline Bottom

                (G 13) Naomi Bottom married Kevin Nollmeyer

                (G 13) Caleb Flack Bottom married Jana Hallmark

                (G 13) Miriam Flack Bottom

        (G 11) Terri Flack (3/17/1957-...) married Mark Okeson

            (G 12) Joshua Okeson married April (last name was not available)

                (G 13) Lily Okeson

                (G 13) Natalie Okeson

                (G 13) Emily Okeson

                (G 13) Aimee Lynn Okeson married Byron Freund

                    (G 14) Oden Freund

(G 14) Monica Eleanor Freund married
Vilmar Alves

(G 15) Mac Alves

(G 15) Eli Alves

(G 11) Nerissa Flack (3/16/1971-...) married
Mark Allen Nichols

(G 12) Anna Nichols

(G 12) Lane Nichols

(G 12) Shea Nichols

(G 12) Kyra Nichols

(G 12) Aden Nichols

(G 12) Iann Nichols

(G 12) Rhia Nichols

(G 11) Coral Flack (10/10/1974-...) married
Matthew Heyl on 6/1/1996

(G 12) Corbin Andrew Heyl (3/27/2000-...)

(G 12) Luke Justus Heyl (7/12/2002-_)

(G 12) Mia Jo Heyl (12/20/2005-...)

(G 12) Rebecca Annalee Heyl (10/20/2007-...)

(G 12) Emmanual Joseph Heyl (1/11/2011-...)

(G 10) Jane Eleanor Flack (5/4/1936-...) married
Bill Marlow

(G 10) Nora Jean Flack (10/31/1940-...) married
Edward Montayne

(G 10) Diane Joyce Flack (5/12/1944-...) married
Glenn Fahr

(G 10) Carey Gene Flack (11/6/1947-...) married
Rose Banbridge

(G 10) Denise Lynn Flack (4/2/1951-...)

(G 9) George M. Lownes, Jr. (12/9/1923 – 10/31/1997)
married Anna Somer Neil on 9/13/1947

(G 10) Ellen Louise Lownes (10/1/1948-...) married
Ed Gilmore

(G 11) Scott Gilmore

(G 11) unknown (name was not available)

(G 11) unknown (name was not available)

(G 10) William George Lownes (1/9/1952-...)
married

(G 10) John Alfred Lownes (5/20/1955-...) married

(G 10) Cynthia Anna Lownes (6/19/1957-...)
married Glen (last name was not available)

(G 8) Hannah Lownes (10/17/1886 – 9/16/1927)
(husband's name was not available)

(G 9) Margaret Elizabeth Lownes (2/17/1926 -...)
married Wesley Charles on 11/13/1954

(G 10) Allen Wesley Charles (8/25/1957-...)

(G 10) Norman Glenn Charles (7/26/1963-...)

(G 10) Bruce Samuel Charles (6/2/1966-...)

(G 8) Helen Jones Lownes (4/17/1894 – unk). married
Albert Cornell, Helen then married Roscoe L.
Horner

(G 9) James Martin Cornell (6/25/1917 – 5/10/1935)

(G 10) Margaret Elizabeth Cornell (2/17/1929-...)

(G 10) Doris Elaine Cornell (5/18/1930-...)

(G 8) Joseph Ewell Lownes (9/4/1896 – 10/3/1973) (twin
to Thomas)

(G 9) Daughter # 1 (name was not available)

(G 9) Daughter # 2 (name was not available)

(G 9) Margaret Evelyn Lownes (5/28/1929-...)
married Ewing Mackey Carson

(G 10) Sandra Louise Carson (10/18/1951-...)

(G 10) Susan Carson (8/16/1954-...)

(G 8) Thomas Russell Lownes (9/4/1896 – 11/15/1973)
(twin to Joseph) married Laura Lownes
(G 9) Daughter # 1 (name was not available)
(G 9) Daughter #2) (name was not available)
(G 6) Joshua Lownes (12/16/1811 – 8/19/1825)
(G 6) Susanna Lownes (12/25/1813 – 2/4/1900)
(G 6) William Elwell Lownes (12/7/1816 – very young)
(G 6) Elizabeth Lownes (12/15/1820 – 4/12/1821)
(G 5) James Lownes (10/16/1775 – 2/8/1844) married Marcy
Betts (unk – 10/23/1837) on 3/13/1802.
(G 6) Eliza Lownes (9/21/1802 – 1/15/1892)
(G 6) William Lownes (12/22/1804 – 8/30/1830)
(G 6) Mary Biles Lownes (1/15/1807 – 4/7/1893)
(G 6) Hannah P. Lownes (12/18/1808 – 9/10/1869)
(G 6) Thomas Betts Lownes (5/25/1811 – 12/24/1880)
(G 6) Esther Lownes (7/21/1813 – 5/28/1838)
(G 6) Sarah A. Lownes (7/14/1815 – 10/16/1823) married
Samuel Cooper.
(G 7) Rachel Cooper married William Pidcuck
(G 6) Rebecca Lownes (7/7/1818 – 1/12/1884)
(G 7) Susanna Rebecca Lownes (7/12/1880 – 6/25/1971)
married Frank Daniels. (Unk - 4/23/1973
(G 8) Ruth Daniels married Art McCollion
(G 9) Jane Ellen McCollion (1/14/1948 -...) married
David Martin
(G 10) Emily Jane Martin (1/5/1977 -...)
(G 4) Rebecca Lownes (2/13/1738 – 1/11/1832) married Caleb
Ash on 4/29/1768
(G 5) Joshua Ash unmarried
(G 5) Joseph Ash married Frances Penrose
(G 6) Joseph Ash married Marie Ashmoad

(G 6) Penrose Ash unmarried

(G 6) Rebecca Ash unmarried

(G 5) Sarah Ash married Alex Elmslio

(G 6) Rebecca Elmslio unmarried

(G 6) Thomas Elmslio unmarried

(G 6) William Elmslio unmarried

(G 6) Ann Elmslio unmarried

(G 6) Elizabeth Elmslio unmarried

(G 5) Alice Ash married Benjaman Jones, Jr.

(G 6) Elizabeth Jones married Robert Taylor

(G 7) Benjaman James Taylor unmarried

(G 7) Anthony Taylor married Caroline F. Johnson

(G 7) Alice Jones Taylor unmarried

(G 7) Sarah Taylor

(G 6) Alice Jones married Benjamin (last name was not available)

(G 5) Caleb Ash unmarried

(G 5) Thomas Ash who married Sarah Chapman

(G 5) Elizabeth Ash died young

(G 5) William Ash died young

(G 4) James Lownes (8/22/1740 – 12/10/1831) married Sarah Pancoast on 11/3/1763 Then married Ann Robinson (unk – 6/6/1833) on 7/14/1803

(G 5) Mary Lownes (8/6/1764 – 6/22/1803) married Thomas Chapman

(G 6) Marianna Chapman (9/1/1784 - unk) unmarried

(G 6) Charles Chapman (9/21/1785 – 8/27/1821 in India) married Charlotte Christte

(G 7) Charlotte Chapman

(G 7) Charles Chapman

(G 7) Fredrick Wiltshire Chapman (Unk – 1821)

(G 6) Elizabeth Chapman (3/2/1787 – unk) married Samuel Harvey

  (G 7) Thomas Harvey

  (G 7) Louise Harvey

(G 6) Charlotte Chapman (4/23/1788 – unk) married Thomas Ingalls

(G 6) John James Chapman (1/10/1790 – unk) unmarried

(G 6) Sarah Chapman (8/12/1792 – unk) married Thomas Ash

  (G 7) Mary Ash

  (G 7) Joshua Ash

  (G7) Charlotte Ash

  (G 7) Charles Ash

(G 6) Louise Chapman (5/24/1794 – unk) unmarried

(G 5) Sarah Lownes (8/17/1766 - unk) married John Scott Pleasants on 4/29/1790

  (G 6) Sarah Pleasants

  (G 6) George Pleasants

  (G 6) Mary Hewes Pleasants

  (G 6) Fredrick Woodson Pleasants

  (G 6) Eliza Ann Pleasants

  (G 6) Charles Scott Pleasants

  (G 6) Louisa Pleasants

  (G 6) James Pleasants

  (G 6) Fitzhenry Pleasants

  (G 6) Cyrus Rodaphus Pleasants

(G 5) Hyatt Lownes (8/26/1769 – 10/27/1821) married Elizabeth Emmery on 8/2/1793

  (G 6) George Emmery Lownes

  (G 6) James Pancoast Lownes

  (G 6) John Lownes

(G 6) Margaret Lownes

(G 6) Elias Lownes

(G 6) Betsy Ann Lownes

(G 5) John Lownes (9/21/1771 – 8/1/1800) unmarried

(G 5) Deborah Lownes (2/20/1774 - unk) married Samuel
  Pleasants on 7/18/1795

  (G 6) Lucinda Pleasants

  (G 6) Sally Ann Pleasants

    (G 7) infant (name was not available)

  (G 6) Samuel Madison Pleasants

  (G 6) Christian Pleasants

  (G 6) Madison Pleasants

  (G 6) Edwin Chapman Pleasants

  (G 6) Ellen Pleasants

  (G 6) Charlotte Pleasants

  (G 6) Mary Galego Pleasants

(G 5) James Lownes Jr. (8/21/1776 – 8/20/1820) married Sarah
  Donaldson on 5/26/1797

  (G-6) Caleb Pancoast Lownes (12/26/1792 – 3/6/1836)
    married Ann Minges on 1/2/1826

    (G-7) Thomas Chapman Lownes (5/24/1827 – 3/4/1902)
      married Sarah Frick (4/15/1832 – 2/24/1899) on
      4/25/1850.

      (G-8) Adaline Lownes (6/29/1851 – 8/16/1906) married
        William J. Thompson on 11/17/1877

        (G-9) William Thompson (1887 – 1/2/1925)

      (G 8) Henry Lownes (2/6/1854 – 8/20/1861)

      (G 8) Charles Thomas Lownes (9/8/1856 – 8/21/1927)
        married Mary C. Heist (unk – 11/28/1930) on
        9/8/1880

        (G 9) Morris Lownes (4/5/1884 – 2/3/1892)

(G 9) John Barton Lownes M.D. (1887 – 2/22/1957) married Kathryn Weis

(G 8) Anna Frick Lownes (7/1/1861 – 12/2/1949) married Irvin Peltz Williams (8/1/1852 – 1/4/195?) on 1/11/ 1882 (Anna twin to Samuel)

(G 9) Bertha L. Williams (11/21/1884 – unk) married A. Wesley Poley (12/21/1883- unk) on 3/27/19?

(G 10) Arlene G. Poley (7/10/1911-unk) married Raymond W. Kantner on 6/7/1942

(G 11) Bonnie Jill Kantner (4/20/1946 -...) married Samuel Kehrer (5/17/1944-...) on 10/15/1966

(G 12) Kristine Kehrer (6/28/1970-...)

(G 10) Audrey Anna Poley (2/28/1914-...) married Ivan F. Bennett M.D. on 9/23/1944

(G 11) Ivan Stanley Bennett (1/27/1949-...)

(G 11) Judith Ann Bennett

(G 10) Alma W. Poley (9/15/1915-...) married Robert L. Kendig on 4/29/1939

(G 11) Robert Kendig, Jr. (8/24/1944-...)

(G 11) Kathleen Kendig (2/6/1946-...) married Donald A. Borden on 8/28/1971

(G 11) Jon Thomas Kendig (3/2/1949-...) married Janice Ellen Kroupa on 8/26/1972

(G 9) Myrtle L. Williams (7/16/1896- unk) married John Charles Dyson on 9/15/1921.

(G 10) John Dyson (2/21/1923-...) married Diane Cook (3/29/1930)-...) on 10/22/1949

(G 11) James Douglas Dyson (3/2/1955-...)

(G 8) Samuel Lownes (7/1/1861 – 11/29/1932) married Lillian Perch. (Samuel twin to Ana Frick)

(G 9) Florence Lownes

(G 9) Elmer Lownes died in infancy.

(G 8) Lewis M. Lownes (8/15/1867 – 3/19/1933) unmarried

(G 8) Robert C. Lownes (4/24/1869 – 11/15/1912) Married Anna C. Bean, (1865 – 1895) then married Susan Trombower Gotals (1860- 12/14/1925) in 1898

Children of Robert Lownes and Anna Bean

(G 9) Clarence Lownes (9/29/1884 -...) married Mamie Stover

(G 9) Harry Lownes died young

Child of Robert Lownes and Susan Trumbower Gotals

(G 9) Ruth Lownes married Frank W. Scholl

(G 8) Ida Parker Lownes (3/11/1870 – 10/18/1930) married William Blackwood Thomason on 8/1/1900

(G 8) Walter B. Lownes (9/25/1872 – 4/28/1935) married Anna Clark in 1894

(G 9) Walter Bowen Lownes Jr. (6/10/1889 – 9/1967) married Florence Prinold on 1/23/1918

(G 10) Joyce Prinold Lownes (8/4/1920 – 5/28/2018) married Henry (Hank) Augustus Hoyt II (9/1/1914- 12/16/1967) on 5/11/1949. Second marriage Hamilton Leftwich Robinson (11/13/1917 - unk) on 5/20/1972

(G 11) Joanne Linda Hoyt (2/19/1950-...) married David Allen Young (2/23/1953 -...) on 12/31/1983

(G12) Brian David Young (8/9/1985-...) married Dorothy Kangah Gyeni (7/7/1989 -...) on 8/9/2014

(G 12) Timothy Ryan Young (5/18/1989-...) married Christine Noel Glendening (4/24/1987-...) on 9/17/2016

(G 11) Pamela Elizabeth Hoyt (5/16/1951-...) married James Leon Schmutz on 6/13/1970

(G 12) Catherine Joy Schmutz (11/10/1976-...) married Peter Andrew Sutton on 8/21/2004

(G 13) Julia Kathleen Sutton (4/16/2009-...)

(G 13) Nina Elizabeth Sutton (7/6/2011-...)

(G 12) Christian James Schmutz (5/14/1978-...) married Caryn Elizabeth Herzog on 7/12/2002

(G 13) Ezekiel Christian Schmutz (8/7-2007-...)

(G 13) Nehemiah Christian Schmutz (3/28/2010-...)

(G 13) Malachi Christian Schmutz (6-11-2012-...)

(G 13) Amariah Faith Schmutz (3-30/2017-...)

(G 12) Jonathan David Schmutz (12/25/1982-...) married Cheryl Elizabeth Lucas on 1/5/2008

(G 13) Lucas James Schmutz (9/13/2008-...)

(G 13) Jude Thomas Schmutz (4/15/2014-...)

(G 13) Annabeth Florence Schmutz (7/27/2018-...)

(G 12) Carolyn Joanne Schmutz (3/27/1985-
...) married Matthew Keith Lenard
on 9/8/2018

(G 12) Jeremiah Wesley Schmutz
(12/31/1988-...) married Ashley Rose
Couch on 6/23/2012

   (G 13) Titus James Schmutz (6/14/2014-...)

   (G 13) Francis David Schmutz (7/22/2016-...)

   (G 13) Winry Rose Schmutz (7/30/2019-...)

(G 11) James Warren Hoyt (7/23/1956 -...)
married Amalia de los Angeles Beltran
de Lopez on 9/15/1979

(G 12) James Warren Hoyt Jr. (12/1/1981-
...) married Julia Lindsey Ragan on
1/28/2012

   (G 13) Jenna Rose Hoyt (1/12/2015-...)

(G 12) Jonathan Richard Hoyt (12/28/1982-...)

(G 12) Michael Justin Hoyt (11/29/1987 –
11/27/2017)

(G 11) Henry Augustus Hoyt III (5/10/1959-
...) married Janice Allison Board
(4/15/1959-...)

(G 12) Jacqueline Allison Hoyt (8/20/1992-...)
married Ross Pallansch on 8/31/2019

(G 10) Charlotte Lownes (11/14/1921 – 3/16/2005)
married Grant Olewiler (6/29/21 –
3/30/2017) on 3/13/1942

(G 11) Suzan Jill Olewiler (2/11/1944-...)
married Walter Strader (1/20/1943-_)
on 6/20/1964

(G 12) Vance Strader (2/21/1967-...) married Annie (last name was not available) then married Cathy (last name was not available) then married Debbie (last name was not available) (4/8/1962-...) on 1/25/2014

Children of Vance and Annie

    (G 13) Hannah Strader (9/16/1991...)

    (G 13) Jack Strader (5/22/1994-...)

    (G 13) Alex Strader (4/4/1996-...)

(G 12) Matthew Strader (7/23/1969-...) married Rebecca (5/28/1968-...) (last name was not available)

    (G 13) Tobias Strader (8/13/2002-...)

    (G 13) Samuel Strader (4/17/2004-...)

(G 12) Chad Strader (12/27/1971-...) married Kristina (last nane not was available) (8/7/1968-...) married on 4/1/2019

    (G 13) Ethan Strader

(G 11) Megret Olewiler (10/7/1948-...) married Rev. Dave Ransome Bransby on 8/4/1967

(G 12) Andrew David Bransby (8/2/1969-...) married Francis Marie Bilhohn Sulliam (6/8/1961-...) on 4/4/1998

    (G 13) Caitlyn Ruth Bransby (3/11/1995-...) Andrew adopted Francis Bilhorn daughter Caitlyn Ruth (3/11/1995-...)

    (G 13) Naomi Bilhorn Bransby (3/5/1999-...)

(G 13) Dawn Bransdy (3/10/2000-_)

(G 13) AndrewLukeBransdy(3/13/2002-_)

(G 12) Rebecca Bransby (1/19/1972-...) married Jay Forbes (10/12/1961-...) on 12/7/1998

(G 13) Tuck Forbes (1/11/2003-...)

(G 13) Jorie Forbes (6/24/2004-...)

(G 12) Suzan Beth Bransby (2/26/1975-...) married C. J. Rebstock on 12/7/1998 then Peter Morrison

(G 13) Kasey Rebstock (1/5/2004-...)

(G13) Nora Rebstock (9/7/2007-...)

(G 12) Michael Bransby (12/8/1976-...) married Priscilla Payan (5/18/1979-...)

(G 13) Evangeline Bransby (3/21/2009 -...)

(G 13) Jack Bransby (11/15/2010-...)

(G 13) Isabeau Bransby (11/19/2013-...)

(G 13) Michael Finn Bransby (1-7-2017-...)

(G 12) Anna Bransby (1/11/1983-...) married Ronald Merrell on (4/17/2004)

(G 13) Braddock Merrell (5/9/2006-...)

(G 13) Brody Merrell (9/14/2007-...)

(G 13) Leilani Merrell (1/9/2014-...)

Megret married Kenneth Westfall on 2/7/2004

Megret: Stepson Adam and Tiffany had two children: Violet and Adeline

(G 11) Lora Olewiler (9/3/1952-...) married James Stewart Moody on 12/7/1974, then married Tom J. Van Dixhorn (10/18/1954-...) on 10/17/1998

(G 12) Will Stewart Moody (9/4/1983-...)

(G 12) Lora Leanne Moody (8/4/1985-_) married Ed Cannon IV (10/10/84-...) on 10/17/1998)

    (G 13) Ed Cannon V (4/20/2015-_)

(Lora: Stepchildren)

(G 12) Jason Van Dixhorn (11/30/1979-...)

    (G 13) Bryn Van Dickson (unk - ...)

(G 12) Joshua Van Dixhorn (10/6/1981-...) Kathryn (last name was not available) (9/5/1982-...)

    (G 13) Genevieve Van Dixhorn (4/19/2008-...)

    (G 13) James Van Dixhorn (4/3/2011-...) (twin to Felicity)

    (G 13) Felicity Van Dixhorn (4/3/2011-...) (twin to James)

(G 12) Tasha Van Dixhorn (8/2/1986-...) married Ted Leon

(G 11) April Olewiler (4/17/1954-...) married Mark Brandes (3/10/1954-...) on 3/10/1979

(G 12) Kelly Brandes (11/15/1980-...) married Andrew Hartman (12/4/1979-...)

    (G 13) Emma Hartman (2/25/2008-...)

    (G 13) Luke Hartman (8/11/2010-...)

    (G 13) Katherine Brown Holstrom (foster daughter in love)

(G 13) Breanna Cuellar (foster daughter in love)

(G 11) Constance (Conny) Olewiler (6/2/1957-...) married Michael Crisalli (8/2/1954-...) on 1/13/ 1979

    (G 12) Paul Crisalli (12/21/1982-...) married Shannon Lawless (3/13/1984-...) on 5/17/2006

        (G 13) Jamie Lawless Crisalli (8/24/2013-...)

        (G 13) Lucia Lawless Crisalli (8/25/2016-...)

    (G 12) Peter Joseph Crisalli (3/31/1986-...) married Meredith Ann Roberts (3/31/1986-...) on 9/17/2011

        (G 13) Lucas Alexander Crisalli (10/18/2016-...)

        (G 13) Rachel Sofia Crisalli (9/10/2019-...)

(G 11) Grant Miller Olewiler III (4/29/1960-...) married Catherine Ann Cashen (10/17/1962-...) on 7/10/1982

    (G 12) James Miller Olewiler (6/10/1984-...) married Amy Elizabeth Summers (1/30/1984-...) on 11/3/2006

        (G 13) Isaac Miller Olewiler (8/31/2009-...)

        (G 13) Eveyln Faith Olewiler (7/23/2011-...)

        (G 13) Jacob Russell Olewiler (8/4/2013-...) adopted

        (G 13) Levi James Olewiler (5/13/2019-...)

    (G 12) Daniel Olewiler (3/7/1986-...) married Karen Rader (6/11/1986-...)

        (G 13) Jonathan Olewiler (11/15/2014-...)

        (G 13) Alaina Olewiler (9/28/2016-...)

(G 13) Haddon Thomas Olewiler (2/18/2019-...)

(G 12) Heather Olewiler (10/16/1987-...)

(G 12) Emily Olewiler married Joshua Moore

(G 13) Nathan Moore

(G 12) Katy Olewiler (1/20/1993-...)

12) Christine Olewiler (10/11/1999-...) married Jarid Johnson (4/4/1992-...) on 5/13/2017

G 10) Walter Bowen Lownes III (11/27/1926 – 5/14/1991) married Nancy Patricia Delaney (12/13/1931 -...) on 6/26/1953

(G 11) Deborah (Debbie) Ann Lownes (3/11/1955-...) married Rickey Eugene Robb on 5/15/1976, then Stuart Kent Wise on 10/7/1989

(G 12) Heather Elizabeth Robb (2/2/1981-...) married Garrett Matthew Vonk on 7/10/2004

(G 13) Madeline Ann Vonk (4/17/2009-...)

(G 13) Zachary Ryan Vonk (11/13/2011-...)

(G 12) Patricia Jane Robb (2/7/1984-...) married Jacob Robert Pitman on 7/10/2010

(G 13) Elizabeth Marie Pitman (11/5/2011-...)

(G 13) Ethan Robert Pitman (9/29/2015-...)

(G 11) Walter Craig Lownes (4/29/1958-...) married Donna Elaine Mitchell on 4/10/1993

(G 12) Loren Elaine Lownes (10/17/1995-...)

(G 12) Catherine Anne Lownes (5/17/1997-...)

(G 9) Myrtle Lownes (9/7/1895 – 1957) married James Halberstadt

   (G 10) Rae Etta Halberstadt (1/19/1933 -...) married William Conley

   (G 11) Dana Conley (11/4/1956-...)

   (G 11) James Conley (7/3/1963-...)

   (G 11) Laura Conley (2/23/1967-...)

(G 9) Thomas Lownes (1/10/1897 – 7/2/1962) married Jean Barton in Feb.1921

   (G 10) Thomas Lownes, Jr. (10/3/1936-...) married Anne Lampe (2/9/1936-...) on 5/30/1959

     (G 11) Elizabeth Ann Lownes (8/29/1960-...) married Timothy R. Wolfers on 9/14/1991

      (G 12) Robert Sawyer Wolfers (7/8/1996-...)

     (G 11) Barbara Ann Lownes (4/5/1962-...) married Jeffery Lee Fildman on 10/6/1985 (divorced)

      (G 12) Morgan Feldman (10/22/1986-...) married Josh Merkel on 5/24/2014

       (G 13) Mason Merkel (11/29/2015 - ...)

      (G 12) Max Feldman (6/17/1993-...) married Stasey Belcher on 3/20/2009

     (G 11) Thomas Chapman Lownes III (Tucker) (8/31/1967 -...) married Kim E. Noonan

      (G12) Kari Lownes (2/22/1997-...)

      (G 12) Cooper Lownes (12/3/1998-...)

      (G 12) Griffin Lownes (11/30/2000-...)

(G 9) Edna Lownes (8/30/1900 – 1975) married Charles Frederick Slaw (1924)

(G 10) Charles Fredrick Slaw Jr. (9/1924 - 2015) married Jean Roberts in 1947

(G 11) Fredrick Clayton Slaw (3/4/1949-...) married Paula Fredrick on 12/12/1970

(G 12) Bella Slaw (10/1/1971- ...)

(G 11) Edward Clayton Slaw (11/5/1950-...) married Jeanette Forlano on 10/3/1975

(G 12) Jennifer Slaw (2/16/1978-...)

(G 10) Nancy Slaw (19??-...) married R. Koellc (19?? -...)

(G 11) Child number 1 (name was not available)

(G 11) Child number 2 (name was not available)

(G 11) Child number 3 (name was not available)

(G 11) Child number 4 (name was not available)

(G 9) Charles Lownes (11/6/1901 – 11/6/1954)

(G 9) Laura Lownes (10/8/1904 – 8/11/1906)

(G 9) Irvin Lownes (6/1/1908 – 2/14/1983) married Dorothy Deihm (10/26/1908 – 8/9/1992) on 1/11/1932.

(G 10) Irvin Sheldon Lownes Jr. (10/14/1932- ...) married Eileen Becker (1/29/1940 – 12/9/2018) on 6/7/1958 Irvin then married second wife Linda Rawson Pursell (5/4/1943-...) on 9/23/1989.

(G 11) Nancy Jane Lownes (6/16/1959-...)

(G 12) Richard Benjamin Lownes (7/24/1982-...)

(G 12) Jennifer Marie Mathis (11/24/1984- ...) married Edwin Victor Berg III (12/29/1982-...) on 10/15/2011

(G 13) Taylor   Rosemary   Berg
(10/27/2009-...)

(G 13) Riley Alexander Berg (4/17/2012-...)

(G 12) Sean David McClure (9/12/1992-...)

(G 11) Sally Ann Lownes (4/18/1961-...) married
Arthur Karl Butcher (8/30-1954-...) on
4/12/1990

(G 12) Dean Michael Butcher (6/16/1985-
...) married Leeann Frances Carl
(4/2/1989-...) on 7/6/2010 and a chapel
ceremony on 7/12/2011

(G 13) Isabella Rose Butcher (8/2/2012
stillborn)

(G 13) Anabelle   Lynn   Butcher
(9/13/2014-...)

(G 13) Isaac Garrett Butcher (2/8/2017-...)
born in Germany

(G 12) Courtney Lynn Butcher (4/26/1991-...)
married Clayton Park (10/6/1964 -...)
on 5/17/2013 divorced in 6/2016
presently engaged to Michael
Moulton

(G 12) William Sheldon George Butcher
(9/4/1993-...)

(G 11) Paul Thomas Lownes (5/4/1963-...)
married Lisa Marie O'Hara (5/20/1963-
...) on 6/15/1991

(G 12) Joshua Paul Lownes (1/8/1996-...)

(G 12) Austin Gregory Lownes (3/15/1998-...)

(G 12) Ean Patrick Lownes (3/30/2000-...)

(G 11) Bonnie Jean Lownes (10/3/1964-
...) married James Joseph Cameron
(10/10/1957-...) on 10/7/1989

(G 12) James Giles Cameron (3/7/1991-...)
(transitioned to Amanda Cameron)

(G 12) Dorothea Marie Cameron
(4/28/1995-...)

(G 10) Howard Gerald Lownes (7/6/1935-...)
married Verna M. Allebach (8/28/1940 –
12/6/2015) on 6/25/1960

(G 11) Howard Gerald Lownes Jr.
(1/20/1962 – 11/16/2018) married Linda
Schmidt (12/7/1953-...) on 5/12/1990

(G 11) April Lynn Lownes (4/27/1967-...)
married William Hostler (1/3/1961-...)
on 5/27/2000

(G 10) John Brian Lownes (5/16/1942 – 5/31/2004)
married Marlene Murray (11/18/1944-...)
on 3/4/1963

(G 11) Beverly Lynn Lownes (12/20/1963 –
9/30/2014) married Carl Lynn Carter
(5/29/1960-...) 3/29/1980

(G 12) Carl Lynn Carter Jr. (9/13/1980-...)
married Alicia Susanne Clark on
6/16/2001, then married Kimberly
Michelle Duval on 10/28/2011

(G 13) Luke Jordan Carter (9/26/2002-...)

(G 13) Chloe Christian Carter
(1/13/2004-...)

Carl Lynn Carter, Jr. and Kimberly
Michelle Duval's child

(G 13) Collin Reese Carter (3/21/2014-...)

(G 12) Christopher Brian Carter (3/8/1984 – 8/29/2003)

(G 13) Bailey Briann Carter (2/24/2003-...)

(G 12) Chad Carter (10/17/1987-...) married Carrie Carthy McCatrhy

(G13) Sawyer Brooks Carter (3/31/2015-...)

(G 13) Raley Lynn Carter (4/4/2016-...)

(G 11) Kathlyn Edith Seigler Lownes (8/24/1965-...) married James Seigler (10/6/1964 – 7/28/2019) on 7/17/1983

(G 12) James Dean Seigler (6/16/1984-...) married Hannah Walker on 9/17/2016

(G 13) Madison Marie Seigler (7/30/2017-...) twin to James

(G 13) James Siegler (7/30/2017-...) twin to Madison

(G 12) Krystal Lynette Seigler (8/11/1986-...) married Robert Jenkins

(G 13) Haylee Danielle Jenkins (9/22/2010-...)

(G 12) Joshua Dewayne) 1/4/1990-...) married Sheivena (last name was not available)

(G 11) Tobbie Lu Ann Lownes (7/25/1970-...)

(G 8) Morris Lownes

(G 7) Catherine Lownes

(G 7) Robert Lownes

(G 7) William Lownes

(G 7) Mary Lownes

(G 7) James Roach Lownes (1830 – unk) married Euphemia Bisbing (unk – 1882)

(G 8) Sarah Lownes

(G 8) Herbert Lownes

(G 8) Anna Lownes

(G 8) James Oscar Lownes (1861 – 1930) married Hannah (last name was not available)

(G 8) Milton Markley Lownes (8/1896 – unk) married Gladys Williams Dunlap (1900 – unk)

(G 9) Dr. Milton Markley Lownes Jr.(2/26/1925 – 7/9/2001) married (wife's name was not available)

(G 10) Philip Lownes

(G 10) Joanne Lownes

(G 10) Mark Lownes

(G 9) Alice M. Lownes (1928 – unk)

(G 9) Richard Dunlap Lownes Sr. (1930 – 10/24/2016) married Nancy Morrison

(G 10) Richard Dunlap Lownes Jr. married Catherine Amwake in 1988

(G 11) Anna Lownes

(G 11) Amanda Lownes

(G 10) Ruthann M. Lownes

(G 10) Robert S. Lownes

(G 10) Randall K. Lownes married Margie (last name was not available)

(G 11) Wesley Lownes

(G 11) Ryan Lownes

(G 11) Austin Lownes

(G 11) Grant Lownes

(G 11) Harrison Lownes

(G 8) Ella Lownes married a Scheetz (first name was not available)

(G 8) Herbert E. Lownes

(G 6) Sarah Lownes married William Wencks

(G 6) Lydia Lownes married Herman Keller

(G 6) William Donaldson Lownes married Hannah Low

    (G 7) Jane Eliza Lownes married John Eckel

        (G 8) Benjamin Barker Eckel

        (G 8) Caroline Eckel

        (G 8) Edwin Eckel

        (G 8) Sarah Ellen Eckel

        (G 8) Lilla Eckel

        (G 8) Earl Eckel

        (G 8) Mary Eckel

        (G 8) John Eckel

        (G 8) Christina Eckel

    (G 7) Amanda Lownes married Benjamin F. Baker

    (G 7) Son number 1(name was not available)

    (G 7) Son number 2 (name was not available)

(G 5) Caleb Lownes (8/17/1778 - unk) married Jane Steele on 5/21/1807

    (G 6) Andrew Jackson Lowndes (8/23/1822 - 3/16/1892) married Mary Ann Bucknall (7/27/1822 – 8/2/1910) on 1/7/1846

        (G 7) Mary Lowndes (1/25/1859 – 12/4/1939) married Albert Sidney Johnson Owens (3/7/1863 – 3/29/1937) on 8/23/1887

            (G 8) Mary Lowndes Owens (11/16/1888 – 4/15/1975) married John Collinson Jr. (12/31/1886 – 12/14/1950) on 2/21/1917

(G 9) John Collinson III (5/24/1918 – 7/7/1989) married Mary Clagett Magruder (unk – 8/12/2012) on 8/28/1943

    (G 10) Mary Catherine Collinson (7/14/1944 - …)

(G 6) James Lowndes

(G 6) George Steel Lowndes married Kate Williams

(G 6) Ann Lowndes

(G 6) Kevin Birkhead Lowndes

(G 6) Samuel Pleasants Lowndes (1816 – unk) married Julia Catherine Dougherty (4/1/1830 - unk)

    (G 7) Mary Ellen Lowndes (10/12/1845 – 1929) married Lester Arrowsmith

        (G 8) Lester Arrowsmith (7/31/1879 - unk)

        (G 8) Halstead Arrowsmith (2/10/1882 - unk)

        (G 8) Jennie Arrowsmith (9/17/1886 - unk)

    (G 7) Jennie Lowndes

    (G 7) Henry Lowndes

    (G 7) James Lowndes

    (G 7) Sarah Lowndes (1863 – unk)

    (G 7) Rueben Lowndes (1872 - 1916) married Nellie Verbeck (1874 – 5/15/1911)

        (G 8) Raymond Gerald Lowndes (3/19/1897 – 10/30/1972) married Bridget Ruddy (1903 – unk)

            (G 9) Raymond Gerald Lowndes Jr. (9/29/1930--…) married Rita Sears on 6/25/1955

                (G 10) Patricia Lowndes (7/9/1961-…) married Ruben Arrieta on 9/18/1986

                    (G 11) Colton Arrieta (2/22/1985-…)

                    (G 11) Kyle Arrieta (1986-…)

                (G 10) Margaret Lowndes (10/2/1962-…)

                (G 10) Jennie Lowndes (1/1/1964-…)

(G 11) Jennifer Lowndes (1986-...)

(G 10) Raymond Gerald Lowdnes III (9/1/1969-...)

(G 9) Donald Lowndes (9/22/1936-...) married Josephine P (last name was not available) (11/20/1939-...) on 4/25/1959

    (G 10) Donna Lowndes (2/6/1960 -...) married George Dombroski (7/28/1958-...) on 5/10/1986.

        (G 11) Daniel Dombroski (1989-...)

    (G 10) Debra Lowndes (2/26/1961-...) married Glenn Barron on 9/20/1986

        (G 11) Matthew Barron 1(1989-...)

    (G 10) Albert Lowndes (1963-...)

    (G 10) Marjorie Lowndes (1964-...)

    (G 10) Dorothy Lowndes (1970-...)

(G 8) Albert Lowndes (3/16/1899 – 8/20/1969) married Lillian O'Keefe (1896 – 1970)

(G 8) George Lowndes (3/30/1901 – 1989) married Sophia Rimminsland (1899 - 1989) on 6/6/1923

    (G 9) Dorothy Lowndes (1934-...)

        (G 10) Donald Lowndes

        (G 10) Susan Lowndes

        (G 10) William Lowndes

            (G 11) Kyle Lowndes (12/11/1966-...)

        (G 10) Margaret Lowndes (10/2/1962-...)

(G 6) Araminta Steel Lowndes (1828 – unk) married Francis J. Barnes (1809 -1882)

(G 7) Alice Barnes

/

(G 7) Jane E. Barnes (1839 – unk)

(G 7) Fannie M. Barnes (1843 – unk)

(G 7) Addie Barnes (1847 -1913)

(G 7) Ella Barnes (1849 – unk)

(G 7) George Barnes (1831 – unk)

(G 7) Bella Barnes (1855 - unk)

(G 7) Ella G. Barnes (1856 – unk)

(G 5) Jane Lownes (6/30/1780 – 11/1/1823)

(G 5) Joseph Lownes (2/21/1783 – unk)

(G 5) William Lownes (3/23/1785 – unk) married Arian Wormly Glynn

  (G 6) Josiah Hewes Davis Lownes married Arrabella Sinton on 5/14/1834

  (G 7) Joseph Henry Lownes

  (G 7) Sarah Lownes

  (G 7) Josiah Hewes Lownes

  (G 7) Chas Lownes

  (G 7) Danison Lownes married Nancy Catherine Gamble

    (G 8) Robert Lownes

    (G 8) Glynn Lownes

    (G 8) Chas Lownes

    (G 8) Henry Grattan Lownes

    (G 8) Edward Brackinridge Lownes

    (G 8) Elise Gamble Lownes

    (G 8) Cary Gamble Lownes

    (G 8) Letitia Edwards Lownes

  (G 6) Mary Glenn Lownes married G.L. Donison on 5/12/1831

  (G 6) Charles. Lownes

  (G 6) Chapman Lownes

  (G 6) Virginia Radcliffe Lownes married F. G. Annen on 11/18/1834

  (G 6) Jane Dado Lownes married Mr. Root

(G 6) John Henry Augustus Lownes

(G 6) Margaret Ann Lownes

(G 6) Willianna Lownes married Mr. Miller (first name was not available)

(G 6) Sarah Lownes

    (G 7) Laura Beth Lownes unknown died at age 6

(G 4) Mary Lownes (12/18/1742 – 6/22/1803) married John Bacon on 2/24/1764

    (G 5) John Lownes (1779 – 1859)

        (G 6) Mary Ann Lownes

    (G 5) child number 2 (name was not available)

(G 4) Jane Lownes (9/19/1745 - unk)

(G 3) Hannah Lownes (11/13/1695 –7/2/1785) married Nehemiah Allen Jr. on 8/31/1718

(G 3) James Lownes Jr. (1697 – 1785) married Sarah Forrester on 6/27/1736

Note: John signed a Loyalty Oath of Allegance in 1778 in York County, Pennsylvania (Document # 414)

(G 4) John Lown (1740 – 1824) married Catherine Baumgartine (1760 – after 1824) in 1789

    (G 5) John Lown Jr. (1791 – unk)

    (G 5) Henry Lown (1/25/1794- 9/24/1849) married Esther High (5/22/1795 – 5/17/1877) in 1815

        (G 6) John Lown (1817 – 1895)

        (G 6) James Lown (1821 – 1903)

        (G 6) Phillip Lown (1824 – 1900) married Martha Van Velset in 1848

            (G 7) Frank Lown (18** - 1940) married Nora Naden (1884 – 1974) in 1915

                (G 8) Frank Phillip Lown (1917 – 1993) married Mary Rauterkus in 1944

(G 8) Wendall Naden Lown (1921) married Anita (last name waq not avilable) in 1955

(G 6) Katherine Lown (1827 – unk) married Elwin Highley in 1846

(G 6) Lewis Lown (1829 – 1862)

(G 6) Mary Ann Lown (1831 – 1856) married Abram Wright in 1853

(G 6) Jane Lown (1833 – 1913)

(G 6) Henry Lown Jr. (1835 – 1912) married Mary W. Hughcs in 1865

(G 6) Martha Lown (1837 – 1865) married David Rees in 1858

(G 6) Jacob Lown (4/21/840 –2/18/1903) married Mary Ann Rees (1843 – 1906) on 5/27/1866

  (G 7) Albert "Bert" Lown (unk – 1929) married Maud Eschleman (1877 – 1954)

    (G 8) Floyd Lown married Alma Lee (last name was not available)

    (G 8) Glenna Lown (1897 – 1954)

    (G 8) Pauline Lown (1905 -1956) married Leo Schaller

  (G 7) Sarah J. Lown (1867 – 1955) married Wilson Brooks (1866-1917) in 1887

    (G 8) Oscar Brooks married Amy (last name was not available)

    (G 8) Ernest Brooks married Eliza (last name was not available)

    (G 8) Jay Brooks married Ruth (last name was not available)

    (G 8) Ralph Brooks married Elizabeth (last name was not available)

    (G 8) Helen Brooks married Howard Saltzgaber

(G 8) Alice Brooks was unmarried

(G 8) Mary Brooks married Ward Cooper

(G 8) Harold Brooks married Juanita (last name was not available)

(G 7) Rees Rees Lown (9/2/1870 – 7/10/1939) married Olive Lanah Mason (11/20/1875 – 1/20/1961) on 10/31/1894

(G 8) Bernie Colman Lown (1897 – 1986) married LuLu Augusta Tippet (1893 – 1984) in 1919

(G 9) Martha Ann Lown (1923 – 2008) unmarried

(G 8) Emory Lester Lown (11/1/1901 – 8/4/1969) married Lena M. Baker (1/19/1901 – 11/14/1985) in 1924

(G 9) Gordon Leo Lown (7/29/1930 – 2/22/1975) married Patricia A. Leek (1932 - 2019) in 1952

(G 10) Steven L. Lown (1955-...) married Katherine L. Gatsch (1951-...) in 1984

(G 11) Patrick Logan Lown (1987-...) married Raynee Gutting (1984-...) in 2017

(G 11) Larissa "Lacey" Lauren Lown (1989-...) married Matthew Lawrence Hanford (1989-...) in 2014

(G 11) Maxton Loren Lown (1990-...)

(G 10) Barton Leo Lown (1957-...) married Bethany L. Bean (1953-...) in 1989

(G 11) Laura Louise Lown (1991-...)

(G 11) Lindsay Louise Lown (1994-...) married Nathan Baker in 2017

(G 9) Eldon Cyril Lown (1934-...) married Marilyn R. Woods (1934-...) in 1956

(G 10) Gary R. Lown (1957-...) married Kim (last name was not available)

(G 11) Justin R. Lown

(G 11) Erin F. Lown

(G 10) Jeff A. Lown (1959-...) married Melodie (last name was not available)

(G 11) Michael Lown

(G 10) Susanne Kay Lown (1960-...) married Russell L. Robson in 1989

(G 11) Michael Robson

(G 11) Thomas Robson

(G 10) Mark Lown (1962-...)

(G 8) Ceetta Lown (1905 – 1988) married Owen James Cooper (1902 – 1930), then married Gerald Hall then married James Pleasant

(G 9) James Reese Cooper (1926 – 1988) married Wilma Cave (1929 - unk)

(G 10) Linda Cooper (1949-...) married Chamblis (first name was not available)

(G 10) Teresa Cooper (1965-...) married M. Keith Ward in 1982

(G 5) Nancy Lown (1796 – unk) married Snyder (first name was not available)

(G 5) Frances Lown (1798 – unk) married McBride (first name was not available)

(G 5) Martha Lown (1798 – unk) married Smith (first name was not available)

(G 3) Susannah Lownes (6/13/1703 – 3/12/1739) married out of unity 8/29/1731 Phila. MM

(G 3) Rebecca Lownes (9/18/1705 – 3/12/1799) married Job Yarnall on 8/13/1737

(G 3) Mary Lownes (11/7/1712 – 1765) married Phillips Coudemas 11/27/1743

(G 2) George Lownes (Quaker) (10/11/1668 – 6/25/1740) married
Mary Bowers (8/20/1675 - 1718) married on 6/25/1701

(G 3) Jane Lownes (3/10/1702 - unk) married Johathan Maris then
married Joseph Burn on 1744

(G 4) Richard Maris (1727 – unk)

(G 3) Esther Lownes (7/2/1703 – 11/11/1747) married Samuel Ogden
(10/30/1695 – 11/14/1748) on 3/26/1720

(G 3) Anne Lownes (8/1/1707 – 12/19/1780) married George Maris
II on 9/14/1732

(G 4) Richard Maris

(G 3) George Lownes II (2/28/1708 – 10/26/1793) married Elizabeth
Mordegai Maddock (1717 – 3/10/1788) on 5/21/1734

(G 4) Slater Lownes married Eleanor Cox on (8/31/1778)
(G 5) Clarissa Lownes (unk - 3/24/1837)

(G 4) Rebecca Lownes (7/10/1830 – 1845)

(G 4) Curtis Lownes (1759– 10/23/1810) married Grace Lownes
(1/26/1761 – 10/5/1813) on 12/21/1794)

(G 5) John Lownes (3/10/1796 – 7/8/1829) married Rebecca
Crosby (1796 – unk) on 1/13/1820

(G 6) Curtis Lownes (1829 – 7/18/1831) died at age 3

(G 6) Sarah Crosby Lownes married Crosby P. Morton on
9/19/1839

(G 7) Susannah Crosby Morton married J. Frank Black
on 2/16/1865

(G 6) Hannah Lane Lownes married William W. Maddock
on 3/10/1843

(G 7) Lownes Maddock married Elizabeth Worrall of
Ridley on 1/22/1872

(G 7) William Maddock married M. Hannah

(G 8) Willie Maddock died in infancy

(G 5) Agnes Lownes (5/13/1797 – 5/19/1871) married Edward
Levis in 1821

  (G 6) Elizabeth Levis (4/5/1819 – 4/29/1886) married Philip
Brooks (1821 – 1903)

    (G 7) Agnes Brooks (7/23/1844 – 1914)

(G 4) George Bolton Lownes (1793 – 1834) married Hannah
Lawrence

(G 4) Mary Lownes married Andrew Reynolds

(G 4) James Lownes

(G 4) Jean Lownes

(G 4) Sarah Lownes

(G 4) Rebecca Lownes

(G 4) Francis Lownes

(G 4) Esther Lownes

  (G 5) Joseph Lownes was a jeweler

  (G 5) Curtis Bolton Lownes married Agnes (last name was
not available)

(G 3) Benanuel Lownes (Quaker) (1720 – 8/1/1767) married Alice
Williamson (1714 – 1812) on 5/20/1744

  (G 4) Benanuel Lownes II (10/26/1773 –11/29/1773) unmarried

  (G 4) Sarah Lownes (1760 – 1804) married Ebenezer Reynolds

    (G 5) Son (name was not available)

  (G 4) Alice Lownes (1758 – 1801) married William Temple (unk)
then married John Pennock

    (G 5) Thomas Temple

    (G 5) Mary Temple

    (G 5) William Temple

    (G 5) Alice Temple

    Alice Lownes and John Pennock's children

    (G 5) Marshall Pennock

    (G 5) Ruth Pennock

(G 4) Mary Lownes (1761 – 1846) married William Levis (unk) then married Joseph Taylor, brother to Elizabeth Taylor

   (G 5) Alice Levis married Mr. Thomas (first name was not available)

   (G 5) William Levis

Mary Lownes and Joseph Taylor's children

   (G 5) Joseph Taylor

   (G 5) Sarah Taylor

   (G 5) Lownes Taylor

(G 4) George Lownes III (Quaker) (1764 – 1796) married Elizabeth Taylor (sister to Joseph Taylor) on 7/29/1789

   (G 5) George Lownes IV granted certificate to Wilmington MM on 2/24/1814

   (G 5) Maria Lownes

   (G 5) Sarah Lownes

(G 4) Joseph Lownes (unk – 6/20/1780)

(G 4) Hannah Lownes (unk – 2/25/1746)

(G 4) Hugh Lownes (Quaker) (unk – 1814) married Rebecca Rhodes (unk -1830)

   (G 5) Benanuel Lownes III

   (G 5) Elizabeth Lownes II–

   (G 5) Sydney Lownes

   (G 5) Joseph Lownes (Quaker) (1/17/1797 – 4/8/1872) marriaed Rachel Massey, (unk – 1830) then married Priscilla Pratt (unk – 1872)

Children of Joseph Lownes and Rachel Massey

   (G 6) Rebecca Lownes III (9/4/1809 – 11/20/1859) never married

   (G 6) Hugh Lownes III (10/11/1811 – 10/20/1834) never married

   (G 6) William Lownes (6/4/1814 – 5/9/1837) never married

(G 6) Phineas Lownes (4/1/1816 – 7/1/1856) married Emily Lewis

    (G 7) Anna Lownes (12/19/1842 – unk)

    (G 7) Phineas William Lownes (11/16/1851 – unk) married Eunice Stevens

        (G 8) Edward Phineas Lownes (11/22/1879 – 1/6/1896)

        (G 8) Edith B. Lownes (11/3/1883 – unk)

        (G 8) Harry P. Lownes

    (G 7) Emily Lownes (7/3/1855 – unk) married Dr. Walter Browning

        (G 8) Walter Browning Jr. (10-1882 – unk)

        (G 8) Eleanor Browning

(G 6) Massey Lownes (9/23/1819 – 6/10/1863) married John Jackson (second cousin)

    (G 7) Deborah Jackson

    (G 7) Elizabeth Jackson

    (G 7) John Jackson married Massey Lownes

    (G 7) Israel Jackson married Joseph Taylor

        (G 8) Joseph Taylor

    (G 7) Harlum Jackson

(G 6) Joseph Lownes (10/12/1827 – 4/21/1913) married Minerla Webb (9/20/1832 – 1872) on 11/19/1852

    (G 7) William Lownes married Eunice (last name was not available)

(G 6) GeorgeBoltonLownesII(Quaker)(1/25/1825–8/21/1923) married Rachel (Rebecca) Webb on 1/12/1849

    (G 7) William Henry Lownes III (1/9/1850) married Florence Ida Thayer (7/11/1854 – unk) on 10/13/1881

        (G 8) Nathan Thayer Lownes (5/16/1883 – 5/16/1950) married Breta Clara Dohan on 4/3/1907

        (G 8) Rebecca Lownes (8/26/1884 – unk)

(G 8) Emily Lownes (6/20/1887 – unk)

(G 8) Charlotte Lownes (9/1/1895 – unk)

(G 7) George Bolton Lownes III (8/9/1851 – 4/14/1909) married Elizabeth Cummings, then second marriaiage Mary Datesman

    (G 8) Edward Datesman Lownes

    (G 8) George Bolton Lownes IV

(G 7) Mary Moore Lownes (8/24/1854 – unk) married S. Edgar Levis

    (G 8) Florence Levis (10/11/1881 – unk) married Trainer (first name was not avaiable)

        (G 9) Banncroft Trainer

        (G 9) Mary L. Trainer

    (G 8) Ogborn Levis (2/1/1885 – unk)

    (G 8) George B. Levis (10/23/1890 – unk)

    (G 8) Hannah Darlington Levis (3/2/1895 – unk) married Elwood Garrett

        (G 9) Florence Garrett

        (G 9) Mary Garrett

(G 7) Hannah Darlington Lownes (4/6/1856 – 4/11/1930)

(G 7) Edward Lownes I (8/22/1860 – 6/4/1900) married Viola Healy (3/25/1866 – unk)

    (G 8) Viola Healy Lownes (3/26/1886 – unk)

(G 7) Rebecca Lownes (11/24/1861 – 2/11/1929)

(G 7) Francis "Frank" Lownes (Quaker) (7/6/1863 – 1951) married Eliza Rogers (3/6/1877 – 7/26/1940) on 10/21/1896

    (G 8) John (Jack) Lownes (Quaker) married Hannah Hannum

        (G 9) Sarah Lownes

        (G 9) Margaret Lownes

(G 9) John Roger Lownes

(G 9) Rebe Lownes

(G 8) Margaret Lownes (Quaker) (7/7/1897 – unk) married Dagmar Conover

(G 9) Margaret Conover

(G 9) Frank Conover

(G 9) Ann Conover

(G 7) MinervaWebbLownes(Quaker)(6/7/1865–2/11/1929)

(G 7) Jane Carpenter Lownes (4/16/1867 – unk) married John Webster on 10/9/1890

(G 8) Edward Webster (4/26/1852 – unk)

(G 8) Mary Rebecca Webster (11/5/1855 – 10/8/1895)

(G 8) Harold Smedley Webster (3/29/1897 – unk)

(G 8) Lydia Smedley Webster (10/5/1900 – unk)

(G 8) John Webster Jr.

(G 7) Joseph Lownes (Quaker) (7/24/1858 – 11/9/1943) married Jennie Worrell Powel (1/16/1877 – 4/14/1950) in 1905

(G 8) Joseph Lownes Jr. (12/12/1907 – 11/19/1992) married Grace Hamilton Custer (3/22/1910 – 8/81998) on 9/5/1930

(G 9) JosephDonaldLownesIII(4/10/1932–6/22/2018) married Carol Ann Haworth (5/25/1933 – 2/6/2019) on 9/12/1953

(G 10) Bette Jane Lownes (8/16/1957-...) married George A. Ferris (3/28/1955 -...) on 10/9/1982

(G 11) MarkJosephFerris(1/31/1994-...)married Alexandria Morgan (8/6/1994 - ...)

(G 10) Linda Lee Lownes (12/16/1959-...) married Gregory Thomas Hytha (4/12/1960-...) on 7/2/1983

(G 11) Robert Maxwell Hytha (6/29/1990-...)
Married Kathanne Marris on 10/6/2018

(G 11) Alexander Miles Hytha (11/9/1992-...)

(G 11) Carrie Evangeline Hytha (4/25/1995-...)
married Noah Morgan on 6/20/2018

(G 11) Christopher Gregory Hytha (6/28/1997-...)

(G 10) Donna Mae Lownes (5/13/1965-...) married Paul Andrew Brady (5/2/1963-_) on 8/25/1990

(G 11) Daniel Joseph Brady (4/25/1994-...)

(G 11) Brian Robert Brady (10/23/1996-...)

(G 11) Steven Michael Brady (5/17/1998-...)

(G 9) George Bolton Lownes (4/12/1937-...) married Kay Kachel (4/11/1937-...) on 5/17/1958

(G 10) George Bolton Lownes Jr. (2/19/1959-...)

(G 10) Jeffrey Steven Lownes (7/13/1961-...) married Jennifer (divorced)

(G 11) Carly Grace Lownes (6/25/2000-...)

(G 10) Gregory Douglas Lownes (3/2/1965-...)

(G 10) Gary Martin Lownes (7/27/1966-...)

(G 9) Kenneth Hugh Lownes (3/7/1939-...) married Judith Urian (11/7/1938-...) on 8/7/1965

(G 9) Jane Ann Lownes (1/31/1941-...) married Charles Gallagher (3/8/1938-...) on 3/8/1958 second marriage Maetin Shea on 10/17/1980

(G 10) Susanne Gallagher (8/30/1958-...) married Robert Allen Murray (10/23/1957-...) on 12/10/1977

(G 11) Jill Murray (9/17/1993-...)

(G 11) Robert Murray Jr. (9/9/1995-...)

(G 10) Charles Kirk Gallagher (3/20/1962-...) married Marianne (last name was not available) (divorsed)

(G 10) Sandra Lynn Gallagher (7/10/1963-...) married Christopher Mantin on 4/30/1988

   (G 11) Brielle Mantin (2/13/1991-...)

   (G 11) Jamie Mantin (9/6/1994-...)

(G 10) Jennifer Jane Gallagher (3/24/1969-...) married John Barnhart (6/16/1985-...) on 12/19/1992

(G 9) Bruce Thayer Lownes (11/22/1948-...) married Paula Pastorius

(G 10) Nathaniel Dean Lownes (6/30/1982-...)

(G 10) Rebecca Jane Lownes (6/1/1984-...) married (name was not available)

(G 10) Joseph Lownes (12/25/1987-...)

(G 10) Sarah Grace Lownes (11/14/1992-...) married (name was not available)

Children of Joseph and Priscilla Pratt

(G 6) Elizabeth Pratt Lownes (11/22/1841 – 11/7/1886)

From the History of Chester County, Pennsylvania

Page 494

Written by John Hill Martin Esq. 1877
(copied from Charlotte Lownes Olewiler's book, *The Gawsworth Quakers Hugh and Jane Lowndes* published in 1978)

Among the original purchases of land in England who settled in Chester, and some of whose descendants are now residence there, will be found the name of Jane Lowndes, now Lownes, of whom Dr. Smith says, p.480, she "came from Cheshire, where she had suffered persecutions in the distraught of her goods, in 1678, for attending Friends' meeting at Newton and Selsby. She was the widow of Hugh Lownes, and was accompanied to this country by three sons, James, George, and Joseph. James married Susannah Richards in 1692, and George, married Mary Bowers, a woman from New England in 1701. Jane, on her first arrival, located her purchased land in Springfield Township, upon which a cave is marked by a stone planted by her descendants in 1799, which bears the date of the patent for the land (1685). The meeting records show the presence of Jane Lownes here in May 1684, and she probably had arrived here a year earlier. It was usual to occupy lands a long time before they were patented. I remember well in my boyhood visiting Rebecca Crosby Lownes, who lived in Springfield on part of the above mentioned tract, and her daughter Hannah Lane Lownes."

James and Susanna Lownes had four children, Joseph, b. 1693; Hannah, b. 1695; James, b. 1697, and Susannah. The family removed to Philadelphia in 1711. Mary Lownes, wife of George, was, perhaps, a daughter of Benanuel Bowers, who suffered persecution in New England. Her children were Jane, Esther, Ann, George, Jr., married in 1734, Elizabeth, daughter of Mordecal Maddock, of Springfield; and his brother, Benanual, married in 1774, Alice Williamson, daughter of John and Sarah, of Newtown.

In the account of the Cowpland family given here in before, (p. 273) it is stated that John Lownes, son of Joseph and Sarah, of Philadelphia, married Agnes Cowpland, a daughter of Caleb and Sarah, of Chester, on the 27th of the 8th mo. 1753; their children, Caleb, Sarah, Joseph, David, Grace, who married Curtis Lownes; Agnes, who died in infancy; and Agnes (2), who died in 1793, age 16 or 17 years. George Lownes, and Elizabeth, his wife had three sons, Boulton, Joseph and Curtis. Boulton married Hannah Lawrence, a Quaker lady. He died without issue. He gave one of his farms to Isaac Newton, afterwards U.S. Commissioner of Agriculture. Joseph was for some time a Jeweler, in Chestnut east of 4th Street, Philadelphia. Curtis married his distant relative, Grace Lownes, as above. John Lownes was born in 1723, and his wife, Agnes, Aug. 4, 1727. His mother was, probably a sister to her father's first wife, and a daughter of William Tidmarsh. Also in the family Bible: Agnes Lownes, d. May 2, 1775; her husband John Lownes, d. Aug. 13, 1807. George Lownes, d. 1793; his son Curtis, d. Oct. 23, 1810. Grace Lownes, the wife of Curtis, d. Oct.5, 1813. Emily Lownes, a daughter of Curtis and Grace, was b. Sept. 19, 1803; d. Jan. 1804. Margaret, b. Feb. 17, 1805; d. Oct. 21, 1810. Curtis, b. Sept. 19, 1803; a twin brother of Emily, d. April 2,1821.

John Lownes, son of Curtis and Grace, born March 10, 1796, was a farmer, of Springfield. He married Rebecca, daughter of John and Sarah Lane Crosby, of Ridley, Jan. 13, 1820, and died July 8, 1829, leaving surviving, his widow and two daughters, Sarah Crosby, who married Crosby P. Morton, Sept. 19,1839, and had one child, Susannah Crosby, who m. J. Frank Black, of Chester, Feb. 16, 1865. The other daughter, Hannah Lane, m. William W. Maddock, of Ridley, March 10, 1843, and their son Lownes, m. Elizabeth Worrall, of Ridley, Jan. 22, 1872; they have a son William. William and Hannah had one other child, Willie, who died in infancy. John and Rebecca had a son, Curtis, who died at the age of 3 years, July 18, 1829.

Agnes Lownes, daughter of Curtis and Grace, who was married Dec. 21, 1794, became the wife of Edward Levis. She was b. May 13, 1797; date of marriage is not given, only 181-?; she d. May 19, 1871. Elizabeth Lownes, daughter of Curtis and Grace; b. Dec. 19, 1708; m. Samuel Huggins, May 4, 1829; she is now dead. Esther, another daughter of Curtis and Grace, was born Oct. 12, 1810. Nothing further is said regarding her in the Bible.

Hugh Lownes, son of Benanuel and Alice, of Springfield, was married in 1794, to Rebecca, daughter of James Rhoads, of Marple. Their son, Joseph, b. 1,17,1797, died 4,8, 1872, was twice married; and had children, Rebecca, Hugh, William, Phineas, Massey, George Bolton, Joseph and Elizabeth, born in Springfield.

"Pocket-wallet Facts about Your Springfield Township, Delaware Co., Pennsylvania"

(Copied from Charlotte Lownes Olewiler's book, *The Gawsworth Quakers Hugh and Jane Lowndes,* published in 1978)

(Where Gracious Living prevails through out the year... celebrating nearly three centuries of fine community life).

Founding of the Township is dated from the year 1683 when Jane Lownes, a widow and her sons and daughter occupied a cave adjacent to the Crum Creek Valley in Springfield.

Early settlers were the Quaker Pioneers who received their land-grants from Wm. Penn, the proprietor. Many came over with him on the "Welcome" in 1682, taking up their tracts in the wilderness a few years later. Jane came over in 1680 on the *"John and Mary."*

Springfield Road is one of the oldest highways in the country having been first open to the public on December 9, 1687. Baltimore Pike, the famous Route 1, formerly the Delaware County Turnpike, was first used in 1701. It was paved with logs in some sections.

Benjamin West, the great colonial artist, was born in Springfield in 1738 in a house now part of the Swarthmore College campus. He painted over 3,000 canvases, yet there is not a painting by him anywhere in

Springfield where he was born. Swarthmore Boro was created in 1893, and Morton Borough in 1898, out of Springfield Township.

John Edgar Thomson, known as the "Father of the Pennasylvania Railroad," was born in Springfield in 1801. He was one of the world's greatest engineers and helped to develop the locomotive, studying under George Stephenson, the English inventor of the vehicle. His father, John Thomson, helped build the first railroad in this state along with Thomas Leiper. The railroad was used to haul stone from the Leiper Quarries to Ridley Creek.

The Lenni-Lenape or Delaware Indian Tribe inhabited the area before and after the white settlers arrived. Even to this day, arrowheads and other artifacts are found in Springfield Township, many in gardens. The Township Historical Museum has a large collection.

Springfield became a "Township of the First Class" in 1924 and presently has seven wards. Population today approaches the 26,500. In 1920, 1998 persons lived on the township. This would indicate that Springfield has a desirable reputation as a "good place in which to live."

There are thirty men on the Township Police Force. All five of our prowl cars are equipped with tow-way radio, making them minutes away from your telephone. All police cars carry emergency equipment including oxygen tanks. They implement the Springfield Ambulance Corps and its modern equipment which has used over three thousand times since it was started in 1948. The Springfield Police Department, maintains around-the clock service to the community and the telephone, KI 4-1100, is the one of the busiest in Delaware County.

Twelve Citizen's Advisory Boards and Commissions assist in the governing of the Township. All the appointed members serve without remuneration.

Springfield Township has nine park areas in the process of development and use and several being held until funds available for their maintenance. Along with the municipally-leased countty club,are notably one after our beloved Jane Lownes. Along with the municipally-leased country club, three hundred areas or more will be dedicated to the recreation and health of the citizens. Springfield will always be a "green town" since lands dedicated for park purpose cannot be used otherwise at any time.

Springfield's volunteer fire company is one of the most active and well equipped in Delaware County with six modern pieces of equipment, its own Fire Hall, and training program. There are 185 fire hydrants in the township with new ones being installed as areas become built up.

There are almost 1150 electric streetlights in the township places according to the plans of Philadelphia Electric Company. which maintains them. There are over 56 miles of township roads with almost that many miles of State highways in Springfield Township. There are six public schools, three parochial schools, and several privately or church-run kindergardens.

There are eighteen churches in Springfield, the oldest being the Springfield Freinds Meeting founded in 1686.

Springfield has a municipally-supported public library. It has a garden club, women's club, Lion, rotary, optimist, and other service clubs, American Legion, Veterans of Foreign Wars, Masonic Lodge, Knights of Columbus, DeMolay, and fraternal organizations. It has an adult school, Great Books Group, athletic association (with hundreds of kids), and church and business groups along with its Junior Chamber of Commerce. These activities denote a well-rounded community devoted to the American "way of life" for which many Springfield men have given their lived in the service of their country. It puts its faith in God and a wonderful past, looking forward to an even greater future.

(Distributed as a public service by Jim Davis, Treasurer, Springfield Township who is very grateful to this wonderful community for the privilege of living in it). Sincerely Yours, Jim Davis 18 N. Norwinden Drive, Springfield, Kingswood 3-3921.

Excerpts from Springfield Township

(Copied from Charlotte Lownes Olewiler' book, *The Gawsworth Quakers Hugh and Jane Lowndes,*published in 1978)

By Janes Milburn Davis

Township Commissioner of Springfield Township Commissioner of Springfield Township, President of the Historical Society of Springfield. Curator of the Springfield Township Museum, Delaware County, Pennsylvania.

... Even at this early period, the inhabitance were eager to assume their civic responsibilities -- a clarion call to service that Springfield citizens today never fail to heed. Farming and grazing of cattle were the principal operations of the inhabitants of the township. Each cattle owner had his own brand and the strays that wandered off into the virgin format were usually returned unless destroyed by wolves. These predatory beast became so numerous that in 1687 a bounty was offered by the authorities for their destruction.

The white newcomers had little trouble with the Indians. This was no doubt owing to the wise and just principles inaugurated by Penn in all his dealings with the natives. The local tribes belonged to the Lenni-Lenape family, more frequently termed the Delaware Indians, since they inhabited the Sylvan Delaware River Valley. They maintained several villages or wigwams in the Springfield locale and one large settlement was situated on Lownes Run, a small stream flowing into Crum Creek. The Delawares were an ancient tribe designated by the other Indians as a "grandfather tribe" and reciprocated the fairness of the Quaker dealers with them. There actions proved them to be peace-loving and sagacious. The historian can but conjecture what would have happened to the gentle Quakers had they decided to settle in lands occupied by the war-like Iroquois further north. Penn's colony might have become a great tragedy instead of a "great experiment" in colonization. Some have cast aspersions on the bravery of the Delawares because of their conquest by the Iroquois. Nothing could be less deserved by the courageous Delawares for the truth is that the Delawares held off well-armed invaders who had been fully equipped with fire-arms through their trading with the French. The local tribes were armed only with stone-age weapons -- bows and arrows, but even so it took the Iroquois twenty years to make victory certain. In this struggle of gunpowder versus raw courage, the Delawares proved themselves to the satisfaction of the historian. Even today, arrowheads and stone implements are discovered in the fields and woodlands of Springfield Township, showing evidence of the former occupancy of the redman.

A tribute must be paid to the early residents for their bravery in facing the dangers of the wilderness. Jane Lownes, a widow with several children, came to Springfield probably about 1683, although the patent for her land bears the date of "second month, tenth, 1685." Not having a dwelling available, the little family lived in a cave until a home could be constructed. The site of the cave was marked by her descendants in 1799 and while the cave has long been filled in, the monument still remains as a reminder of the typical "Pioneer Mother."

It also appears that there was a wilderness trail connecting Springfield with Haverford and some folks made the journey on foot in spite of the isolated location of the settlements. The exact number of inhabitants recorded in the early settlement of the township is not generally known. However, the tax list of 1776 shows that there were sixty persons taxable who paid a total tax of thirteen pounds, fifteen shillings and three pence. Today the population figure is drawing closer to 34,000 persons.

Many of the early settlers are buried in the ancient Quaker Burial Ground, located at the intersection of Old Sproul Road, or as it was known in colonial days, Chester Road, and Springfield Road. Given to the Quakers by Bartholomew Coppock, the Younger in 1686, the two-acre tract contains a possible fivr thousand burials, and while few of the graves are marked today with headstones, those that are marked bear the names of families appearing on the early land-grant lists.

The first meeting house of the sect was probably of logs and erected by the worshipers. It was constructed in 1703 and destroyed by fire in 1737. A second meeting house was built of durable Delaware County stone from local quarries and used until 1851, when the present structure was erected using much of the stone in the new building. During the construction of the present meeting house, the ancient date marker from the previous house of worship disappeared and to this day the search for it continues. Legend has it that it somehow found its way into the sturdy rock wall surrounding the property and eventually the stone may be found.

Springfield Meeting was known as the "backwoods meeting" in Quaker circles because of its isolated location. This situation has been changed in nearly three centuries. In keeping with the great interest of the Society of Friends in education, school was maintained on the site on several occasions, and the small frame building on the grounds today was built in 1835 for the maintenance of a school and library. Because of the great historic significance of the school, the Commonwealth of Pennsylvania Museum and Historical Commission has furnished the official metal marker granted to authentic historic sites and the location will be recorded in the state guide book.

An ancient white oak located in the burial grounds is probably the oldest tree still standing in the township and is a reminder of the dense virgin forests of yesterday that clothed the hillsides.

Townships like Springfield are an integral part of the bone and sinew of the United States. But such elemental parts of a great country are not created overnight, they are the product of slow and painful growth emerging from the mists of time as a well-rounded community. Acknowledging its debt to the past, the Board of Commissioners unanimously passed the resolution given to them on October 23, 1950. It was presented by the Historical Society of Springfield and reads in part, "With the thought in mind that God-fearing people, from many lands representing all denominations of the Christian faith, came to this land of promise to establish new homes and to worship God as they chose, we hereby request the Board of Commissioners of Springfield Township to designate the first Sunday in November of each year as 'Springfield Day' in commemorative of this ancient town, one of the oldest in our country."

The Trial of William Penn(1670)

(Copied from Charlotte Lownes Olewiler's book *The Gawsworth Quakers Hugh and Jane Lowndes*, published 1978).

William Penn, I affirm I have broken no law, nor am I guilty of the indictment that is laid to my charge. And to the end that which the jury, and myself, with these that hear us, may have a more direct understanding of this procedure. I design you would let me know by what law it is you prosecute me, and what law you ground my indictment.

Recorder: Upon the common law.

Penn: Where is that common law?

Recorder: You must not think that I am able to run up so many years and over so many adjudged cases which we call common law to answer your curiosity.

Penn: This answer, I am sure, is very short of my question, for if it be common, it should not be so hard to produce.

Recorder: Sir, will you plead to your indictment?

Penn: Shall I plead to an indictment that hath no foundation in law? If it contain that law you say I have broken, why should you decline to produce that law, since it will be impossible for the jury to determine or agree to bring in their verdict who have not the law produced by which they should measure the truth of this indictment, and the guilt of contrary of my fact.

Recorder: You are a saucy fellow. Speak to the indictment.

Penn: I say it is my place to speak to matter of law. I am arraigned a prisoner; my liberty, which is next to life itself, is now concerned; you are many mouths and ears against me, and if I must not be allowed to make the best of my case, it is hard. I say again, unless you show me and the people the law you ground your indictment upon, I shall take it for granted your proceedings are merely arbitrary. (At this time several upon the bench urged hard upon the prisoner to bear him down).

Recorder: The question is whether you are quilty of this indictment.

Penn: The question is not whether I am quilty of this indictment, but whether this indictment be legal. It is too general and imperfect an answer to say it is the common law, unless we know both where and what it is. For where there is no law there is no transgression, and that law which is not in being is so far from being common that it is no law at all.

Recorder: You are an impertinent fellow. Will you teach the court what law is? It's lex non scripts, that many have studied thirty or forty years to know, and would you have me tell you in a moment?

Penn: Certainly if the common law be so hard to be understood, it's far from being very common; but if the Lord God in his institutes be of any consideration, He tells is that common law is common right, and that common right is the Great Charter privileges, confirmed, 9Hen, III, c 29: 25 Edw. I,c.1:2 Edw. III C,.8: 2 Coke Tst. 56.

Recorder: Sir, you are a troublesome fellow, and it is not for the honor of the court to suffer you to go on.

Penn: I have asked but one question, and you have not answered me, though the rights and privileges of every Englishman be concerned in it.

Recorder: If I should suffer you to ask questions till tomorrow morning, you would be never the wiser.

Penn: That is according as the answers are.

Recorder: Sir, we must not stand to hear you talk all night.

Penn: I design no affront to the court, but to be heard in my just plea, and I must plainly tell you that if you will deny over of that law which you suggest I have broken, you do at once deny me an acknowledged right and evidence to the whole world your resolution to sacrifice the privileges of Englishman to your sinister and arbitrary designs.

Recorder: Take him away. My lord, if you take not some course with this pestilent fellow to stop his mouth, we shall not be able to do anything to night.

Mayor: Take him away, take him away; turn him into the bail-dock.

Penn: These are but so many vain exclamations. Is this justice or true judgment? Must I therefore be taken away because I plead for the fundamental laws of England? However, this I leave upon your conscience, who are of the jury and my sole judges, that if these ancient fundamental laws, which relate to liberty and property, and are not limited to particular persuasions in matters of religion, must not be indispensably maintained and observed. Who can say he hath right to the coat upon his back? Certainly our liberties are openly to be invaded, our wives to be ravished, our children slaved, our families ruined and our estates led away triumph by every sturdy beggar and malicious informer as their trophies, but our pretended forfeits for conscience' sake. The Lord of heaven and earth will be judge between us in this matter.

(The jury, having been exhorted to deliver a verdict of guilty, tried four times to do so, though they were kept all night without food, drink, or heat).

Recorder: What is this to the purpose? I say I will have a verdict (And speaking to Edward Bushel, said: O, you are a factions fellow. I will set a mark upon you, and while I have any thing to do in the city, I will have an eye upon you.

Mayor: Have you no more wit than to be led by such a pitiful fellow? I will out his nose.

Penn: It is intolerable that my jury should be thus menaced. Is this according to the fundamental laws? Are not they my proper judges by the Great Charter of England? What hope is there of ever having justice done when juries are threatened and their verdicts rejected? I am concerned to speak and grieved to see such arbitrary proceedings. Did not the lieutenant of the Tower render one of them worse than a felon? And do you not plainly seem to condemn such for factious fellows who answer not your ends? Unhappy are those juries who are threatened to be fined and starved and ruined if they give not in verdicts contrary to their consciences.

Recorder: My lord, you must take a course with that same fellow.

Mayor: Stop his mouth, jailer, bring fetters and stake him to the ground.

Penn: Do your pleasure: I matter not your fetters.

Recorder: Till now I never understood the reason of the policy and prudence of the Spaniards in suffering the Inquisition among them. And certainly it will never be well with us till something like the Spanish Inquisition be in England.

Penn: I demand my liberty, being freed by the jury.

Mayor: No, you are in for your fines.

Penn: Fines for what?

Mayor: For contempt of the court.

Penn: I ask if it be according to the fundamental laws of England that any Englishmen should be fined or amerced but by the judgment of his peers of jury, since it expressly contradicts the Fourteenth and Twenty-ninth Charter of England, which say no freeman ought to be amerced but by the oath of good and lawful men of the vicinage?

Recorder: Take him away, take him away. But 'tis no wonder since the Spanish Inquisition hath so great a place in the Recorder's heart. God Almighty, who is just, will judge you all for these things.

They haled the prisoners into the bail-dock and from thence sent them to Newgate for non-payment of their fines, and so were their jury.

"Blue Church" Marks 125th Anniversary

January 24, 1957

By Helen Nylund

(Copied from Charlotte Lownes Olewiler' book, *The Gawsworth Quakers Hugh and Jane Lowndes*, published in 1978)

When Mrs. Hugh Lownes, a Quaker widow fleeing religious persecution, settled with her three sons and a daughter in a Springfield cave for the winter of 1684, she could not know that one day a descendant would establish a church, not far from her primitive home, commemorating her struggle for freedom.

Known as the "Blue Church" because of the lights cast by its blue limestone construction, the Lownes Free Church, oldest church building in Springfield, this year will mark its 125th anniversary. Active members in the Protestant union church today total one hundred twenty.

The church was built of Pennsylvania blue limestone, which would turn blue in the rain. Although the building is now covered in white stucco, the colorful name has remained. The church was built in 1832 by George Bolton Lownes, a descendant of Jane Lownes who is considered an original settler of Springfield. George dedicated an acre and a third on Baltimore Pike and requested in his will that a church and burial ground be erected there. A provision of his will stated that the church must be free for the use of any who would worship here.

Through the years, Methodist, Presbyterian, and Baptist clergymen have been heard from the pulpit of the church, which is open to all denominations providing only that orthodox ministers conduct its services.

These were the provisions of George Bolton Lownes in 1832 when he set apart burial ground and a tract on his farm for the church he built that year.

Two years later, Lownes died and was buried near the entrance of his church. In his will, he left $400 to the church with the investment interest to be used for building and ground maintenance.

But by 1870, the church was so dilapidated that Mrs. M.E. Parker undertook the task of raising funds to repair it. As a result, $1200 was raised and the church was rededicated January 8, 1871, with the Rev. Henry G. Weston of Crozer Theological Seminary preaching the sermon.

The renovated building then had a floor covered with matting and reversible wooden benches in substantial iron frames. The simple rectangular edifice with a pitched roof has a door shaded by ancient horse-chestnut tress.

In the north repose the ashes of Mr. Lownes. A plain slab bears his name, age and the inscription, "Where he was born, there he lived and died. An honest man and a useful citizen." In scribed also is a passage from Job: "I know that my Redeemer liveth." In August, 1955, the slab was moved from the wall to the ground for preservation.

On the opposite side of the porch, a tomb bears the name of a favorite cousin of the founder. These tombs together served for many decades as rustic seats for the congregation waiting for services to begin. One corner of the church-yard marks the resting place of many early settlers.

The Blue Church was closed during the Depression, but regular services were resumed in 1933. In 1948, the church was reorganized with sixty seven charter members. Two years later it was incorporated.

Below are two pictures. First is a picture of George Bolton Lownes's grave marker, the second is a picture of the church he built.

The Blue Church
Picture taken Nov. 17, 2016

Official Pennsylvania Emblem The State Coat of Arms

(Copied from Charlotte Lownes Olewiler.s book, *The Gawsworth Quakers Hugh and Jane Lowndes,* published in 1978)

The Pennsylvania Coat of Arms was seldom used until after the Declaration of Independence when the state's coat of arms appeared on state paper money issued in 1777. This first coat of arms was almost the same as the State Seal without the encircling inscription.

In 1778, Caleb Lownes of Philadelphia prepared a coat of arms, heralding in design, with the shield and crest similar to the shield and crest of the Seal of the State of Pennsylvania; the supporters for the shield and crest were two black horses, harnessed for drawing a vehicle, rearing on their hind legs, and facing each other on either side of the shield, and adorned with symbols of Pennsylvania's strengths, a ship carrying state commerce to all parts of the world; a clay-red plough, a symbol of Pennsylvania's rich natural recourses; and the three golden sheaves of wheat, representing fertile fields and Pennsylvania's wealth of human thought and action. Behind each horse was a stalk of corn; below the shield an olive branch and cornstalk cross limbs beneath; and across the base of the coat of arms was looped a streamer bearing the state's motto, "Virtue, Liberty, and Independence." Atop the coat of arms is a bald eagle, representing Pennsylvania's loyalty to the United States.

In 1874, the general assembly approved a commission to prescribe one official coat of arms for the State of Pennsylvania. In 1875, this commission reported to the general assembly the coat of arms with the heraldic design.

There is still a coat of arms in stone that may be seen, somewhat weathered by time, surmounting the doorway of Congress Hall (6th and Chestnut Streets) Philadelphia, carved, it is believed, around 1790, but without the cornstalks.

About the Nelly Curtis Serving Spoon

from

The National Trust for Historic Preservation

(Copied from Charlotte Lownes Olewiler's book, *The Gawsworth Quakers Hugh and Jane Lowndes,* published in 1978).

We hope this beautiful replica of the Nelly Curtis's service spoon will be a pleasant and useful reminder of your membership in the National Trust for Historic Preservation. Your spoon is crafted in fine silver plate that closely matches the silver patina of the original. Selected and especially crafted exclusively for members of the national trust, your spoon has been diligently reproduced in all its intimate detail by a skilled Massachusetts silversmith. The original spoon was designed by the Lownes Firm in Philadelphia, founded by Joseph Lownes in 1754 (note the "Lownes" hallmark on the back of your spoon).

Lawrence Lewis was George Washington's nephew and Nelly Parke Curtis was Washington's adopted daughter through his marriage to Nelly's grandmother, Martha (Dandridge) Curtis. Nelly and her younger brother, George Washington Parke Curtis, were orphaned at an early age and adopted into the busy life at Mount Vernon on February 22, 1799. Lawrence Lewis and Nelly were married at Mount Vernon.

The original of the handsome spoon on display at Woodlawn Plantation is part of the Lewis-Curtis silver service.

Lownes – Frick-Van Fossen Families

(Copied from Charlotte Lownes Olewiler's book *The Gawsworth Quakers Hugh and Jame Lowndes,* published in 1978)

Generation 7

Thomas C. Lownes b. 5/21/1827 in Philadelphia, MD, m.4/25/1850 Sarah Frick b. 4/15/1832 in Worcester Twp., PA .d 2/24/1899, dt. of Henry & Catherine.

Generation 8

Children of Thomas & Sarah Lownes.

1. Adaline b. 6/29/1851 d. 8/16/1906 m. Wm. Jr. Thompson 11/17/1877
2. Henry b. 2/6/1854, d. 8/20/1861
3. Charles T. b. 9/8/1856 d. 8/21/1927 m. Mary C. Heist 9/8/1883, d 11/28/about 1930
4. Robert C. b. 4/24/1859 d. 11/15/1912 m. Amanda Bean 1865 – 1895 m. (?) Susan Godshall b. 1860 d. 12/14/1925
5. Anna Frick b. 7/1/1861 d. 12/2/1949 m. 1/11/1882 Irvin Peltz Williams
6. Samuel Lownes b. 7/1/1861 d. 11/29/1932 m. Lillian Parch
7. Lewis M.. b. 8/15/1867 d. 3/19/1933 unmarried

8. Ida Baker b. 3/11/1870 d. 10/18/1930 m. Wm. Blackwood Thomson 8/1900
9. Walter B. b.9/15/1872 d. 4/28/1935 m. Anna Clark in 1894 in Phila.

Generation 9

Children of Adaline Lownes & Wm. J. Thompson: Wm. B. 1887 d. 10/2/1925 in California. No descendants
Children of Charles & Mary Heist Lownes

1. Morris b. 4/5/1884 d. 2/3/1892 no descendants
2. John Barton Lownes M.D. b. 1887 d. 2/22/1957 m. Kathryn Weis. He was "A noted urologist, one of the founders of Philadelphia Urological Society. A writer of many valuable articles on urinary diseases." No descendants.

Children of Robert & Amanda Lownes

1. Harry died in infancy
2. Clarence B. b. 9/29/1884 m. Mamie Stover b. 8/3/1883

Ch. of Robert & Sue: Ruth B. m. Frank W. Scholl, no descendants
Children of Anna & Irvin P. Williams

1. Bertha L. b. 11/21/1884 m. A. Wesley Poley 3/27/19-- b. 12/21/1883
2. Myrtle L. b. 7/16/1896 m. John Charles Dyson 9/15/1921 descendants. listed under Gen. 10

Children of Samuel of Highlands, N. J.

1. Florence b.--m.--d.—
2. Elmer, died in infancy

Children of Lewis M. none, unmarried

Children of Ida B. & Wm. B. Thomson none

Children of Walter B. & Anna Clark

See separate sheet

Lownes – Frick – Van Fossen Families

Generation 10

Descendants thru Bertha L. & A. Wesley Poley:

1. Audrey Anna b. 2/28/1914 m. Ivan F. Bennett M.D. 9/23/1944
2. Alma W. b. 9/15/1915 m. 4/29/39 Robert L. Kendig
3. Arlene G. b. 7/10/1911 m. 6/7/42 Raymond W. Kantner

Descendants thrugh Mrytle & John Dyson

1. John C. Dyson b. 2/31/1923 m. 10/22/1949 Diane L. Cook b. 3/29/1930

Generation 11

Ivan Stanley Bennett b. 1/27/1949

Judith Ann Bennett b. 1/5/1951

Robert L. Kendig, Jr. b. 8/24/1944

Kathleen Kendig b. 2/6/1946 m. Donald A. Borden 8/28/1971

Jon Thomas Kendig b. 3/2/1949 m. Janice Ellen Kroupa 8/26/1972

Bonnie Jill Kantner b. 4/20/1946 m. Samuel Kehrer 10/15/1966

Generation 12

Kristine Kehrer b. 6/18/1970

James Douglas Dyson b. 3/2/1955 (born 100 years after his great-grandfather, Irvin P. Williams)

Thomas C. Lownes married Sarah Frick, daughter of Henry and Catherine

Henry Frick, Jr. of Worcester m. Catherine Van Fossen at Wentz Reformed Church, Worcester Co. PA

Henry Frick (Henrich) 2/26/1776-3/25/1855 m. Anna — 10/21/1781 – 6/10/1852. Buied Dutch Ref. Ch. Worcestor Co. PA. (Worc. Evang. Cong.)

Henrich Frick 7/21/1748-7/21-1828 arrived Phila. on ship "*Union*", 9/30/1774; m. 2/11/1777 Barbara Schnyder (German Ref. Ch. Phila. 1748-1802. Will prov. 4/22/1828 ments. ch. Henry, Susanna, Catherine, grch. Mary Sweabolt, stepson Jacob Beyer. A Phillipina Wyant (Weyand; Wieand) Beyer (Boyer) 11/10/1737-9/22/1814 (da. Wendel and Margaretta Fisher Weyand) m. (1) 11/7/1758 Andrew Beyer (s. Abraham & Rosine (Jackel) Beyer. She m. (2) Henry Frick after 11/5/1774. Henry Frick, Jr. administrator of Wendel Wyant, Sr's will, Montg. Co. PA., 9/13/1831. Henry Frick and Anna – had a da. Phillipina (b. 7/1/1818). Is this H. F. his father?

Henry Frick married Catherine Van Fossen, dt of Joseph & Sarah Rittenhouse Van Fossen. 8 Ch.

Joseph Van Fossen 2/2/1775 – 12/28/1853 m. Sarah Rittenhouse b. 1778 buried Whitpain Cem. b. Worcester, Wheelwright. Wife lif. 1850, Wor. Twp.

Leonald Van Fossen 1748 – 1833 m. Mary Tyson 1753 – 1833. Blacksmith. Liv. Worcester, Purch. Land from Conrad 5/5/1777. Wheelwright 10/8/1797. Will prov. 11/23/1833. Burd. Lower Providence Presby. Ch.

Montg. Co. Pa. Perkiomen, Skippack. He burd.Skippack Menonite B. G. (?)

Cunrad (Conrad) m. Ankin (Ann Bon (Bun) Yeomen, Worchester, Phila. Co. Will prob. 6/2/177-. Ankin (da of Peter Bon by lat wife) Elizabeth Op de Graef (Peter petitioned for road from Farmer's Mill to Skippack, 1713) Conrad m. (2) Garetze (Gurthan) Jansen, (da. of Claus Jansen). 1711 Memb. Ref. Congreg. Ch. Skippack 1711. Will of Peter Prov. 8/12/1745.

Arnold Van Vossen m. Mary – (Sellen?) Crefeldt, Germany. To Phila. 1684; settled Germantown 12/21/1700. Skippack (Bebber's Twp.) Wm. Penn conveyed to Govert Remke, Lenart Arets and Jacob Isaac Van Bebber, all of Crefeld, each 1000 acres, 6/11/1683. Crefeld Purchasers, 13 families assembled 6/18/1683, sailed 7/24 on ship "Concord", Wm. Jeffries, Master, landing Phila. 10/6/1638; Founded Germatown, Org. Mennonite Ch. 1703; log cabin on land donated by Arnold Van Vossen. Ch. Membs. Peter Conrad, Mary Sellers, Henry Sellers, Margaret Tyson, Arnold Arnold Kuster, Elizabeth Kuster, Hermanus Kuster, Arnold Van Vossen, Conrad Johnson (Jansen) and wife. 1st minister, Wm. Rittenhouse.

Ref. "The Messenger" Mennonite Church paper March – April 1958:

Feb. 10, 1702, Arold Van Fossen delivered to Jan Neuss on behalf of the Mennonites a deed for three square perches of land for a church. On it a log cabin was built. The quantity of land was later increased, since in 1714, Sept. 5, Van Fossen conveyed thirty four perches "for a place to erect a meeting house and for a place to bury their dead." Arnold and Mary moved to what is now Worcester Township (Skippack Pike) 1702. Retained membership in Germantown Mennonite Ch. (The first church was log; the second building was stone and was still standing in 1972).

APPENDIX IX

Lownes and Donaldson

Hinshaw Vol. VI Henrico M.M. Va.

(Copied from Charlotte Lownes Olewiler.s book, *The Gawsworth Quakers Hugh and Jane Lowndes,* published in 1978)

Lownes 196, 197, 415, 528, 529, 762, (218, 593), 218 Winston Donalson 487 (510) P. 510 Hough Fam.

Page 196, 197:

1793, 7.6 James & Joseph prof Fairfax M.M. Va. Acc.

1794, 12, 6 Deborah & William s James, rocf Fairfax M.M. Va. Trtco the Swamp P.M.

1796, 4.6 Deborah (now Pleasants) dis. mcd

1803, 3.5 William, minor, gct Alex. M.M. rq of his father, James Lownes (rem)

1803, 3.5 James, Richmond City dis m his niece of affinity

1804, 9.1 James con disorderly m. & rq rst; placed on probation

1805, 4.6 James con disorderly m; acc & rst

1806, 2 mo. Ann, form of Phila. M.M. lately dis for disorderly; m. rst

1806, 6.7 Ann, wife James, rocf Phila. M.M. Pa. & rtco Richmond P.M. (cert dtd 1896, 6.7)

1807, 8.1 William uc of this M.M. at the rg of the Alexandria M.M. of which he was a mbr. for joining in military operations

1810, 2.3 James co Richmond P.M.

1810, 11.3 Ann co Richmond P.M. resigned 1815,11,21

1816, 2.28 James released as overseer of Richmond P.M.

1816, 4.6 James released as overseer of Richmond Mtg. (rem)

1821, 4.7 James sued by James Winston both members Richmond P.M.

1830 9.4 James & wife Anna gct Phila. M.M. (rem) Hopewell M.M. Va.

1780 5.1 James & wife Sarah & ch Mary, Sarah, Hyat, Deborah & Caleb, rocf Phila. M.M. dtd 1779,12,31

Henrico M.M. (also called Curles, New Kent, Upper, Upland, White Oak Swamp & Weyanoke M.M. established price to 1699)

Sarah, dt of James & Sarah Lownes of Alexandria, Va. M 29/4/1790 at Alexandria MH Va. John Scott Pleasants s of Jacob, dec & Sarah Pleasants of Henrico Co. Va. (see Pleasants)

William, minor s of James, gc 23/8/1794 White Oak Swamp M.M. Va. on request of father; clear.

Fairfax M. M. Va. P 487

Donaldson, Elizabeth (form Hough) rpd mod 6 mo. 1815; dis 31/7/1816 "after long care"

Lownes

1783,8,30 James & w Sarah Pancoast & ch. Sarah, Hyatt, John, Deborah, James, Caleb, Jane & Joseph, gct Fairfax 1783,8,2 Mary (form Lownes) rpd mou; dis Alexandria M.M. p 762

Lownes

William, s of James, rocf White Oak Swamp M.M. Va. 21/4/1803, dtd 3/3/1803; "We are informed (25/6/1807) that he has rem within the verge of White Oak Swamp M.M. Va., & has been performing military duty there," dis 22/10/1807

Hinshaw

Lownes, Fairfax M.M., Va. P 528, 529

Deborah (dt of James Lownes Sr) "removed & settled" gc 23/8/1794 White Oak Swamp M.M. Va. On req of father; clear. Hyatt dis 25/5/1793 mou in 3 mo. Last. James roc 24/4/1784 Croched Run M.M. 30th 8 mo. 1783; also for w Sarah & 8 ch. Sarah, Hyat, John, Deborah, James, Caleb

C. p 53: - James Lownes & 4 ch; John, Deborah, Joseph & William, gct White Oak Swamp M.M. Va. 26/1793; all are clear; but John, Deborah & William were gct White Oak Swamp M.M. Va., 23/8/1794; on req of their father (James, Sr.) James Jr. & Caleb were gct Phila. M.M. 22/12/1792. James, Jr. & Caleb (sons of James Sr. & w Sarah Pancoast, the latter evidently dec) gc 22/12/1792 Phila. M.M. Pa. on req father (Note: This cert. is addressed "To the Middle Monthly Meeting of Friends in Phila." See H-v2, p 587

Lownes

Penna,. New Jersey vol 2 Hinshaw

Lownes 391, 586, 753, 893, 964, 1012, 1055 (799, 782, 805)

Page 391

Agnes dt. of John d. July 27,1788

Agnes w of John, brd May 3, 1775 age 48

Agnes buried Sept. 22, 1793 age 20

Edmund s of David, brd 4/21/1801 age 5

Edward & Hannah

Ch: Thomas Burns b. Oct 5, 1818

Hannah Ann b. May 12, 1820

Eleanor buried Nov. 14, 1807 age 50

Hannah, dt. Of Jos. d. May 25, 1746

Hannah, w of Edward, d. June 5, 1820 age 24

James Jr. d. Dec. 16, 1743

James d. June 18, 1759 aged

John, s of John d. Aug. 11, 1765 age wo mo.

John, brd. Aug. 15, 1807 age 84

Joseph, d. Oct. 12,1762

Rachel (Lowns), dt. of James d. 8/13/1739

Samuel, s of James, dec. 3/29/1751

Sarah, dt of John, d. 9/17/1757

Susannah Lowns, dt of James d. 3/12/1739

Thomas Burns, s of Edward, d. 6/8/1819 age 8 mo.

. . . . . . s of Joseph, Jr. d. 12/5/1758

Page 586,587

1712,3,30 James (Lowns) and fam. rocf Chester M.M. held at Middletown
dated 1712,1,31

1718,8,31 Hannah rmt Nehemiah Allen Jr.

1721,4,30 Joseph rmt Sarah Tidmarch

1731,8,29 Susannah, p rpd mou

1736, 6,27 James Jr. con mou

1737,8,13 Rebecca dt of James, Phila., Pa. m Joh Yarnall, s of Phillip,
Chester Co., Pa. at Phila. M.

1743,11,27 Mary Phillips (late Lowns) con mcd

1744,3,24 Ann, dt. of Joseph, Passiunk Pa, m John Page, s of George,
Phila.

1745,7,12 Dusanna (Lowns) dt. Of Jos. Phila. Pa. m James Lindley, Phila.

Vol 11 Hinshaw Phila. MM

1753,8,24 John gct Chwster M.M. to M.

1754,2,22 Anna, w of John rocf Chester M.M. dated 1753,12,31

1757,10,20 Sarah dt of Jos., Phila. Pa. m Jonathan Shoemaker, s of Jacob,
Phila., Pa.

1757,12,15 Joseph, s of Joseph, Phila. M Hannah Robinson, dt of Edward,
Phila. Pa., Mtg.

1761,5,7 Hannah, dt of Joseph, Phila. Pa. m Joshus Pancoast, s of Samuel, Phila. Pa. at Phila. Mt.

1762,5,6 Wm. S of Joseph, Phila. Pa. m Rebecca Elwell, dt of David, Phila.

1763,11,3 James, s of Joseph, Phila. Co. Pa. m Sarah Pancoast, dt of Wm. Phila.

1768,4,29 Rebecca Ash (late Lownes) con mcd (page 578)

- - - - Benanual, s of Benanual, rocf Chester M.M. held at Providence dated 1770,3,23

- - - - Hugh, s of Benanual, rocf Chester M.M. at Providence, dated 1774,4,27

1774,2,24 Mary, dt of Jos. & Sarah, m Job Bacon, s of John & Eliz. Phila.

1779,12,31 James & w Sarah & ch. Mary, Sarah, Hyatt, John, Deborah, James & Caleb, gct Hopewell M.M. Va.

1782.1.25 Caleb gct Wilmington M.M. Caleb (Lowns) rocf Wilmington M.M. Dated 1785,3,16

1786,1,12 Joseph, s of John and Agnes, Phila. Pa. m Esther Middletown, dt of Abel and Mary at Phila. Mtg.

1789,2.24 Joseph & w Esther, gct SD MM

1790,5,28 Caleb, gct Abington MM tr m

1790,12,31 David gct Friends in Grace Church St. or elsewhere in London

1790,12,31 Margaret w of Caleb rocf Abington M.M. dated 1790,12,27

- - - - David (Lowns) rocf Piel M.M. London dated 1791,10,5

- - - - James & Caleb sons of James rocf Fairfax M.M. dated 1792,12,22

1795,3,27 Grace dis mou

1795,8,28 David dis Joining with others in a military expedition

1796,12,30 Caleb (Lowens) & w Margaret & ch John, Edward & George gct N.D.

1797,5,26 James, dis mou (Sarah Donaldson – 18 yrs. 4 mo & 16 days of age

- - - - Joseph, rocf N.D. MLM dated 1800,12,23

1801,6,26 Ellen rocf M.M. dated 1801,4,27

1803,7,29 Ann (late Robinson) dis mcd with a man whose former w was her aunt

1806,2,28 Ann con mcd to person whose former w was her aunt

1806, 5,2 Ann gct White Oak Swamp, Henrico Co. Va.

1807,7,2 Caleb Jr. dis N.D. mou

1809,9,28 David gct N.D. M.M.

- - - - George rocf S.D. m.m. dated1810,10,24

1814,2,24 George, minor gct Wilimington

1817,3,27 Edward F. & w Hannah P. rocf S.D. M.M. 1817,2,26 Phila. M.M.

Lownes

1829,2,26 Edward F. Dis mou

1832,3,29 Sarah Burns & gr dt Hannah Ann Lownes Minor gct S.D. M.M.

- - - - Hugh M. rocf Chester M.M. dated 1832,2,25

Phila. M.M. Hicksite Page 893

Lownes

1829,3,18 Mary recrg

1830,6,3 Mary dt. Of David & Elizabeth Phila. M Richard K. Betts s of Sam. & Grace, Phila. At Cherry St. M.H.

1888,7,18 Marianna rocf Makefield M.M. dtd 1888,6,7

1900,4,18 Marianna gct Gwyedd M.M. Falls M.M. page 964

Mary, dt of Joseph & Sarah Ann b. April 3,1837

No death announcement in Poulson Daily Advertiser 1807 – 1814 for James Lownes (his wife Sarah Donaldson mar. second time David McCord April 1807)

Ph 29A:I Ph 23A: 2 Ph 23A:3

Falls M.M. p 1012

Lownes

1776,9,4 Wm (Lowness) & Rebecca & ch Joseph, Mary Daniel, Wm. & James rocf S. D. M. M.

1783,12,3 Joseph, s of Wm. Gct S. D. M. M.

1784,5,13 Wm. S of Joseph, Buck Co. m Rachel Fell, dt of Jos. Bucks Co. at Upper Makefield M.M.

1785,7,6 David s of Wm. gct N.D.M.M.

1786,4,5 Mary gct S.D. M.M.

1786,4,5 Wm. & s Wm & James gct S.D

1789,6,3 Mary rocf S. D. M. M.

1789,6,3 Wm. & s Wm. & James rocf S.D.

1790,7,7 Joseph rocf Buckingham M.M.

1790,9,16 Joseph s of Wm. Bucks Co. m Merriam Betts dt of Elizabeth dt of Zachariah, Bucks Co. at Makefield M.M. Pa

1790,11,18 Mary, dt of Wm. Bucks Co. m Robert Knowles s of John, Bucks Co. at Makefield M.M. Pa.

1790,12,16 Wm. Bucks Co. m Mary Whitson Bucks Co. at Makefield M. H. Pa.

1795,5,6 Wm. Jr. gct Wrightstown M. M. to m Susannah Stoke

1795,9,9 Susannah (Lowness) rocf Wrightstown M.M.

1800,3,5 Wm. Jr. gct Buckingham M. M. to m Sarah Cantby

1800,6,4 Sarah (Lowness) rocf Buckingham M.M.

1801,11,4 Joseph & w Miriam & sm ch Charles, Bethula, Rebecca & Josiah gct Baltimore M. M.

1812,3,18 James s of Wm. & Rebecca, Bucks Co. m Mercy Betts dt of Zacharis & Mary, Bucks Co. Makefield M.H.

1803,4,6 Wm.. dis disunity

1819,5,7 Mary gct Buckingham M.M.

Falls M. M. Orthodox P. 1055

Lownes

1828,11,6 Eliz dis jh (or Elizabeth)

1828,11,6 Mercy dis jh

1828,11,6 Rebecca dis jh

1828,11,6 Sarah dis jh

1828,11,6 Thomas dis jh

1828,11,6 Wm. Jr. dis jh

1831,11,10 Joseph Jr. gct Buckingham M.M.

1834,12,4 Esther dis jh

1834,12,4 Hannah Pancoast dis jh

1834,11,4 Susan dis jh

1834,11,4 Thomas Betts jh

1838,4,6 Rebecca (Lowness) dis jh

1839,5,5 Mary gct Buckingham M.M.

1839,5,5 Sarah Ann Cooper & ch Elias Paxson Lownes & Jos Lownes gct
Buckingham M.M.

1870,3,10 Beulah dropped from

From the Records of the Parish Church St. James, Gawsworth, Eng.

(Copied from Charlotte Lownes Olewiler's book, *The Gawsworth Quakers Hugh and Jane Lowndes,* published in 1978)

Baptized 2/20/1551 Humprey, s of Hugh (great-great grandfather of Hugh?)

Born 7/1563 Ellen, dt of Thomas

Bapt. 7/18/1564 Peter, s of Hugh of Rode

Bapt. 2/4/1565 Alex s of Thomas of Rode

Births:

8/14/1573 Thomas s of Roger Lowndes

1581 Elizabeth, dt of Peter

9/25/1595 Thomas s of Thomas of Morton

3/23/1596 Alice dt of John of Rodes

9/30/1598 Edward s of Edward of Rodes

1/23/1600 M. dt of John of Rodes

4/2/1612 Mary dt of John of Rodes

12/21/1612 Kathy, dt of Ed. Of Rodes

1614 Edward s of John of Rodes

2/26/1612 Margaret dt of John of Rode

12/31/1616 M. dt of John of Rode

3/14/1618 Ellen dt of John of Rode

10/6/1619 Ann dt of Edward of Rode

9/10/1620 John s of John of Rode

3/11/1621 Urian s of Edward of Rode

2/6/1622 Helen dt of John of Rode

5/2/1624 E. son of John of Rode

9/19/1647 Rebecca dt of Ed Jr. of Rode

9/13/1649 Mathew s of Edward of Rode

1610 Christopher Sherwin m Joan Lowndes

Burials

1599 Widow Lowndes

1597 Alice dt of John Lowndes

7/29/1597 Edward Lowndes, single man

5/17/1611 Peter Lowndes of Rods

8/26/1612 Peter Lowndes & Alice, wife

1/2/1612 Em Lowndes of Rodes

12/3/1657 Urian, s of Edward of Rodes

4/8/1667 Mary of N. Rode

From the Courthouse Records
Of Chester, Cheshire County, England

Marraiges:

1557 January 24 Hugh Lowndes and Thomasin Brodhurst, Presburie Parsh

1557 January 23, Thomas Lowndes of Rodes and Marie Lyon, Presburis Parish

1574 August 1, Thomas Lowndes and Joane Kelsall

1589 December 26, Thomas Lowndes and Anne Davenport

Encyclopedia of American Quaker Genealogy Hinshaw Vol. II 1938

(Copied from Charlotte Lownes Olewiler's book, *The Gawsorth Quakers Hugh and Jane Lowndes,* published in 1978)

Page 391 Philadelphia M.M.

Agnes, dt John, d 7-27-1768

Agnes, w John, bur 5-3-1793 age 48

Agnes, bur 9-22-1793 age 20

Edmund, s David, bur 4-21-1801, age 5

Edward & Hannah

Ch: Thomas Burns b 10-5-1818

Hannah Ann b 5-12-1820

Eleanor bur 11-14-1807 age 50

Hannah, dt Joseph, d 5-25-1746

Hannah, w Edward, d 6-5-1820 age 24

James, Jr. d 12-16-1743

James d 6-18-1759, very aged

John, s John d 8-11-1765 age 20 m

John bur 8-15-1807 age 84

Joseph d 10-12-1762

Rachel [Lowns], dt James, d 8-13-1739

Samuel, s James, dec, d 3-29-1751

Sarah, dt John, d 9-17-1757

Susannah [Lowns], dt James, d 3-12-1739

Thomas Burns, s Edward, d 6-8-1819 age 8 m

—-, Joseph, Jr., d 12-5-1758

Page 586 Philadelphia M.M.

1712, 3-30, James [Lowns] & fam rocf Chester MM, held at Middletown, dated 1712-1-31

1718, 8,31. Hannah rmt Nehemiah Allen, Jr.

1721, 4,30. Joseph rmt Sarah Tidmarch

1731, 8,29. Susanna, Jr. rpd mou

1736, 6,27. James, Jr. con mou

1737, 8,13 Rebecca, dt James, Phila.,PA.,m Job Yarnell, a Philip, Chester Co.,Pa. at Phila. Mtg

1743, 11,27 Mary Phillips (late Lownes) con mcd

1744, 3,24. Ann, dt Joseph, Passiunk, Pa., m John Page, s George, Phila., at Phila. Mtg

1745, 7,12 Susanna [Lowns], dt Joseph, Phila., Pa., m James Lindley, Phila., Pa., at Phila. Mtg

1753, 8,24. John gct Chester MM to m

1754, 2,22. Agnes, w John, rocf Chester MM dated 1753-12-31

1757, 10,20. Sarah, dt Joseph, Phila., Pa., m Jonathan Shoemaker, as Jacob, Phila., Pa., at Phila. Mtg.

1757, 12,15. Joseph, s Joseph, Phila., Pa.,m Hannah Robinson, dt Edward, Phila., Pa., at Phila. Mtg.

1761, 5,7. Hannah, dt Joseph, Phila., Pa., m Joshua Pancoast, s Samuel, Phila., Pa., at Phila. Mtg.

1762, 5,3. Wm., s Joseph, Phila., Pa., m Rebecca Elwell, dt David, Phila., Pa., at Phila. Mtg

1763, 11,3. James, s Joseph, Phila., Co., Pa., m Sarah Pancoast, dt Wm., Phila., at Phila. Mtg

1768, 4,29. Rebecca Ash (late Lownes) con mcd

——, --,-- Benanuel, s Benanuel, rocf Chester MM, held at Providence, dated 1770- 3- 23

——, --,-- Hugh, s Benanuel, rocf Chester MM held at Providence, dated 1772-4-27

1774, 2,24 Mary, dt Joseph & Sarah, m John Bacon, s John & Elizabeth, Phila., Pa.,at Phila. MH

1779, 12,31 James & w, Sarah, & ch, Mary, Sarah, Hyatt, John, Deborah, James & Caleb gct Hopewell MM, VA

1782, 1, 25 Caleb, gct Wilmington MM

——, --, -- Caleb [Lowns] rocf Wilmington MM dated 1785, 3,16

1786, 1,12 Joseph s John & Agnes, Phila., Pa., m Esther Middleton, dt Abel & Mary, at Phila. MM

1786, 2, 24 Joseph & w Esther, gct SD MM

1790, 5, 28 Caleb gct Abington MM to m 1790, 12, 31. David gct Friends in Grace Church or elsewhere in London

1790, 12, 31 Margaret, w Caleb, rocf Abington MM, dated 1790, 12, 27

——, --, -- Daivd [Lowns] rocf Peel MM, London dated 1791, 10, 5

——, --, -- James & Caleb, s James, rocf Fairfax, MM dated 1792, 12, 22

1795, 3, 27 Grace dis mou

1795, 8, 28 David dis joining with others in a military expedition

1796, 12, 30 Caleb [Lowns] & w, Margaret, & ch, John, Edward, & George, gct ND MM

1797, 5 es dis mou

——-, --, -- Joseph rocf ND MM, dated 1800, 12, 23

1801, 6, 26 Ellen rocf Chester MM, dated 1801, 4, 27

1803, 7, 29 Ann (late Robinson) dis mcd with a man whose form w was her aunt

1806, 2, 28 Ann con mcd to person whose form w was not her aunt

1806, 5, 2.Ann gct White Oak Swamp, Henrico Co., Va.

1807, 7, 2.Caleb, Jr. dis mou

1809, 9, 28 David gct ND MM

——, --, -- George rocf SD MM, dated 1810, 10, 24

1814, 2, 24 George, minor, gct Willington MM

1817, 3, 27 Edward F. & w, Hannah P., rocf SD MM dated 1817, 2, 26

Page 753 Philadelphia MM (Orthodox)

1829, 2, 26 Edward F. dis mou

1832, 3, 29 Sarah Burns & gr dt, Hannah Ann Lownes, minor, gct SD MM

——, --, -- Hugh M. rocf Chester MM, dated 1833, 2, 25

Page 779 Philadelphia MM (Hicksite)

Clayton Allen, s Enoch & Rachel (Ward), b 11-9-1814 d 4-17-1887 bFH; m
Ruth Anna Lownes, d 1-25-1877, age 58, bFH (nmtm)

Page 782 Philadelphia MM (Hicksite)

Richard Kinsey m Mary Lownes, dt David & Elizabeth (Keegan), d 8-20-
1832, b WG ch. Hannah Lownes b 3-27-1831

Page 805 Philadelphia MM (Hicksite)

David Knowles, s Jacob & Rachel (Buckman), d10-16-1876 bFH; m Eliza
W. Lownes

Page 893 Philadelphia MM (Hicksite)

1829, 3, 18 Mary recrq

1830, 6, 2.Mary, dt David & Elizabeth, Phila., m Richard K. Betts, s
Samuel C. & Grace, Phila. at Cherry St. MH, Phila.

1888, 7, 18 Marianna rocf Makefield MM, dtd 1888, 6, 7

1900, 4, 18 Marianna gct Gwynedd MM

Mary, dt Joseph & Sarah Ann, b 4, 3, 1837

Page 1012 Falls MM

1776, 9, 4 Wm. [Lowness] & w, Rebecca, & ch, Joseph, Mary, Daniel, Wm. & James, rocf SD MM

1783, 12, 3 Joseph, s Wm., gct SD MM

1784, 5, 13 Wm., s Joseph, Bucks Co., m Rachel Fell, dt Joseph, Bucks Co. at Makefield MH

1785, 7, 6 David, s Wm., gct ND MM

1786, 4, 5 Mary gct SD MM

1786, 4, 5 Wm. & s, Wm. & James, gct SD MM

1789, 6, 3 Mary rocf SD MM

1789, 6, 3 Wm. & s, Wm. & James, rocf SD MM

1790, 7, 7 Joseph tocf Buckingham MM

1790, 9, 16 Joseph, s Wm., Bucks Co., m Merriam Betts, dt Zachariah, Bucks Co. at Makefield MH, PA.

1790, 11, 18 Mary, dt Wm., Bucks Co., m Robert Knowles, s John, Bucks Co. at Makefield MH, PA.

1790, 12, 16 Wm., Bucks Co., m Mary Whitson Bucks Co., at Makefield MH, PA.

1795, 5, 6 Wm., Jr. gct Wrightstown MM, to m Susannah Stokes

1795, 9, 9 Susannah [Lowness] rocf Wrightstown MM

1800, 3, 5 Wm., Jr. gct Buckingham MM, to m Sarah Canby

1801, 11, 4 Jodeph & w, Mirian, & small ch Charles, Bethula, Rebecca & Josiah, gct Baltimore MM

1802, 3, 18 James, s Wm. & Rebecca, Bucks Co., m Mercy Batts, dt Zachariah & Mary, Bucks Co., at Makefield MH

1803, 4, 6 Wm., Jr. dis disunity

1819, 5, 7 Mary gct Buckingham MM

1828, 11, 6 Eliza dis jH (or Elizabeth)

1828, 11, 6 Mercy dis jH

1828, 11, 6 Rebecca dis jH

1828, 11, 6 Sarah dis jH

1828, 11, 6 Thomas dis jH

1828, 11, 6 Wm., Jr. dis jH

1831, 11, 10 Joseph, Jr. gct Buckingham MM

1834, 12, 4 Esther dis jH

1834, 12, 4 Hannah Pancost dis jH

1834, 12, 4 Susan dis jH

1834,12, 4 Thomas Betts dis jH

1837, 4, 6 Rebecca [Lowness] dis jH

1859, 5, 5 Mary gct Buckingham MM

1859, 5, 5 Sarah Ann Cooper & ch, Elias Paxdon Lownes & Joseph Lownes, gct Buckingham MM

1870, 3, 10 Beulah dropped from mbrp

Card File Data from Swarthmore College Museum

All cards have at the top c mm, ccp

Card 2 V3 p 108 1753-12-31 Lowns, Agnes wf of John gct Phila

Card 2 V 2 p 353 1744-9-26 Lowns, Alice, w of Bennanuell, rocf Goshen m.m. (?) dated

Card 3 V 4 p 13 1779-3-26 Lownes, Alice med to Buckley (see Alice Buckley)

Card 3 V1 p 139 1732-9-14 Lowns, Ann (m George Maris)

Card 2 V 7 p 69 1861-9-30 Lownes, Anna; disf jqsm

Card 2 V2 p 348 1744-5-30 Lowns, Benanuel, gct Goshen (?) mm to Mary Alice Williamson, dt of John

Card 2 V1 p 33 1770-3-23 Lownes, Benanuel, s of Benanuel, decd, get Phila m.m.

Card 2 V8 p 221 1897-2-22 Lownes, Edward; off acc for m.m.

Card 2 V 4 p 463 1778-8-31 Lownes, Eleamor (cox) dt of John, decd w of Slater

Card 2 V 4 p1 1778-10-26 Lownes, Eleanor disf

Card 2 V2 p 212 1734-8-25 Lowns, Elizabeth (for Maddock, dt Mordeca mcd to George Lowns, Jr.

Card 2 V 2 p 214 1734-9-25 Lowns, Elizabeth, w of George, Jr. disf med

Card 1 V1 p 73 Lownes, Elizabeth d 8-25-1868 dt Hugh

Card 3 V 4 p 373 1793-7-29 Lownes, Ellen rst (ack accptd for now)

Card 2 V1 p 257 1801-4-27 Lownes, Ellen gct Phila m.m.

Card 2 V6 p 338 1853-2-28 Lownes, Emily L. disf j a soc

Card 3 V1 p 63 1720-3-26 Lownes, Esther m Samuel Ogden

Card 2 V8 p 321 1903-8-31 Lownes, Francis, mou

Card 2 V8 p 325 1903-10-26 Lownes, Francis, off acc for now

Card 2 V1 p 65 1701-5-28 Lownes, George & Mary Bowers, am

V1 p 66 1701-6-25 Lownes, George & Mary Bowen, amistm,ma

Card 1 V1 p 17 Lowns George (b —d —) m Mary Bowers

Ch:
1. Jane b 1-10-1702
2. Esther b 7-2-1703
3. Ann b 8-1-1707

4. George b 2-20-1709

Card 2 V1 p 98 1779-1-25 Lownes, George, s of Benanuel, decd, get Concord m.m.

Card 2 V4 p 103 1782-6-24 Lownes, George; rocf Concord M.M. (?) dated 2-27-1781

Card 2 V1 p 118 (c) 1782-7-29 Lownes, George, s of Benanuel, decd, get Kennett m.m.

Card 2 V2 p 323 mr 1784 –- ?Lownes, George, rocf Kennett m.m. dated 4-15-1784

Card 2 V4 p 207 1787-1-27 Lownes, George, mcd

Card 2 V1 p 177 (c) 1789-6-29 Lownes, George, get Kennett m.m.

Card 2 V1 p 257 1801-4-27 Lownes, George, a minor, get Goshen m.m.

Card 2 V6 p 296 1848-12-25 Lownes, George b,, get Kennett m.m. (?) to marry Rebecca Webb

Card 1 Lownes, George B (b1-25-1825; d 8-21-1923) s of Joseph & Rachel Massey, m 1-12-1849 at Kennett m.m.

Rebecca Webb (b 3-24-1826; d 11-5-1852, dt of Alban & Hannah (Darlington)

Ch:
V 1 p159 1. William Henry b 1-9-1850
2. George Bolton b 8-9-1851, d 4-14-1909 bu Redlands, CA
3. Mary b no date

4. Hannah D b 4-6-1856, d 4011-1930
5. Joseph b 6-24-1858
6. Edward b 8-22-1860, d 6-4-1900
7. Rebecca b 11-24-1861, d 909-1862 bu Spr
8. Francis b 6-7-1863
9. Minerva b 7-7-1865, d 8-21-1929
10. Jane C b 4-15-1867 m 10-9-1890 John H. Webster, Jr.

Card 2 V5 p 101 1806-7-28 Lownes, Hannah (f Lawrence) mou (no further mention)

Card 2 V? p 520 1806-8-25 Lownes, Hannah (f Lawrence), off acc for mou

Card 1 V1D p 59 Lownes, Hannah b 12-26-1842

Card 2 V1 p 32 (c) 1772-4-27 Lownes, Hugh, s of Benanuel, decd, get Phila m.m.

Card 2 V4 p 46 1780-6-26 Lownes, Hugh; rocf Phila M.M. for N.D. dated 8-24-1779

Card 2 V4 p 59 1781-1-29 Lownes, Hugh; disf taking the test & collecting military taxes

Card 2 V1 p 325 mp 1784-4-26 Lownes, Hugh; slg complying "with Requestions for caring on warlike purposes & likewise took a test" was dis, rtb rst

Card 2 V4 p 146 1784-5-31 Lownes, Hugh, rst

Card 1 V2 p 11 Lownes, Hugh (b —;d—; s Benanuel, decd, Chester Co., PA) m 1784-10-21 at Springfield, PA., Rebecca Rhoads (b—d—;, dt James, decd, Chester Co. PA.)

Ch:

V1 p 105 1. Joseph b 1-17-1787

2. Benanuel b 2-19-1790 d?? 18665 bu spl

3. Elizabeth b 1-18-1793

4. Sidney b 1-13-1796 d 10-16-1843 bu spr

Card 2 V4 p 151 1784-8-30 Lownes, Hugh s of Benanuel, decd, & Rebeckah Roads, of James, decd, &

V4 p 153 1784-6-28 Lownes, Hugh & Rebekah Roads, amist ma

V4 p 155 1784-10-25 Lownes, Hugh & Rebekah Roads, rm

Card 2 V8 p 146 1808-9-26 Lownes, Hugh, dis

Card 2 V6 p 112 1833-2-25 Lownes, Hugh M., s of Joseph;get Phila M.M.

Card 1 V1 p 10 Lows, Joseph (b—; d—) m Susannah Richards

Ch.

1. Joseph b 1-30-1693

2. Hannah b 11-13-1695

3. James b 1-3-1698

Card 2 V1 p 29 1692-9-7 Lows, James & Susannah Richards, and

V1 p 30 1692-10-5 Lows, James & Susannah Richards, amist, ma

Card 2 p 195 1712-1-31 Lownes, James: get Phila m.m. & Susannah

- From wom.mins/ she makes the rg for a cert for herself jointly with her husband to Phila M.M. 12-25-1711. In mins. For 1-31-1712 it is stated that a cert is granted to James (James) Lownes & wf —. Men's mins. Fail to mention her.

Card 3 V1 p 103 1726-4-19 Lownes, Jane m Jonathan Maries. (See Jonathan Maries)

Card 2 V4 p 414 1795-4-27 Lownes, Jane & George, ch of Ellen; rec rq

Card 2 V2 p 246 1799-10-28 Lownes, Jane, a minor get Phila M.M. for N.D.

Card 3 p 273 1890-10-9 Lownes, Jane C. m John H. Webster, Jr. see John Webster, Jr.

Card 2 p 104 1753-8-27 Lowns, John, rocf Phila M.M. to marry Agnes Cowpland

Card 1 V1 p 271 Lows, John (b—; d—; s Joseph & Sarah, Philadelohia, PA. m 175308-27 at Providence MH, PA Agnes Cowpland (b 6-4-1627; d —-; Caleb & Sarah, Chester Co. PA.)

Card 2 V3 p 103 1753-7-30 Lows, John, s of Joseph & Agnes Cowpland, dt of Caleb, ami
    V3 p 104 1753-8-27 Lowns, John & Agnes Cowpland amst m.m.
    V3 p 105 1753-9-24 Lowns, John & Agnes Cowpland rm

Card 2 V3 p 428 1775-11-27 Lowns, Joseph, disf "being concerned in military preparations & combinations repecting government"

Card 2 V5 p 145 1808-8-29 Lownes, Joseph, mov

Card 1 Lowns, Joseph (b—;d—) m Rachel
    Ch.
    V1 p 105 1   Rebecca b 9-4-1808
            2. Hugh b 10-11-1811
            3. William b 6-4-1814
            4. Phineas b 4-1-1817 m Emily Lewis
    V1 p 127 5   Massey b 9-23-1819
            6. George Bolton b 1-25-1825 m Rebecca Webb
            7. Joseph b 10-12-1819 m Minerva Webb

Card 2 V5 p 151 1808-11-28 Lownes, Joseph, off acc mou

Card 2 V6 p 195 1839-10-28 Lownes, Joseph & Prisilla Pratt, ami
    V 6 p 196 1839-11-25 Lownes, Joseph & Priscilla Pratt, amist ma
    V6 p 197 1839-12-30 Lownes, Joseph & Priscilla Pratt, rm

Card #1 V2 p 210 Lownes, Joseph (b1-17-1787; d—; s Hugh & Rebecca,
both decd, Delaware CO., PA) m 1839-12-12 at Springfield MH, PA
Priscilla Pratt (b—;d—; dt
Thomas & Hannah, both decd, Delaware Co., PA

    Ch.

    V1 p 137 1. Elizabeth (b11-20-1841, d 11-2-1886)

Card 2 V6 p 336 1853-12-27 Lownes, Joseph, gct Kennett m.m. (?) to
marry Minerva Webb

Card 1 V2 p 60MB Lownes, Joseph (b 10-12-1827, d 4-21-1913) s of Joseph
& Rachel (Massey) m 1-13-1852 at Kennett M.M.
Minerva Webb (b 9-20-1832; d 11-16-1916, dt of Alban & Hannah
(Darlington)

Card 1 V1D p 75 Lownes, Joseph d 1872 bu spr

Card 2 V8 p 16 1885-6-30 Lownes, Joseph, appointed an overseer

Card 2 V8 p 372 1905-12-25 Lownes, Joseph Jr., mou off acc.

Card 3 V1 p 233 1744-9-22 Lownes, Mary m Isaaac Hubberd, see Isaac
Hubberd

Card 2 V1 p 99 1779-1-25 Lownes, Mary, dt of Benanuel, decd, get
Concord M.M.

Card 2 V7 p 320 1879-10-27 Lownes, Mary M.l rel rq (reg. made because of her engagement to a person not a member

Card 2 V2 p 216 1843-8-10 Lownes, Massey m John Jackson

Card 2 V6 p 347 1853-12-26 Lownes, Minerva W., w of Joseph Jr.; rocd Kemmett M.M. dated 12 m 1853

Card 2 V6 p 206 1840-10-26 Lownes, Phineas & Emily Lowis; ami
V6 p 208 1840-11-30 Lownes, Phineas & Emily Lewis amist ma
V6 p 209 1840-12-28 Lownes, Phineas & Emily Lewis rm

Card 1 V2 p 212 Lownes, Phineas (b 4-1-1817; d --; s Joseph & Rachel, the latter decd, both of Delaware CO., PA) m 1840-12-10 at Springfield MH, PA, Emily Lewis (b —;d —; dt John & Elizabeth, Delaware, CO., PA.

Ch.

V1 p 155 1. Anna b 12-19-1842
V1 p 161 2. William b 11-30-1850

Card 2 V6 p 338 1853-2-28 Lownes, Phineas, disf j a scc

Card 1 V1D p 75 Lownes, Priscilla d 1878 bu sp

Card 2 V5 p 235 1812-12-28 Lownes, Rachel (w of Joseph) & minor ch Rebecca & Hugh rec rq

Card 2 V6 p 302 1849-7-30 Lownes, Rebecca W,; rocf Kennett M.M. (?) dated 7 m 1849

Card 3 V2 p 32 1789-5-14 Lownes, Sarah m Jacob Reynolds

Card 2 V? p 315 1838-9-24 Lownes, Sidney appntd Treasurer, in place of Phebe R. Garrnet

Card 2 V7 p 236 1875-10-27 Lownes, William, disf jng Baptists

Card 2 V7 P 400 1883-12-31 Lownes, William, mov

Card 2 V8 p 21 1884-11-24 Lownes, William H, disg mov

APPENDIX XIII

Abbreviations

b	born	mbr	member
bCLB	buried Central Laurel	mbrp	membership
bF	buried Fallsington	mcd	married contrary in discipline
bFH	buried Fair Hill	MH	meeting house
bLH	buried Laurel Hill	MM	monthly meeting
bMR	buried Marshall Road	mou	married out of unity
bNLH	buried North Laurel Hill	mtg	meeting
bs	buried Salem	NDMM	Philadelphia MM for the Northern District
bSLH	buried South Laurel Hill	nmtm	not member of this meeting
Bswg	buried South Western Ground	prc	produced a certificate
Bur	buried	pref	produced a certificate from
bWC	buried Woodland Cemetery	QM	quarterly meting
bWG	buried Western Ground	rec	receive, received
Bwlh	buried West Laurel Hill	recrq	received by request
cert	certificate	relrq	released by request
ch	child, children	rem	remove, removed
com	complained, complained of	rm	reported married
con	condemned	rmt	reported married to
d	died	roc	received on certificate

449

dec	deceased	rocf	received on certificate from
dis	disowned, disowned for	rpd	reported
dt	daughter, daughters	rq	request, requests, requested
fam	family	rqc	requested certificate
form	formerly	rqct	requested certificate to
gc	granted certificate	rst	reinstate, reinstated
gct	granted certificate to	s	son, sons
h	husband	SDMM	Philadelphia MM for the Southern District
Jas	joined another society	w	wife
jH	joining Hichsites	wd	widow
jO	joining Orthodox	WDMM	Philadelphia MM for the Western District
Ltm	Liberated to marry, left at liberty to marry		
M	marry, married, marrying, marriage		

The Dirary

These pages were copied from Charlotte Olewiler's book *The Gawsworth Quakerss Hugh and Janes Lownde*

84

was a widower at the time having mar...
...ried Ann ...hew ... ...
...wife ... ... their second ...husband
& they legal - six children

Charles McCord -
George W.   oldman   "
John Boggs   "
Louis Labue   "
Susiana McCord (Aunt Susan)
Margaret Boggs McCord (Aunt Mary)

Sarah Lowndes had a son Wm Donaldson
Lowndes, my Grandfather who married
Hannah Long of Boston from whence
the town of Lowell derives it name.
He was a graduated physician but
discontinued the practice -

They had two daughters
Jane Eliza Lowndes   my mother
Araminta   "

Jane married John Eckel my father
Araminta   "   Benjamin F Potter -

John Eckel & Jane had nine children
Caroline M L died Nov 19, 1913 at 82 John R -
Edwin F   Christina
Sarah Ellen died from July 14 - 1890 - 38
Lilla
Earl age 62   Heart disease died Jan 26th 1917 Polyclinic Hospital
Mary died Aug 7- 1902 - Peritonitis - aged 45
Ida V.

Aunt Susan's mother & Betsy Ross's mother were own sisters

Aunts Boggs — was Betsy's sister Sarah's child she was born the month the flag was made Jan 10 1776 & died June 18 76. Sheid 100 yrs & five months old — she had one son John Boggs who died before her aged 75 yrs.

Aunt Boggs was born the month the flag was made —

Betsy Ross's sister Hannah Grecom (nee) Lorring made the first rag carpet ever made in America.

Betsy Ross & Hannah Lorring were two of the sweetest old Quaker ladies & their lawn in their white caps came from England & cost $10.00 per yd.

William Donaldson my great great grand father was a ship builder & owned a large vessel. He & Capt Ashburn went out & fought in the Revolutionary war were captured & put in Mill prison & were released & exchanged when Cornwallis surrendered. Capt Ashburn died of joy when the news reached the prison & was buried over in England & John Claypole came over in the same ship with Wm Donaldson when the exchange of prisoners took place & he T.l. was who broke the news to Betsy Ross that her husband died.

Claypole became Betsy's third husband.
Betsy had once been engaged to Capt. Ross.
Ross married Eliza Ashburn — & Ross
by Claypole —

A baker who sympathized with the
Americans in Mill prison kept
them informed of the news of battles
by notes slipped in the loaves
of bread. He was caught & hung
for a traitor —

Arthur Donaldson, my Great, Great Grandfather's
brother, an engineer, helped to make
the famous cheveaux (horse of iron) de frise
which sank the English ships that
came up the Delaware River —

The chain is in the Museum on Glen
Island, New York. Saw it myself summer 1902 —

My Great Great Great Grandfather Samuel
Griscom an austere Quaker helped to
build the State House, Carpenters Hall.
He was a lumber merchant & had a lot
of carpenters, his yard extended from
13 to 4 — and from Arch to Race. He had
the first brick house & built the first
College in Phila — Front & Vine
The house second above walnut +

Aunt Susans mother & Betsy Ross's
~~mother were~~ own sisters

Aunts Boggs - was Betsy's sister Sarah's
child she was born the month the flag was
made Jan 1st 1776 & died June 1876. She was
100 yrs & five months old - she had one son
John Boggs who died before her aged 75 yrs.

Aunt Boggs was born the month the flag was
1 month —

Betsy Ross's sister Hannah Griscom (nee) Lossing
made the first rag carpet ever made in
America)
Betsy Ross & Hannah Lossing were two of
the sweetest old Quaker Ladies & their
lawn in their white caps came from
England & cost 400 pds yd.

William Donaldson my great great grand
father was a ship (which Aunt & owned
a large vessel) He & Capt Ashburn went
out & fought in the Revolutionary war
were cap. tured & put in Mill prison
& were released & exchanged when
Cornwallis surrendered. Capt Ashburn
died of joy when the news reached
the prison & was buried over in
England & John Claypole came
over in the same ship with Wm.
Donaldson when the exchange of
prisoners took place & It is. T.J.
was who broke the news to Betsy
Ross that her husband died.

List of Lownes Personnel in the Armed Forces of America

Husband of Mary Lownes Thomas Chapman was an officer in the Revolutionary War (8/22/1764 – 6/22/1803)

Joseph Lownes II (unk – 3/20/1780) was in Revolutionary War with a final rank of major

Hugh Lownes II (unk – 1814) was dismissed from meeting for military action in the Revolutionary War 1781

William Lownes (date not known) was in the Revolutionary War and was captured and released Spent time in the Mill Prison in England

Joseph Lownes of the George Lownes branch was a Major in 6th Company, 3rd Battalon, May 14, 1777 in the Revolutionary War

Caleb Pancoast Lownes (12/26/1792 – 2/23/1836) was killed at the Mexican takeover of the Alamo.

Thomas Chapman Lownes (5/21/1827 – 3/4/1902) enlisted in the Army in Company E. 4th Regiment, Pennsylvania Volunteers, Gar. 1861 was in the Civil War.

Henry Lown (1/25/1794 – 9/24/1849) was in the war of 1812.

Jacob Lown (1840 – 1903) Civil War 113 Regiment Ohio Volunteer Infantry Co. F

Thomas Lownes (1/10/1897 – 7/2/1962) drafted in World War I (war ended before he had to serve)

Gordon L. Lown (1930 – 1975) Korean War

Charles David Lownes (12/27/1949 – 5/4/1970) killed in action in Vietnam

Joyce Lownes (8/4/1920 – 6/2/2018) enlisted in U.S. Women's Army in 1942

Walter B. Lownes MP in Germany 1945 – 1946

Irvin S. Lownes, Jr. (10/14/1932-...) served in the U.S. Army

John Brian Lownes (5/16/1942 – 5/31/2004) served in the U.S. Army

Howard G. Lownes, Jr. (1/20/1962- 11/16/2018) Enlisted in the Air Force served from 1980 – 1984

Dean Michael Butcher (6/16/1984-...) presently serving in the U.S. Army in Germany

Maps

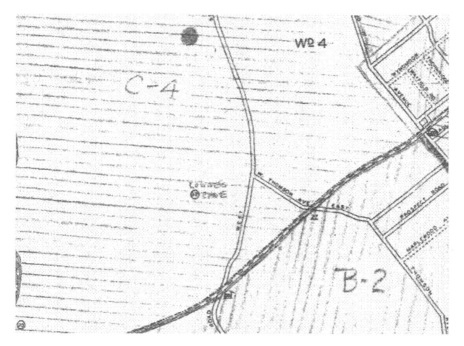

Old Map showing approximate location of The Cave

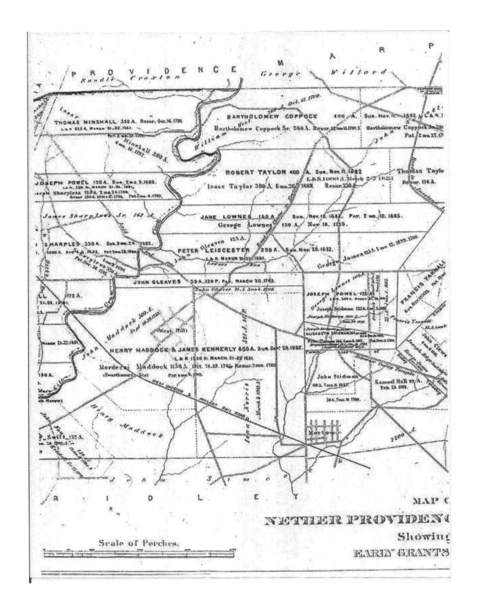

Scale of Perches.

MAP OF

NETHER PROVIDENCE

Showing

EARLY GRANTS

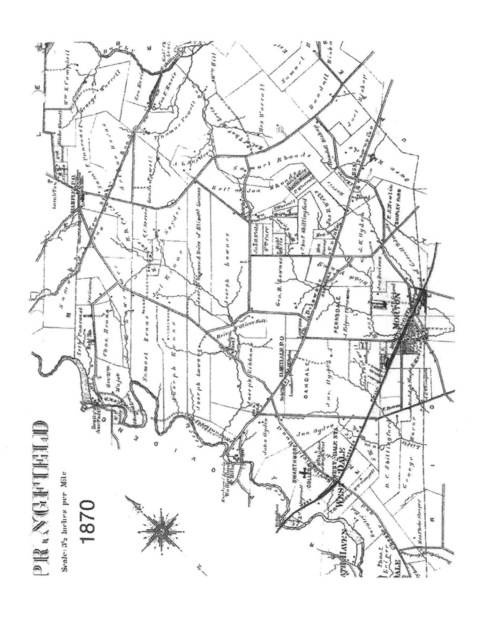

PR₄NGₑFTₑₑD

Scale: 3½ Inches per Mile

1870

This map shows Lownes Alley in Philadelphia in 1777.

Chronology

(Copied from Charlotte Lownes Olewlier's book *The Gawsworth Quakers Hugh and Jane Lowndes* published in 1978)

Shakespeare	1554 – 1616
Birth of George Fox	1624
Accession of King Charles I	1625
Begin Puritan migration to Massachusetts	1630
Hugh Lowndes was born	1635
Jane (Stretch) Lowndes was born	1636
First Civil War in England	1642 –1646
Isaac Newton	1642 - 1727
Milton wrote his Areopagatics	1644
2ND Civil War in England	1648
King Charles I executed	1649
First printed Quaker material	1652
Oliver Cromwell – Lord Protector of England	1653 -1658
Quakers refused oath ofAbjuation	1655
First Quaker to America	1656
Death of Cromwell	September 1658
Hugh Lowndes and Jane (Stretch) Lowndes were married	October 2, 1658
60,000 Friends in England	1658
4 Quakers hanged in Boston	1659 -1661
Bunyan starts Pilgrim's Prog. In prison	1660

Joseph Lowndes was born	1660
King Charles II restored Quaker Act	1660 –1661
Act of Conformity	1662
Anniversary of massacre of Hugeonots in France	1662
Hannah Lowndes was born	1662
First Conventicles Act against non-cofform	1664
70,000 Londoners die in the Plague	1665
James I. Lowndes was born	1665
Great Fire of London	1666
William Penn converted	1666
Milton wrote Paradise Lost	1667
Penn in Tower for blasphemy	1668
George Lowndes was born	1968

Hugh and Jane preaching and persecuted

APPENDIX XVIII

References

Charlotte Lownes Olewiler's Book "The Gawsworth Quakers Hugh and Jane Lowndes

Courthouse Records of Chester, Cheshire County, England

Chester County Book page 483

Old Swedes Church Wilmington CDelaware

History of Chester page 494

National Trust for Historic Preservation

"The Messenger" Mennonite Church paper March – April 1958

Springfild Historical Musium

Swathmore Historical Musium

Montogomery County Historical Musium

Hinshaw Volumne II 1936

Hinshaw Volumne VI Henrico M.M. VA.

Hinshaw Index 1999

Quaker Meeting Houses

Diary of Ida Eckle pages 83 to 86 dated July 20, 1903

Linda Lownes Hytha / Bettie Ferris Family Data

Ancestry.com